FORGING
the
TRIDENT

Titles in the Series

Studies in Naval History and Sea Power

Christopher M. Bell and James C. Bradford, editors

Studies in Naval History and Sea Power advances our understanding of sea power and its role in global security by publishing significant new scholarship on navies and naval affairs. The series presents specialists in naval history, as well as students of sea power, with works that cover the role of the world's naval powers, from the ancient world to the navies and coast guards of today. The works in Studies in Naval History and Sea Power examine all aspects of navies and conflict at sea, including naval operations, strategy, and tactics, as well as the intersections of sea power and diplomacy, navies and technology, sea services and civilian societies, and the financing and administration of seagoing military forces.

FORGING
the
TRIDENT

THEODORE ROOSEVELT
AND
THE UNITED STATES NAVY

Edited by
John B. Hattendorf *and* William P. Leeman

Naval Institute Press
Annapolis, Maryland

Naval Institute Press
291 Wood Road
Annapolis, MD 21402

Library of Congress Cataloging-in-Publication Data
Names: Hattendorf, John B, editor. | Leeman, William P, editor.
Title: Forging the trident : Theodore Roosevelt and the United States Navy / edited by John B. Hattendorf and William P. Leeman
Other titles: Theodore Roosevelt and the United States Navy
Description: Annapolis, Maryland : Naval Institute Press, [2020] | Series: Studies in Naval History and Sea Power | Includes bibliographical references and index.
Identifiers: LCCN 2020022992 (print) | LCCN 2020022993 (ebook) | ISBN 9781682475348 (hardback) | ISBN 9781682475560 (ebook) | ISBN 9781682475560 (epub)
Subjects: LCSH: Roosevelt, Theodore, 1858–1919. | United States—History, Naval—20th century. | United States—Politics and government—1933–1945. | United States. Navy—History—20th century. | Roosevelt, Theodore, 1858–1919—Influence.
Classification: LCC E757 .F67 2020 (print) | LCC E757 (ebook) | DDC 359.00973/09041—dc23
LC record available at https://lccn.loc.gov/2020022992
LC ebook record available at https://lccn.loc.gov/2020022993

28 27 26 25 24 23 22 21 20   9 8 7 6 5 4 3 2 1
First printing

CONTENTS

PREFACE AND
ACKNOWLEDGMENTS

Battleships served a power-projection role for the United States during Theodore Roosevelt's presidency. Today aircraft carriers perform that power-projection role; they include the *Nimitz*-class supercarrier USS *Theodore Roosevelt* (CVN 71), commissioned by the U.S. Navy in 1986 to honor the twenty-sixth president of the United States. Few people have had as profound and multifaceted an impact on the U.S. Navy as Theodore Roosevelt did during his time as Assistant Secretary of the Navy and as commander in chief. An accomplished naval historian before embarking on a political career, Roosevelt used naval history and heritage as a way to capture the interest and secure the support of the public, the press, and his fellow politicians for an expanded and mightier American fleet. Roosevelt's appropriation and glorification of America's naval past to educate his fellow Americans and enhance U.S. naval power in his own time forms the central theme of this book. Drawing inspiration from *FDR and the U.S. Navy* (New York: St. Martin's Press, 1998), an excellent collection of scholarly essays edited by Edward J. Marolda that examines Franklin D. Roosevelt's lifelong interaction with the Navy, we decided to produce a similar book focusing on Theodore Roosevelt, FDR's distant cousin and idol.

This volume is a cooperative effort between faculty members in the Department of History at Salve Regina University and the John B. Hattendorf Center for Maritime Historical Research at the Naval War College, both in Newport, Rhode Island. A key element in the development of the book was a conference workshop held at Salve Regina University's Pell Center for International Relations and Public Policy on 26 January 2019. At Salve Regina University, Jim Ludes, the executive director of the Pell Center, supported this project from its beginning and generously provided the venue for the workshop, while Teresa Haas, the office and events manager at the Pell Center, expertly handled the logistics. Special thanks go to Sally McGinty and the rest of the McGinty family for their generous financial support of the Department of History's activities through the John E. McGinty Fund in History, which provided funding for the workshop. At the Hattendorf Center, David Kohnen, the director, arranged funding support for travel to the workshop, and Mark Fiorey, the deputy director, handled the travel arrangements. At the Naval Institute Press, Glenn Griffith expressed immediate interest in publishing this volume and gave valuable advice as the manuscript moved toward publication.

William Leeman would like to thank Salve Regina University for awarding him a semester-long sabbatical to complete work on the book. His student Makenzie Sadler helped with the preparation of the book manuscript during the final stages. His Department of History colleagues Timothy Neary and John Quinn have offered advice, support, enthusiasm, and encouragement for this project since its inception. His parents, Barbara and William Leeman, have provided unwavering support and encouragement for this book, as they have for all of his previous historical endeavors.

The positions expressed in this book are each author's own and do not necessarily represent those of Salve Regina University, the Naval War College, the U.S. Navy, or the Department of Defense.

INTRODUCTION

Theodore Roosevelt, the Navy, and Newport

John B. Hattendorf

It should not be surprising that faculty members from two institutions located in Newport, Rhode Island—the U.S. Naval War College and Salve Regina University—chose to publish a collection of scholarly essays on Theodore Roosevelt and the U.S. Navy. Theodore Roosevelt visited Newport four times in his lifetime, and the Navy was the focus of each of his visits, in 1888, 1897, 1908, and 1913.

The story of the Naval War College's connection with Theodore Roosevelt originated even before there was a Naval War College. The war college's founder, Rear Adm. Stephen B. Luce, had long had an interest in school ships and had written a number of articles on this subject in the 1860s. One of his well-known achievements was helping to bring the sloop of war *St. Mary's* to New York as a training ship in 1874, thereby creating the basis for what continues today as the State University of New York Maritime College at Fort Schuyler. An antecedent to this pioneering effort in education for the merchant marine occurred when the New York City Department of Public Charities and Correction acquired the former New York–to–Havre sailing packet *Mercury* to use as a reform school ship in 1869.[1] The State Commissioners of Public Charities based her at their industrial reform school at Hart's Island, off Pelham, New York. During the period that *Mercury* was in use for this purpose, Luce became the senior member of an inspection board to examine the ship. Through that connection he met the commissioners, one of whom was the businessman and philanthropist Theodore Roosevelt Sr. (1831–78). Through him Luce came to know his son, Theodore Jr., who entered Harvard in 1876 with a growing interest in naval history.[2]

In 1883, the twenty-two-year-old Roosevelt published his first book, *The Naval War of 1812*. Five years later, in 1888, Rear Admiral Luce, having established the Naval War College and served as its first president, from 1884 until 1886, was back at sea in command of the Navy's North Atlantic Squadron. Writing from his flagship at Barbados on 13 February 1888, Luce told Roosevelt that he was impressed with the impartiality in his new book and the care that he had shown in examining original source materials: "There is no question in my mind that the work must be accepted as the very highest authority we have on the subject. It teaches the naval student the great value of naval history when written in a spirit of fairness."[3] Luce went on to tell Roosevelt,

> We are now giving some attention to the subject of naval history, or what may be called a philosophical study of Naval history; and on that part relating to the war of 1812 your work must be our text book. The Navy Department in recognizing the necessity for an advanced course of study for our officers, in which they will lead to draw from the lessons of the past, the true policy of the future[,] has recently opened a Naval College on an island in Narraganset Bay.... May we not hope that the study you have given to the early history of the Navy will lead you to take some interest in an institution now struggling through the ills of infancy?[4]

Luce's letter to Roosevelt contained an invitation to meet the new president of the Naval War College, Capt. Alfred Thayer Mahan. In October 1888, Roosevelt made his first visit to Newport and the Naval War College, meeting Mahan and lecturing on the War of 1812.[5] Thus, Luce's invitation created an important friendship and led to an interesting and valuable correspondence between Roosevelt and Mahan, two important figures in American history.[6] Mahan, who would serve twice as president of the college, 1886–89 and 1892–93, was to maintain a close relationship with Roosevelt for the rest of his life. In 1897, nearly a decade later, Roosevelt returned to Newport for his second visit, not having forgotten the work of the college in the intervening years. In 1890, he wrote a highly favorable review of Mahan's *The Influence of Sea Power upon History, 1660–1783*.[7]

William McKinley took the oath of office as president of the United States on 4 March 1897. Two days later, McKinley's choice for Secretary of the Navy, John D. Long, took office, but it was six more weeks before the new administration filled the second-highest position in the Department of the Navy; finally, on the urging of Senator Henry Cabot Lodge of Massachusetts, McKinley appointed Theodore Roosevelt to the post. Roosevelt retained the position for just over a year after taking office on 19 April 1897, as the first of three assistant secretaries of the Navy to serve under McKinley. In his new position, it was not long before Roosevelt encountered the work of the Naval War College. Since 1893–94, its students and staff had been studying and writing on the range of strategic situations that the nation faced. Summarized and placed on file with the Office of Naval Intelligence, the work done in Newport became the nucleus of the country's first naval contingency plans. In December 1896, the outgoing administration of Secretary of the Navy Hilary Herbert had been satisfied with neither the plans developed in the Office of Naval Intelligence nor those from the Naval War College and had created a special board to consider the matter. When Long and Roosevelt took over, they established another board. The findings of these boards had little direct bearing on what later transpired, but the major thrust of the Naval War College's work had been established: the belief that advanced planning, detailed preparations, and rational consideration of problems were essential to rapid execution in the event of a war.[8]

With such ideas very much in mind, Roosevelt found an opportunity to go back to Newport as a friend of the Naval War College. At the invitation of the college's president, Assistant Secretary Roosevelt was the principal speaker for the opening of the Naval War College's new academic year on

2 June 1897. Roosevelt took as his theme what he called "Washington's Forgotten Maxim": "To be prepared for war is the most effective means to promote peace."[9] Addressing the members of the college's staff and student body, along with commanders of other local military and naval commands, in the lecture room of what is now Luce Hall, Roosevelt argued for the creation of an American fleet of battleships as a deterrent to war. The *New York Times* summarized his remarks, "[W]hile torpedo boats and cruisers were useful, the possession by the United States of twenty battleships would make war altogether unlikely."[10] Roosevelt's lengthy address contained a wide range of headings: "Battleships Safer Than Arbitration," "Love of Flag and Love of Country," "The Martial Glories of England," "Unreadiness to Fight and Readiness to Bluster," "Preparation Would Have Prevented the War of 1812," "Monroe Doctrine Idle without a Powerful Navy," "Diplomacy Useless without Force," "A Navy Would Not Render Us Overbearing," and the "Need of Heroism in a Nation."

Today, Roosevelt's speech brings to the historian's mind Winston Churchill's declaration in Parliament on 13 May 1940 that he "had nothing to offer but blood, toil, tears and sweat."[11] Forty-three years before Churchill spoke in the House of Commons, Roosevelt had declared in Newport, "We ask for a great navy, partly because we think the possession of such a navy is the surest guarantee of peace, and partly because we feel that no national life is worth having if the nation is not willing, when the need shall arise, to stake everything on the supreme arbitration of war, and to pour out its blood, its treasure, and its tears like water, rather than submit to the loss of honor and renown."[12] Roosevelt closed by saying, "Let me repeat that we ask for a great navy, we ask for an armament fit for the nation's needs, not primarily to fight, but to avert fighting. Preparedness deters the foe, and maintains right by the show of ready might without the use of violence. Peace, like freedom, is not a gift that tarries long in the hands of cowards, or of those too feeble or too shortsighted to deserve it; and we ask to be given the means to insure the honorable peace, which alone is worth having."[13]

Roosevelt was aware that during the first fifteen years of the Naval War College's existence agencies within the Navy had made repeated attacks on it, attempting to take over its facilities and location for their own purposes. One of the college's long-standing opponents had been Capt. Francis W. Dickens, commander of the Recruit Training Station at Newport from 1894 to 1896, who had firmly believed that there was no need for sailors to be educated beyond basic training or for officers to be educated beyond the Naval Academy. Practical, "on the job" experience, he thought, was all that mattered.

In 1897, Dickens became acting chief of the Bureau of Navigation (to which the college reported) and launched another attack. In the first half of the 1880s, two other new organizations had developed with aims related to those of the new Naval War College: the Office of Naval Intelligence and the Office of Naval Records and Library. Dickens focused on the cooperation that had developed between these agencies and the Naval War College in war gaming and war planning to argue that the college was unnecessary and duplicated the work of the others. Dickens demanded that the college be closed, its staff be ordered to the Office of Naval Intelligence in Washington, and war gaming be left to the fleet.[14]

In response, the president of the Naval War College, Caspar Goodrich, wrote directly to Roosevelt as the assistant secretary to secure his support. In an impassioned letter, Goodrich declared that "to suggest or even to appear, in a remote way, to suggest that preliminary reading and study are unnecessary to success in naval warfare is to ignore the essential facts in the lives of both Nelson and our great Farragut, who were earnest students of the history and literature of their profession and even noted for intellectual activity."[15] In response, Roosevelt strongly supported both the college and the Office of Naval Intelligence, directing Goodrich to defend the college's viewpoint publicly. In November 1897, the *Army and Navy Register* published the exchange of letters between Roosevelt and Goodrich, effectively quashing Dickens' attack.[16]

After leaving office as Assistant Secretary of the Navy in 1898 and participating in the Spanish-American War, Roosevelt served as governor of New York from 1899 through 1900. After the death of Vice President Garrett Hobart in 1899, he was persuaded to run for vice president in the presidential election of 1900. McKinley was reelected, and Roosevelt took office on 4 March 1901. Six months later, Roosevelt succeeded to the presidency following McKinley's assassination on 14 September. Roosevelt was to remain keenly interested in naval affairs, working through six different secretaries of the Navy over his seven and a half years as president, between September 1901 and March 1909.

Early in his presidency, Roosevelt's attention was attracted to the ideas of Lt. William S. Sims on improving naval gunnery. In November 1902, Roosevelt appointed him inspector of naval gunnery and promoted him to lieutenant commander; in 1907, Sims was made naval aide to the president, as a commander. Sims had many suggestions to improve the service, several of which involved more efficient naval administration. This latter issue had long been on Admiral Luce's mind as well, and the topic had been discussed at the Naval War College for many years. In particular, Luce and the college had come to advocate an office of naval operations under a senior officer who would supervise the combat functions of the fleet. Several secretaries of the Navy had been sent Luce's letters and articles. A Senate committee was convened, but there was no direct action to improve the situation and little public interest in the matter.

When Roosevelt sent the Great White Fleet off on its round-the-world cruise in December 1907, the Navy suddenly became a major subject of public attention. Taking advantage of this, Sims at the White House encouraged Henry Reuterdahl, an American (Swedish-born) editor at *Jane's Fighting Ships*, to publish an article titled "The Needs of the Navy." Appearing in the January 1908 issue of *McClure's Magazine*, the article reached a wide audience and created a great deal of discussion. When Admiral Luce read the article in Newport, he saw that many of the problems that Reuterdahl and Sims were pointing out could be solved by more efficient military direction within the Navy Department. In the spring of 1908, Luce began to correspond directly with Sims about the subject. Through Sims, Luce's ideas and those of the Naval War College reached Roosevelt.

The discussion focused on a major issue among navies at the time. During the first decade of the twentieth century, several navies had turned to construct battleships with a main battery of the heaviest available guns. The revolutionary all-big-gun HMS *Dreadnought* became at her launch in 1906 the most famous and successful of the designs, giving her name to the whole trend in warship construction. However, two earlier American battleships, *Michigan* and *South Carolina*, designed in 1905, had been part of this same trend and represented distinct innovations of their own.[17] It was at the same time that Sims' predecessor as naval aide to the president, Cdr. Albert L. Key, wrote to the president pointing out design flaws in the battleship *North Dakota*, then under construction at the Fore River shipyard in Quincy, Massachusetts. *North Dakota* and her sister ship, *Delaware*, were the U.S. Navy's response to detailed information it had obtained on *Dreadnought*, the next iteration of American warship design, with others following.

The Navy Department, wrestling with a wide range of design problems to keep U.S. battleships in the forefront of naval competition, was finding that it needed to make design compromises to balance a number of attributes, most importantly armament, propulsion machinery, and armor. Changing the interrelationships among these attributes resulted in warships with quite different capabilities and weaknesses. Controversies developed over warship design, revolving around these matters.

To deal with the general issues and the specific ones that Commander Key had raised in relation to *North Dakota*, Roosevelt appointed a commission of distinguished officers to convene at the Naval War College. Roosevelt traveled to Newport on 22 July 1908 to open the conference of the commissioners. There, arriving in the presidential yacht *Mayflower*, he received all the fanfare the Navy could provide. As *Mayflower* entered Narragansett Bay, Fort Adams, the battleship *Mississippi*, the stationary training ship *Constellation*, and the gunboat *Dolphin* each fired twenty-one-gun salutes. Shortly after *Mayflower* came to anchor, the senior naval officers in the area went out in full-dress uniform to pay their official respects. The president of the Naval War College, Rear Adm. John P. Merrell, was the first to arrive on board, bringing with him in his barge Cdr. William F. Fullam, commandant of the Naval Training Station. Shortly afterward, the battleship *Mississippi*'s swift motor launch brought her commanding officer, Capt. John C. Frémont, a future rear admiral and son of the famous soldier, explorer, and politician.

As the official calls on the president were taking place, a large swarm of small craft began to gather to try to get a glimpse of the president. So many boats gathered that the yacht sent a signal to the Naval Training Station to send a steam cutter to clear the way for the president and others to go ashore. After a path had been made, Admiral Merrell made his departure from *Mayflower* with a thirteen-gun salute. Shortly afterward, the president entered *Mayflower*'s launch to another set of twenty-one-gun salutes from *Mississippi, Dolphin,* and *Constellation.* The launch made her way, through billowing clouds of gun smoke that momentarily filled the harbor, to the landing at Coasters Harbor Island, where Rear Admiral Merrell and Commander Sims greeted the president. Merrell and the college's officers escorted Roosevelt from the landing across the slope of Dewey Field to a flagpole before which the naval apprentices had been drawn up in formation. Roosevelt briefly addressed the recruits.

Entering the Naval War College, heavily guarded by a cordon of Marines, Roosevelt proceeded to the lecture hall to open the conference. In the audience were nine rear admirals, some of them bureau chiefs from Washington, as well as numerous others officers, including Commander Sims and Commander Key, officers in charge of Navy yards, members of the Naval Construction Board, and inspectors of new warship construction, all of whom had been ordered to attend. They constituted the largest group of senior officers ever gathered at the Naval War College up to that point, yet there was still some uncertainty in their minds as to what the event was about. On reaching the podium, Roosevelt announced that he had come to speak not to the audience that had gathered but to the American people. Roosevelt proceeded with an address that proclaimed the country's need for a hard-hitting and effective Navy.[18]

In it Roosevelt asserted that "no fight was ever won yet except by hitting and the one unforgiveable offense in any man is to hit soft." Going on, he pointed out that "the Monroe Doctrine, unbacked by a navy, is an empty boast, and there exist few more contemptible characters, individual or National, than the man or nation who boasts and when the boast is challenged fails to make good." In reference to the Great White Fleet, Roosevelt declared, "The voyage of the sixteen battleships around

South America, through the Strait of Magellan, from Hampton Roads to Puget Sound—that was the most instructive object lesson that had ever been afforded as to the reality of the Monroe Doctrine."[19] Roosevelt concluded his major address to the nation, pointedly delivered through the Naval War College, proclaiming that adequate sea power was a necessity as an effective guarantor of peace.

Roosevelt's second objective in convening the conference then became apparent. He asked that the room be cleared of the press and everyone but the military and naval officers present; Roosevelt intended that the remainder of the conference be a cloistered meeting of officers. Its task, as the *New York Times* reporter described it, "was plainly to give countenance to the claims recently advanced by so many of the navy that our present system of naval administration is inherently wrong."[20] The reporter from the *Army and Navy Journal* inferred that the formal address "was primarily formal platitudes carefully framed for public consumption, while the real purpose of the meeting behind closed doors and with double guards, was known to be specific discussion of controversial forms of construction and the safeguarding of the lives of officers and men of the American Navy."[21]

Roosevelt left the city at this point, but closed-door discussions continued for nearly a month. The Naval War College's final "Battleship Conference Report," which the president received on 21 August, recommended modifications to *North Dakota* and *Delaware* and an entirely different system of turret distribution in the next class of battleships. More importantly, the conference by its very existence marked the end of the Bureau of Construction's exclusive domination of warship design.[22] Indeed, as the *New York Times* reporter had perceived, the conference's concern was much broader than warship design: the fundamental problem of American naval administration.

After President Roosevelt left Newport, he kept well aware of what was happening there. Sims remained in Newport (having found accommodations for the duration of the conference at the Newport Reading Room, still in operation today on Bellevue Avenue). From there Sims regularly reported the conference's progress to Roosevelt, then staying at his home at Oyster Bay, Long Island. Sims also had numerous opportunities to discuss broader professional issues with Admiral Luce and others at the Naval War College.

Following a discussion with Sims in the midst of the conference, Luce wrote directly to Roosevelt recommending that the president convene a commission to study reorganization of the Navy Department. Within two days, Roosevelt indicated his interest in Luce's suggestion. Meanwhile in October, Luce published "The Fleet" in the *North American Review*, further stirring interest in reforming the Navy Department.[23] On 27 January 1909, the president announced the appointment of former Secretary of the Navy William H. Moody as the chairman of a commission to consider a reorganization. The members of the board included two congressmen and five admirals, including Luce, Mahan, and Robley D. Evans, who had commanded the first stage of the voyage of the Great White Fleet. The board completed its work and submitted its report at the end of February 1909, less than a week before Roosevelt left office. Roosevelt immediately forwarded the Moody Board's recommendation to the Senate, but it took no action.

The new Secretary of the Navy in the administration of President William Howard Taft, George von Lengerke Meyer, took an interest in the topic shortly after taking office. He established a board under Rear Adm. William Swift to develop specific plans for a reorganization. In November 1909, Secretary Meyer established without congressional authorization a system of "aids" (aides), who were to act as professional uniformed assistants to the Secretary of the Navy and, as a group, would constitute an advisory council and act as a general staff. This new arrangement did not go as far as Luce and many others at the Naval War College wanted. Luce's concept came more fully into fruition five years later, in 1915, when Congress established the Office of the Chief of Naval Operations.[24]

Theodore Roosevelt's fourth and final visit to Newport took place on Navy Day, 1913. (It would be nearly a decade before the Navy League of the United States established America's first national Navy Day on Theodore Roosevelt's birthday, 27 October 1922.) This occasion in Newport, on 2 July 1913, was an event of the Progressive "Bull Moose" Party, called by its organizers "Navy Day" in honor of Roosevelt, the principal speaker. In the three-way 1912 presidential election, Roosevelt had lost to the Democratic Party candidate, Woodrow Wilson, but had come in a strong second. Roosevelt remained active in Progressive Party politics, moving toward the 1914 midterm elections.

The event was held in a large tent set up on Newport's Easton's Beach next to the convention hall. Attendees enjoyed a clambake in the hall before the speeches began. The crowd was not as large as some had anticipated, but an estimated eight hundred to a thousand enthusiastic supporters streamed to the beach from trains, steamboats, trollies, and automobiles. Aside from Roosevelt, several Progressive Party leaders were present. Among them was former Senator Albert J. Beveridge of Indiana, the party's intellectual leader. Rear Adm. Charles J. Badger, commander, U.S. Atlantic Fleet, and Rear Adm. William B. Caperton, commander, 2nd Naval District, were also present with a number of officers and men.[25]

Once again, Roosevelt's speech focused on preparedness. He argued that the United States must maintain its naval strength. "Congressmen who vote against two battleships a year, he said 'are on a level with men who voted against fortifying Hawaii and our stations in the West Indies. These men are unfit to represent the American people and their actions invite national disaster and humiliation.'"[26] Roosevelt pointed to China as an example of a country that had allowed itself to become impotent in war: "We cannot abandon our rights as the Chinese have. It would be idle to insist upon our own rights, unless we are ready to back up our words with our deeds, and that to do this it is necessary to keep our navy of adequate size and at the highest pitch of efficiency."[27]

After the speeches, Roosevelt proceeded to the Naval Training Station, passing through the center of Newport. Many shops displayed American flags and several shop windows displayed "Teddy bears," the largest of them at J. T. O'Connell's on Long Wharf. The Army-Navy YMCA stretched a large American flag across its building, covering three tiers of windows, while two other flags covered two-thirds of the width of the building.[28] Rear Admiral Caperton and Capt. Roger Welles of the Naval Training Station greeted Roosevelt as he came down Training Station Road, lined with guards at attention. Roosevelt then proceeded to the reviewing stand on Dewey Field, where the apprentice seamen honored his presence with battalion drill. A large crowd from town observed the events. Afterward, he was entertained at a reception in the station's administration building, before proceeding to dinner at Harbor Court, the summer home of Mrs. John Nicholas Brown, and finally leaving for New York by the day's last Fall River Line steamer.[29]

Theodore Roosevelt's four visits to Newport, dealing as they did with the issues of naval history, education, empire, politics, and preparedness, are emblematic of the themes that the contributors to this book discuss in larger context and more detail.

Notes

1. "Saluting NY Reform Ship as SUNY Maritime College Ancestor," New York Correction History Society, http://www.correctionhistory.org/html/chronicl/schoolship/Hart%20Island%20start%20of%20Fort%20Schuyler%20Marine%20Academyo.html.
2. John D. Hayes and John B. Hattendorf, eds., *The Writings of Stephen B. Luce* (Newport, R.I.: Naval War College Press, 1975), 33.
3. Luce to Theodore Roosevelt [TR], 13 February 1888, in *Selected Correspondence and Papers of Rear Admiral Stephen B. Lucew U.S. Navy*, ed. John B. Hattendorf and Pelham Boyer (Newport, R.I.: Naval War College Press, forthcoming).
4. Luce to TR.
5. John B. Hattendorf, B. Mitchell Simpson III, and John R. Wadleigh, *Sailors and Scholars: The Centennial History of the Naval War College* (Newport, R.I.: Naval War College Press, 1984), 28.
6. Richard W. Turk, *The Ambiguous Relationship: Theodore Roosevelt and Alfred Thayer Mahan* (Westport, Conn.: Greenwood, 1987). The correspondence between Roosevelt and Mahan is on pages 101–72.
7. [Theodore Roosevelt], "The Influence of Sea Power upon History" [book review], *Atlantic Monthly* 66 (October 1890): 563–67.
8. Hattendorf, Simpson, and Wadleigh, *Sailors and Scholars*, 45–47.
9. Theodore Roosevelt, *Address of Hon. Theodore Roosevelt, Assistant Secretary of the Navy, before the Naval War College, Newport, R.I., Wednesday, June 2, 1897* (Washington, D.C.: Government Printing Office, 1897).
10. "Naval War College Opened. Assistant Secretary of the Navy Roosevelt Appeals for a Great Navy," *New York Times*, 3 June 1897, 2.
11. See "Blood, Toil, Tears and Sweat," 1940, *National Churchill Museum*, https://www.nationalchurchillmuseum.org/blood-toil-tears-and-sweat.html.
12. Roosevelt, *Address*, 24; "Naval War College Opened," 2.
13. Roosevelt, *Address*, 24; "Naval War College Opened," 2.

14. Hattendorf, Simpson, and Wadleigh, *Sailors and Scholars*, 49–50.

15. Hattendorf, Simpson, and Wadleigh.

16. "The Future of the Naval War College," *Army and Navy Register*, 20 November 1897, 332.

17. Norman Friedman, *U.S. Battleships: An Illustrated Design History* (Annapolis, Md.: Naval Institute Press, 1985), 51.

18. "President Demands Hard-Hitting Navy," *New York Times*, 23 July 1908, 2, column c.

19. "President Demands Hard-Hitting Navy," 1.

20. "President Demands Hard-Hitting Navy."

21. *Army and Navy Journal*, 25 July 1908.

22. Hattendorf, Simpson, and Wadleigh, *Sailors and Scholars*, 61–64: James R. Reckner, *Teddy Roosevelt's Great White Fleet* (Annapolis, Md.: Naval Institute Press, 1988), 123–37.

23. Reprinted in Hayes and Hattendorf, *Writings of Stephen B. Luce*, 109 ff.

24. Hayes and Hattendorf, 23.

25. "Crowds Dwindle to Fraction," *Newport Daily News*, 2 July 1913, 7, 10; "Roosevelt the Central Figure," *Newport Daily News*, 3 July 1913, 2, 7, 8.

26. "Crowds Dwindle to Fraction."

27. "Crowds Dwindle to Fraction."

28. "Crowds Dwindle to Fraction."

29. "Roosevelt the Central Figure."

1

AN INDISSOLUBLE UNION

Theodore Roosevelt, James Bulloch, and the Politics of Reconciliation

Sarah Goldberger

During a grand tour of the South in October 1905, Theodore Roosevelt made a public pilgrimage to his mother's childhood home in Roswell, Georgia. Upon his arrival at the train station, "the county sheriff and a dozen leading citizens on horseback" escorted the president and his wife, Edith, to Bulloch Hall, a Greek Revival mansion. Bulloch Hall, which features large white columns and a wide veranda, is the quintessential plantation house and bears a strong resemblance to Tara in *Gone with the Wind*.[1] During his two-hour tour, Roosevelt met two former slaves of the Bulloch family, Aunt Grace and Uncle William, and posed for a photograph with them on the front steps.[2] While the occasion may have had personal meaning for the president, the presence of "two old servants of the antebellum days," as one newspaper proclaimed, made him an active participant in the propagation of the mythic Old South, where masters were paternalistic, and slaves happy and loyal. Upon viewing the house and some of his family's furnishings, Roosevelt was overheard saying that he could "hardly bear to leave here," but he traveled by carriage to the town park to deliver a speech to the assembled townspeople.[3]

There was an element of theater in visits of northern Republicans to the South in the late nineteenth and early twentieth centuries, and Roosevelt knew how to play his part. All he had to do was extol his connections to his mother's brothers, who had served in the Confederate navy, praise the service of Confederate veterans, equate the Grey to the Blue, and manage not to upset established race relations (the last of which he had been doing for the last three years). Standing upon the raised platform, Roosevelt recounted the exploits of his uncle Irvine Bulloch, the youngest officer who served on board the commerce raider CSS *Alabama*, and his uncle James, who had built the *Alabama*. He was an "admiral in the Confederate service," Roosevelt said of James Dunwoody Bulloch. "Of all the people whom I have ever met he was the one that came nearest to that beautiful creation of Thackeray—Colonel Newcome."[4] He then exclaimed, "Men and women, don't you think I have the ancestral right to claim a proud kinship with those who showed their devotion to duty as they saw the duty, whether they wore the grey or whether they wore the blue? All Americans who are worthy of the name feel with equal pride the valor of those who fought on one side or the other, provided only that each did with all his might and soul and mind his duty as it was given him to see his duty."[5]

Southern tours were part of the landscape of Republican presidential politics in the post-Reconstruction era. They achieved the immediate objective of securing allies, both Republican and Democratic, in the South, but more strategically they fostered sectional reconciliation, the purpose of which was to reunite the country for the sake of trade and global influence, the settlement of the West, and national stability.[6] Roosevelt's own birth as the son of a Georgia belle and a New York Knickerbocker signified reconciliation in the most intimate way. He used his family's southern heritage, particularly his Confederate uncles, to amend his previous blunders in the South but also to give shape to vision for the United States and its expanding role in the world as a naval power.[7]

Roosevelt's relationship with the South was complicated, vacillating between a personal respect for Southerners and their martial tradition with a clear disgust of their politics, from secession to the disfranchisement of African American voters.[8] His father's Unionism and his mother's southern sympathies and close relationship with her Confederate brothers made it even more complicated.[9] According to Roosevelt's boyhood diary, he spent some of his most enjoyable days in 1869 in Liverpool, the unofficial former European capital of the Confederate diaspora, with Uncle James and his cousins. Both James and Irvine were living in exile in Great Britain with a number of other former Confederates. Although James would return to the United States a few times for business, he was denied amnesty by the United States, as his wartime work for the Confederate navy had included espionage. It was during this visit to Liverpool that Roosevelt had met the son of the former Confederate president, Jefferson Davis. Although Roosevelt's boyhood diary, which was published in 1928, asserts that "some strong words then ensued," one author argues that this line was absent from the manuscript and likely added by the publisher for editorial flourish, given its absence from the original.[10] It would appear that the sons of Confederate expatriates were playmates of a young Roosevelt rather than his bitter rivals.

While it is sheer speculation what Roosevelt learned from his uncle during this visit, he was likely treated to a wealth of sea stories, given the art and culture of storytelling among mariners. James Bulloch's experiences were not limited to the Civil War; he had previously had a fifteen-year U.S. Navy career and after the war another with the U.S. Mail Steamship Company. His adventures included sailing to Brazil and Hawaii, having his ship seized in Cuba with a shipload of cotton, surviving the shipwreck of the *Shark* on the Columbia River, charting the West Coast, and looking the other way when his crew abandoned ship to join the "forty-niners" during the California Gold Rush.[11] In many respects, the Bullochs represented the arc of American history from the American Revolution to the Civil War, with James Bulloch himself in the center of the narrative on antebellum expansionism. Bulloch's stories fell on very fertile ground—the eleven-year-old Roosevelt would have enjoyed hearing how his uncle ran the Union blockade with a cargo hold full of guns. Roosevelt's love of the Navy and the sea undeniably began with his "love and respect" for Bulloch, as he later wrote.[12]

Roosevelt returned again to Great Britain from time to time but most notably on his honeymoon with his first wife, Alice, in 1881. He was working on his naval history of the War of 1812 and spent his days in

Liverpool with the "blessed old sea-captain, talking over naval history." Bulloch had the sort of expert knowledge that Roosevelt needed to answer questions about navigation, sailing, and tactics. It was during that visit that Roosevelt encouraged Bulloch to write about his own experiences and helped him sort through his wartime papers. "I have persuaded him to publish a work," Roosevelt wrote to his mother, "which only he possesses the materials to write about the naval operations abroad during the last war, which were conducted and managed by him."[13]

It was the era of postwar narratives and memoirs, as veterans published their accounts and tried to establish publicly their war records for posterity. But Bulloch had other motives—he was one of the key villains of the "*Alabama* claims," in which the United States famously sued Great Britain for the loss of Union shipping to Confederate commerce raiders that had been built by Britain. The *Alabama* claims dominated the news in the 1870s and contributed to the souring of Anglo-American relations. Britain eventually settled for $15 million. Bulloch's account, *The Secret Service of the Confederate States*, which was published in 1883, served as a vehicle to save the reputation of friends, business associates, and companies as well as to justify his actions, which he claimed were in the interest of states' rights. The two-volume publication, which was not widely read at the time, provides a fascinating account of the business of procurement and the circumvention of the Foreign Entitlement Act and neutrality laws, which prohibited Britain from building warships for belligerents.[14] Bulloch had disguised the purpose of his ships, induced investors to buy into his scheme, and then had the ships armed and crewed in the Azores to wreak havoc on the high seas. His account reveals the degree of effectiveness of the Union blockade, how one could breach it, the resourcefulness of a cash-poor nation, and most importantly, the significance of sea power.[15] It is a fascinating account for someone wanting to create a navy from nothing. What one realizes upon reading these volumes is that Capt. James Bulloch was not only an agent of the Confederate navy but also the architect of the Confederate navy.

Bulloch's account is also a trenchant commentary on the state of U.S. naval affairs in the post–Civil War era. In particular, he argued that policy makers of that period, who sought hegemonic control of the Americas, were unable effectively to invoke the Monroe Doctrine and for one reason only—that they underfunded the Navy. They spent only a few "millions of dollars from year to year," which barely paid for keeping "dockyards in repair" and "a few ships of a bygone type at sea." It was his contention that the Monroe Doctrine could not be applied if the United States was unable to place a fleet "at the required spot and at the critical moment" and control the "highway" between the oceans.[16] Bulloch recommended that "in these times of great armaments, nations who wish to advance their influence, maintain their prestige or even to take part in international discussions with the expectation of being listened to with respect, must demonstrate that they are prepared for attack as well as for defence, that they can strike as well as parry."[17] Long before Alfred Thayer Mahan introduced Roosevelt to his views on sea power, Bulloch schooled him on the importance of navies and how the inability to control one's coastline could be detrimental to a nation-state.

Roosevelt would not return to naval affairs until joining President William McKinley's administration as Assistant Secretary of the Navy in 1897. Previously he had accepted appointments fighting corruption and the spoils system, first with the U.S. Civil Service Commission and then as police commissioner in New York City. A fervent believer in the concept of civil service, Roosevelt ensured that the Navy abided by the reforms that had come to the Navy Department. During the first few weeks as assistant secretary, his correspondence centered on informing patronage seekers that all positions at the Navy yards required a civil service examination. As he tersely wrote to one, "There is no influence of any kind that could advance your chances."[18]

As assistant secretary, Roosevelt was not content simply to respond to job inquiries or report on the preparedness of ships; he also waded into the waters of national policy. His positions, of course, sought to advance American influence in the Pacific and the Americas through a buildup of the Navy. In his correspondence, he identified the Japanese navy as a growing threat to American ambitions in the Pacific and recommended that the United States annex Hawaii. Not surprisingly, he believed the United

States needed to oust the Spanish from Cuba and that national interest required that the "Nicaraguan" canal be built as quickly as possible. As he reported in correspondence with Captain Mahan, now president of the U.S. Naval War College, he wanted a number of new battleships, but the present mood in Washington and the opinion of Secretary of the Navy John D. Long was "to stop building up the Navy."[19]

It was for this reason that Roosevelt traveled to Newport to try to steer the nation and the Navy onto a new course in June 1897. After observing "matters generally" at the Naval War College, he delivered his "preparation speech" to the students and professors.[20] Since the work of the college was predicated upon the concept of studying the past to prepare naval leaders for the challenges of the maritime arena, Roosevelt cited lessons of the Civil War, a conflict with which he was especially familiar:

> We must therefore make up our minds once for the fact that it is too late to make ready for war when the fight has once begun. The preparation must come before that. In the case of the civil war none of these conditions applied. In 1861 we had a good fleet, and the Southern Confederacy had not a ship. We were able to blockade the Southern ports at once, and we could improvise engines of war more than sufficient to put against those of an enemy who also had to improvise them and who labored under even more serious disadvantages.

He warned his already convinced audience, "With a modern military power we shall find its *Merrimac*s already built."[21] The "preparation speech" did not please all, particularly Secretary Long, as Roosevelt confided to Mahan a few days later.[22]

Roosevelt's tenure at the Navy Department was short; he left to join the adventure of war with Spain the following year, doing his part to advance one of the very objectives he had cited in his correspondence as assistant secretary. His triumphant return to civic life as a selfless war hero paved the way for roles in executive leadership, first as governor of New York and then as vice president during McKinley's second term. McKinley's assassination in September 1901 plunged Roosevelt into the presidency of a country still very sectionally aligned and with a vastly reduced southern Republican electorate. While Roosevelt may have loved James Bulloch, who had died six months prior, he would find that there was little to love about the racial politics of the South.

Upon Roosevelt assuming the presidency, southern Republicans immediately approached him on the importance of taking control of the Republican Party in the South. John Wise, a lawyer from Virginia who now lived in self-appointed exile in New York, brought Roosevelt up to date on the sad state of affairs in Virginia—that the commonwealth, like the other southern states, would soon disfranchise black voters. Some Republicans—"Lily Whites," as they were called—believed that this was perhaps a good thing, as it would make white men more likely to join the Republican Party; other Republicans saw the elimination of black voters as fatal to the party. Wise, who considered himself in the latter category, served as the attorney of a group of black plaintiffs who fought disfranchisement.[23] As president, Roosevelt became immersed in the very complex intersection of southern racial politics and federal patronage. Although the majority of federal employment now required civil service examinations, there was still patronage enough to bestow, such as the coveted position of local postmaster.

The issue of patronage would immediately put Roosevelt on a collision course with white Southerners. The first incident happened right away, in the fall of 1901, when Roosevelt invited Booker T. Washington to the White House for the purpose of discussing patronage. Roosevelt was determined to appoint only the most qualified people, and he believed Washington, who was well respected, to be best judge of the African American appointees. The White House dinner given for Washington created outrage in the South; editorials pilloried the president for having created a precedent of racial and social equality. Roosevelt continued to buck the South's racial order with two patronage cases involving African Americans, Dr. William Crum in Charleston, whom he appointed as collector of customs, and Minnie Cox of Indianola, Mississippi, whose tenure as postmistress dated to the Benjamin Harrison administration. In the latter case, a particularly vicious one, the townspeople suddenly demanded Cox's removal and then threatened her life. Suitably frightened, Cox tendered her resignation, which Roosevelt initially refused to accept. When Cox departed, Roosevelt proceeded to close the post office in retaliation.[24] He also refused to retract Crum's appointment despite withering criticism. As Roosevelt explained to Charleston mayor Goodwyn Rhett, Crum was well qualified, and he, Roosevelt, would not "take the position that the door of hope—the door of opportunity—is to be, shut . . . purely upon the grounds of color."[25]

Relations with white Southerners did not improve until after the election of 1904, when Roosevelt began to take a new tack with the South and played at the politics of reconciliation. As the historian David Blight argues in *Race and Reunion*, the process of reconciliation required that Northerners recognize the bravery and honor of those who had fought for the Confederacy.[26] Yet by doing so, they accepted the southern narrative of the war, which divorced slavery from the causes of the war and undermined the significance of black freedom. Roosevelt's first conciliatory effort involved the return of more than five hundred Confederate battle flags that had been discovered years before in the basement of the War Department. A joint resolution approved by the president in 1905 required both private organizations and individuals to return flags to their original states. One newspaper proclaimed that this Memorial Day had even greater meaning than usual, as "the flags go back by order of the federal government under the order of a Republican administration under a Republican president, elected by the greatest majority ever."[27]

The president followed this popular measure by proposing a goodwill tour of the South that fall, including even New Orleans, then suffering from a yellow fever epidemic. The tour included the celebrated visit to his mother's childhood home but also to important industrial cities throughout the South, including the New South boomtown of Birmingham, Alabama. One newspaper cartoonist aptly captured the intent of the tour, depicting Roosevelt building a railroad between North and South with a basket of nails and speeches. The railroad ties were labeled "marriage ties," "fraternal feeling," "commercial interest," and "patriotism." Indeed, these were all either objectives or central themes of his southern tour.

Roosevelt was particularly adept at citing the wartime achievements of his Confederate uncles as a way to appeal to the veterans in attendance. His speech in Richmond, which inaugurated the tour, covered much the same ground as that during his later visit to Roswell, citing his admiral uncle. Roosevelt even claimed that he had the same right as Virginians to stand near Richmond's statues of Stonewall Jackson and Robert E. Lee. Throughout his tour, southern speakers parroted these very sentiments back to him. For example, during his visit to Alabama, the state's former governor exclaimed that Alabamans had "confidence in the . . . unsectional patriotism" of the president, especially his "many kindnesses to confederate veterans." The governor continued, "Had you been born 20 years earlier, and in Georgia where you should have been born, you would have been a gallant leader of a brigade under Forrest or Stuart."[28] Praising Confederate veterans, however, was not a goal in and of itself but a means for promoting American patriotism and national unity. In Montgomery, Roosevelt shared these goals with his audience, exclaiming, "There is no place in the union where the President of the union can feel more at home, can feel more that he is indeed the President of all the union, of a reunited and an indissoluble union, than speaking here under the shadow of the first capitol of the confederacy."[29]

Roosevelt, however, still sought to cultivate the partnership he had fostered with Booker T. Washington and so visited the Tuskegee Institute during his tour. There he praised the work of the students, proclaiming that "ignorance is the costliest crop that can be raised in the Union," and condemned the lawless practice of lynching.[30] Yet, the southern tour was centered on fostering goodwill among Southern whites, a theme that *Puck*, a satirical magazine, emphasized on one of its October magazine covers. Over the caption "Marse Theodore," *Puck* artists depicted Roosevelt donning a Confederate-style beard and riding the Democratic donkey through a field of cotton.[31]

Roosevelt returned to the South nearest Washington—that is, Virginia— in the spring of 1906 for the dedication of a monument at the Portsmouth Naval Hospital cemetery. The monument, erected by the Army and Navy Union, purportedly honored those who had died during the

Spanish-American War. After disembarking at the navy yard in Portsmouth and being greeted by Rear Adm. Purnell Harrington, Roosevelt and his family processed, escorted by a parade of more than four thousand sailors and Marines, Grand Army of the Republic veterans, and Confederate veterans, to the naval hospital. As they passed through the streets, schoolchildren serenaded them with the "Star-Spangled Banner" and "Dixie."[32]

The procession ended in woods near the cemetery, from where the president overlooked the graves of sailors who had died throughout the nineteenth century—not only during the Spanish-American conflict, but also in the Civil War. Not surprisingly, his remarks seemed more focused on the Civil War than on the service of those who had fought in the later war. Of each of the dead from 1861–65 Roosevelt exclaimed that "he had the courage to stand without flinching the bickering of the skirmishes and the hammering of great fights; he had the steadfast endurance to bear with uncomplaining resolution the hunger and the heat and the cold, the scorching days and the freezing nights." He concluded, "They have left us the memory . . . where brother fought brother with equal courage, with equal sincerity of conviction, with equal fidelity to a high ideal."[33] If the 1905 tour of the South had been motivated by politics, Roosevelt's praise of the dead sailors on Memorial Day probably meant something more, given the affection and respect he had for one in particular, though James Bulloch, unlike the sailors in the hospital cemetery, was not buried in the South or even the United States. The Memorial Day ceremony clearly had little to do with the Spanish-American War, but served as a continuation of his conciliatory tour. It also occurred as the Commonwealth of Virginia and the federal government were in the midst of developing the program for an industrial exposition that would promote patriotism and further the nation's commercial and naval interests.

The Jamestown Tercentennial Exposition observed the three-hundredth anniversary of the founding of the English colony with industrial and labor exhibitions and associated historical programming. Located on the waterfront of Norfolk's Sewell's Point, it was also a suitable backdrop for the promotion of naval power. Yet, the original purpose of the Jamestown

Exposition as conceived by Virginians was to project the economic achievements and commercial potential of Virginia, in keeping with the messaging of New South boosterism.[34] Like the 1876 Philadelphia Centennial Exposition and the 1893 World's Columbian Exposition, the Jamestown Exposition looked backward, using a founding moment in American history to measure progress. It was due to the efforts of Norfolk's boosters, journalists, politicians, and businessmen that the state assembly selected that city over Richmond to host the 1907 observance. Not surprisingly, Norfolk developers expected a great payday, in terms of real estate, construction of hotels and buildings, and promotion of the port of Norfolk.[35]

When the official program for the exposition was published in early 1907, it seemed that the original themes of commerce and labor had been superseded by militarism and navalism. The exposition now included robust military demonstrations and displays, such as "reproduction war scenes" from the Civil War, the "greatest naval rendezvous" of visiting warships anchored within sight at Hampton Roads, and militiamen serving as a police force. The avenue where all the exhibit buildings were located was dubiously called the "War Path." As a result, a number of exposition advisors, including the historian Reverend Edward Everett Hale and the pacifist Hull House reformer Jane Addams, launched a public protest. They proclaimed that because of the lobbying by the "military party" in Washington, the Jamestown program was now designed "to intoxicate the American people for six months by a great living picture of war with all of its enticing splendors" rather than its "horror." "We solemnly protest," they added, "the prostitution of a great national festival planned to commemorate our New World birth and the representative achievements of these three centuries into an enterprise which 'will be primarily a military and naval celebration.'"[36]

For navalists, however, the Jamestown Exposition was exactly the right venue for promoting a new American fleet: the Navy had long maintained a yard in Portsmouth, and the Jamestown Exposition grounds at Sewell's Point were located on Hampton Roads, which was deep enough to accommodate the largest ships of the Great White Fleet. Roosevelt specifically invited foreign nations to join the United States by "sending their naval vessels to the said celebration."[37] The historical anniversary of Jamestown, furthermore, lent itself to promotion of sea power, as Jamestown was associated in popular memory with England, a maritime power that had crossed the Atlantic in 1607 in search of trade and empire. It would seem, in fact, that the anniversary of Jamestown was entirely suited to promoting American nationalism, the Navy, and empire. Yet, the commemoration of the anniversary of Jamestown can also be placed in the context of regional politics and the sort of regional patriotism that also characterized the Lost Cause.

The first Jamestown Jubilee dated to 1807, when a group of Jeffersonian Republicans made a pilgrimage to Jamestown Island to observe the two-hundredth anniversary of its founding.[38] Their observance was, in many respects, a regional political answer to Forefathers' Day, which Massachusetts Federalists had been observing since the 1790s. New Englanders, who dominated the early field of American history, promoted the origin myth of Plymouth—a tale of purported religious freedom and republicanism—while undercutting the exploits of John Smith and Virginia's venerable House of Burgesses.[39] As a result, nineteenth-century Virginians increasingly invoked the memory of Jamestown to reassert their state's importance in the national narrative.

The fact that in 1907 the nation was poised to observe the three hundredth anniversary of Jamestown signified a kind of national recognition that Virginia also had a claim to national origins. Lyon Gardiner Tyler, the son of former president John Tyler, a preservationist, and president of the College of William and Mary, published in 1906 in anticipation of the exposition a colonial history titled *The Cradle of the Republic: Jamestown and the James River.* Roosevelt's support of the exposition reinforced such lofty claims. As he expressed to the secretary of the Jamestown Exposition Company, G. T. Sheppard, "The three hundredth anniversary of that event must be commemorated by the people of our union as a whole."[40] Jamestown lent itself to the politics of reconciliation.

On opening day in April, Roosevelt disembarked from the presidential yacht *Mayflower* and was met with a three-hundred-gun salute inaugurating the exposition. He then delivered the keynote address on the Lee Parade Grounds, named for Fitzhugh Lee, the former governor, who had worked on the exposition. Lee was also a veteran of the Civil War and the Spanish-American War and a nephew of Robert E. Lee.[41] There were many other reminders of the Civil War, including an entire exhibit along the War Path on the 1862 battle of the ironclads. In keeping with theme of reconciliation that had dominated Roosevelt's tour in 1906, Roosevelt declared that both sections could feel proud of the "valor" of the Blue and the Grey, that the "mists that once shrouded brother from brother" had cleared, and the country was united.[42] In a letter to his son Kermit, Roosevelt characterized the theater of the day as all very typical, culminating in his "usual speech," but he excitedly detailed how in the *Mayflower* he had reviewed the foreign ships and sixteen American battleships in Hampton Roads. "It was an inspiring sight," he confessed.[43]

Roosevelt returned to the exhibition on 10 June, Georgia Day, visiting the Georgia House, a replica of his mother's home, Bulloch Hall. During Roosevelt's celebrated tour of the South, the president of Georgia's Jamestown commission, W. N. Mitchell, an Atlanta businessman, had proposed that Georgia model its representative "state house" in the upcoming Jamestown Exposition on Bulloch Hall, suggesting even "cultures of shrubbery" and "original furniture."[44] In promoting the idea, Mitchell claimed that the house "will symbolize and herald to the world the lasting union of the North with the South showing that in the blood of the President there is intermingled all the attributes of Southern and Northern chivalry and manliness."[45]

During his visit on Georgia Day, Roosevelt thanked the state for creating a replica of "the house in which my mother passed her youth and where she was married to my father." Instead of dwelling on the Civil War, however, he remarked upon the contributions of his ancestor Archibald Bulloch, who had served as the state's revolutionary governor, and emphasized that the nation was united once more. Roosevelt claimed that because he was "half southern and half northern in blood" and attuned also to the West, he felt a "strong sense of kinship with every portion of our great common country."[46] In a humorous letter to Kermit, he relayed how the crowd "received me with wild enthusiasm," although that would, he predicted, "not in the least interfere with their hating me quite as much a year hence."[47]

Aside from Georgia House, Roosevelt made headlines with his visit to the Negro Exhibition Building, which featured exhibits on African American schools, labor, banks, and businesses. Fairs often exhibited racial displays for the purpose of juxtaposing white industrial achievement with the "primitiveness" of nonwhite peoples. While this Negro exhibition would seem to fit into this narrative, many of its displays, among them Meta Warrick's historical tableaux, presented a powerful counternarrative to such portrayals of African Americans. Warrick, an African American sculptor, depicted the injustice of slavery with dioramas of slaves in chains and fugitives being hunted down by whites, but she also emphasized African American uplift, with depictions of African Americans creating middle-class homes and attending a Howard University commencement ceremony.[48] Impressed, Roosevelt made an additional trip to the head-quarters of the Colored Jamestown Company's offices to congratulate the businessmen on their meaningful contribution, exclaiming, "I assure you my support in your efforts."[49] In many ways, the presidential visit to Georgia House and the Negro Exhibition Building could be said to symbolize between them the difficult waters Roosevelt had waded into with regard to politics and the South—his desire to support individual merit, despite race, versus his need for a patriotic and united country.

Roosevelt used the occasion of the formal closing of the Jamestown Exposition to send the Great White Fleet on its voyage to carry the American flag around the globe, a show of force particularly apt in light of souring relations with Japan. It was a clear day in December, almost 301 years since the *Susan Constant*, *Godspeed*, and *Discovery* set out for America in 1606. Unlike the Jamestown Exposition, not oratory but naval pageantry characterized the occasion, Roosevelt in his yacht leading the fleet out of Hampton Roads and reviewing the ships off the Virginia Capes. Describing the occasion as "a great day" and the crews as all "bully," the event symbolized his mark on the Navy, much as commerce raiders had been for Bulloch. "I feel mighty glad," he reflected, "of all these battleships, now that there is this friction with Japan."[50] While the voyage would not be an unalloyed success—ships would break down, and the like—the Great White Fleet set a new course for the Navy, the United States, and also Virginia.

Ten years later, to meet the expanding requirements of the Army and the Navy during World War I, the federal government purchased thousands of acres of land for training camps and bases. Many of these bases were in the South, where the land was cheap and the weather more suited than elsewhere to year-round training. In 1917, the Navy acquired the Jamestown Exposition grounds for a new naval base, Naval Station Norfolk, Virginia, which would become home to the Atlantic Fleet. The purchase also included Georgia House, along with other exposition buildings. One cannot fail to see the irony in the fact that a replica of the boyhood home of James Bulloch, who used every resource and deceit to fight the U.S. Navy, is now standing on U.S. Navy property. The home, located on what is today known as Admirals' Row, has served as quarters for senior officers and has witnessed gray warships cruising in and out of Naval Station Norfolk for the past century. Despite Roosevelt's disdain for the Confederacy, he respected James Bulloch and his naval acumen, and it was through his uncle that he first came to love and understand the importance of the Navy. As Roosevelt waded into the troubled waters of southern politics, he relied upon the memory of Bulloch and the Civil War to reset relations with white Southerners. Georgia House, now a relic in its own right, is illustrative of how the dynamics of reconciliation and sea power converged in 1907—in a Faustian bargain that ignored the South's racial policies in favor of nationalism and a new navy capable of protecting and projecting American interests.

Notes

1. *Abbeville Press* (S.C.), 15 November 1905. See Molly Haskell, *Frankly, My Dear: Gone with the Wind Revisited* (New Haven, Conn.: Yale University Press, 2009), 130.
2. According to newspaper accounts, Grace had served as a maid to Martha "Mittie" Roosevelt since her young "womanhood," while William Jackson supposedly helped decorate the house when she married Theodore Sr. The

Bulloch/Roosevelt wedding is still emphasized at Bulloch Hall, now a museum, where interpreters annually reenact the December wedding ceremony. See *Wilmington Messenger* (N.C.), 24 October 1905; *Weekly Corinthian* (Miss.), 25 October 1905.

3. *Weekly Corinthian* (Miss.), 25 October 1905.

4. *Wilmington Messenger* (N.C.), 24 October 1905. Colonel Newcome was an army veteran and virtuous patriarch in William Thackeray's novel *The Newcomes: Memoirs of a Most Respectable Family*. He was such a revered literary character that Richard Morton wrote a play about him that debuted in 1906.

5. *Wilmington Messenger* (N.C.), 24 October 1905.

6. See Edward O. Frantz, *The Door of Hope: Republican Presidents and the First Southern Strategy, 1877–1933* (Gainesville: University Press of Florida, 2011).

7. Reconciliation through marriage was a popular theme in late nineteenth-century literature. See Nina Silber, *The Romance of Reunion: Northerners and the South, 1865–1900* (Chapel Hill: University of North Carolina Press, 1993).

8. Gary Gerstle explores the tension between Roosevelt's racial ideology and his civic ideology that pushed the United States to welcome all people and encourage their devotion to the state. See "Theodore Roosevelt and the Divided Character of American Nationalism," *Journal of American History* 86, no. 3 (1999): 1280–1307.

9. During the Civil War, Martha Bulloch implored her husband, who was a Unionist, not to fight the South—against her family. As a result, Theodore Sr. spent the war supporting the Union cause, but not in uniform. Toward the end of the war, Martha purportedly hung the Confederate battle flag in the window of her New York home to boost the morale of Confederate POWs passing on the street. *Washington Times*, 22 October 1905.

10. Theodore Roosevelt, *Theodore Roosevelt's Diaries of Boyhood and Youth* (New York: Charles Scribner's Sons, 1928), 16; Walter E. Wilson, *The Bulloch Belles: Three First Ladies, a Spy, a President's Mother, and Women of a 19th Century Georgia Family* (Jefferson, N.C.: McFarland, 2015), 151–52.

11. Walter E. Wilson and Gary L. McKay, *James D. Bulloch: Secret Agent and Mastermind of the Confederacy* (Jefferson, N.C.: McFarland, 2012), 12–15, 22–24.

12. TR to Martha Bulloch Roosevelt, 14 September 1881, MS Am 1934 (1007), Theodore Roosevelt Collection, Harvard College Library, Theodore Roosevelt Digital Library, Dickinson State University, http://www.theodorerooseveltcenter .org/Research/Digital-Library (accessed 9 January 2019).

13. TR to Martha Bulloch Roosevelt, 14 September 1881.

14. See James D. Bulloch, *The Secret Service of the Confederate States in Europe: Or, How the Confederate Cruisers Were Equipped* (London: Richard Bentley and Son, 1883).

15. Bulloch.

16. Bulloch, 91, 95.
17. Bulloch, 96.
18. TR to John O'Donnell, 22 April 1897, Theodore Roosevelt Papers, Series 2, Letterpress Copybook, vol. 1, Library of Congress.
19. TR to A. T. Mahan, 3 May 1897, Letterpress Copybook, vol. 1.
20. TR to Caspar F. Goodrich, 10 May 1897, Letterpress Copybook, vol. 1.
21. Theodore Roosevelt, *Address of Hon. Theodore Roosevelt, Assistant Secretary of the Navy, before the Naval War College, Newport, R.I., Wednesday, June 2, 1897* (Washington, D.C.: Government Printing Office, 1897), 14.
22. TR to A. T. Mahan, 9 June 1897, Letterpress Copybook, vol. 1.
23. Curtis Carroll Davis, "Very Well-Rounded Republican: The Several Lives of John S. Wise," *Virginia Magazine of History and Biography* 71 (October 1963): 461–87.
24. See Willard Gatewood, "Theodore Roosevelt and Southern Republicans: The Case of South Carolina," *South Carolina Historical Magazine* 70 (October 1969): 251–66; Seth M. Scheiner, "President Roosevelt and the Negro, 1901–1908," *Journal of Negro History* 47 (July 1962): 169–82; Deborah Davis, *Guest of Honor: Booker T. Washington, Theodore Roosevelt, and the White House Dinner That Shocked a Nation* (New York: Simon & Schuster, 2012); Philip F. Rubio, *There's Always Work at the Post Office: African American Postal Workers and the Fight for Jobs, Justice, and Equality* (Chapel Hill: University of North Carolina Press, 2010), 23.
25. Draft of letter from TR to R. Goodwyn Rhett, 8 November 1902, Theodore Roosevelt Papers.
26. David Blight, *Race and Reunion: The Civil War in American Memory* (Cambridge, Mass.: Belknap Press of Harvard University Press, 2001).
27. *Washington Star*, 26 March 1905; *Los Angeles Herald*, 28 May 1905; *Alexandria Gazette*, 24 February 1905.
28. *Richmond Times Dispatch*, 19 October 1905.
29. *Boston Daily Globe*, 25 October 1905.
30. *Windham County Reformer* (Vt.), 27 October 1905.
31. *Puck Magazine*, 18 October 1905.
32. *Richmond Times-Dispatch*, 31 May 1906; *New York Times*, 31 May 1906; *Washington Evening Star*, 30 May 1906.
33. *Washington Evening Star*, 30 May 1906; *Richmond Palladium*, 31 May 1906.
34. Carl Abbot, "Norfolk in the New Century: The Jamestown Exposition and Urban Boosterism," *Virginia Magazine of History and Biography* 85 (January 1977): 86–96.
35. Abbot.
36. "Militarism at the Jamestown Exposition," *Advocate of Peace* 69 (February 1907): 35, 37.

37. *The Official Blue Book of the Jamestown Tercentennial Exposition* (Norfolk, Va.: Colonial, 1907), 75.

38. David James Kiracofe, "The Jamestown Jubilees: 'State Patriotism' and Virginia Identity in the Early Nineteenth Century," *Virginia Magazine of History and Biography* 110, no. 1 (2002): 44.

39. Joseph Conforti, *Imagining New England: Explorations of Regional Identity from the Pilgrims to the Mid-Twentieth Century* (Chapel Hill: University of North Carolina Press, 2001); Harlow Sheidley, *Sectional Nationalism: Massachusetts Conservatives and the Transformation of America, 1815–1836* (Boston: Northeastern University Press, 1998).

40. TR to G. T. Sheppard, 9 March 1904, Theodore Roosevelt Digital Library (accessed 9 January 2019).

41. *Confederate Veteran* 15 (January 1907): 43.

42. *Marion Daily Mirror* (Ohio), 26 April 1907.

43. TR to Kermit Roosevelt, 29 April 1907, MS Am 1541 (186), Theodore Roosevelt Digital Library (accessed 8 January 2019).

44. *Daily Press* (Newport News, Va.), 26 April 1907; *Richmond Times-Dispatch*, 21 October 1906.

45. *Washington Herald*, 21 October 1905.

46. *Bamberg Herald* (S.C.), 14 June 1907.

47. TR to Kermit Roosevelt, 13 June 1907, Theodore Roosevelt Digital Library (accessed 8 January 2019).

48. W. Fitzhugh Brundage, "Meta Warrick's 1907 'Negro Tableaux' and (Re)Presenting African American Historical Memory," *Journal of American History* 89 (March 2003): 1368–1400.

49. Giles Jackson and D. Webster Miles, *The Industrial History of the Negro Race* (Richmond: Virginia Press, 1908), 280.

50. TR to Kermit Roosevelt, 13 June 1907.

2

THE WAR OF 1812

Historical Justification for Roosevelt's Naval Advocacy

Kevin D. McCranie

The Naval War of 1812

"I thoroughly enjoyed Harvard, and I am sure it did me good, but only in the general effect, for there was little in my actual studies which helped me in after life," reflected Theodore Roosevelt in later adulthood. "My failure to do so may have been partly due to my taking no interest in the subjects." In hindsight, he may not have been the most diligent of students. "A very clever and studious lad would," as he later explained, have taken "an intelligent interest in some of the subjects assigned to me." Instead, he became sidetracked by naval history, where "the frigate and sloop actions between the American and British sea-tigers of 1812 were much more within my grasp." By graduation in 1880, Roosevelt had completed two chapters of what became *The Naval War of 1812*, chapters that, he confessed, "were so dry that they would have made a dictionary seem light reading by comparison. Still, they represented purpose and serious interest on my part."[1]

Naval affairs had captivated Roosevelt from childhood. His mother provided a particular influence, regaling him with maritime adventures. He later recalled, "From my earliest recollection I have been fed on tales from the sea . . . about ships, ships, ships, and fighting of ships, till they sank into the depths of my soul."[2] The real-life exploits of two maternal uncles, James and Irvine Bulloch, both of whom had served in the Confederate navy, only deepened Theodore's infatuation. They visited the Roosevelt family during a secret trip to New York following the Civil War; many years later, Roosevelt included vivid recollections of the event in his autobiography.[3] He even thanked his Uncle James in the acknowledgments of *The Naval War of 1812*, as one "without whose advice and sympathy this work would probably never have been written or even begun."[4]

During Roosevelt's undergraduate years at Harvard, what had been his childhood fascination with the Navy burgeoned, and in due time, "when I first began to think, in an independent and consecutive order, for the record at Harvard, I began to write a history of the Naval War of 1812."[5] At Harvard, Roosevelt refined a worldview that included a keen understanding of the importance of navies. Exactly when this thinking became coherent remains unclear, but his views on naval power solidified as he wrote *The Naval War of 1812* and likely motivated the book's completion.

At least two factors pushed Roosevelt toward the War of 1812. First, he wished to use naval history to convey lessons to Americans of his own day. For this, he needed an example from his country's past. There were only three major wars to choose from: the War for American Independence, the War of 1812, and the Civil War. In the late 1870s, the War between the States was less than a decade and a half in the past. It remained too controversial. As for the American Revolution, at its start there had been no navy. By a process of elimination, the War of 1812 emerged. Though less controversial than the more recent conflict, it still had drama, the sources were readily available, and he could translate its history into contemporary message he wished to develop. The second inspiration for writing on 1812 arose from a sense of justness—a visceral desire to refute unsubstantiated claims made by previous writers.[6]

Roosevelt found that "no full, accurate, and unprejudiced history of the war had ever been written." He maintained, "Historical writers have treated it either in connection with a general account of the contest on land and sea, or as forming a part of the complete record of the navies of the two nations." He acknowledged that "a few monographs, which confine themselves strictly to the naval occurrences, have also appeared," but claimed that none "of these works can be regarded as giving a satisfactorily full or impartial account of the war—some of them being of the 'popular' and loosely-constructed order, while others treat it from a purely partisan standpoint." In total, he explained, "No single book can be quoted which would be accepted by the modern reader as doing justice to both sides, or, indeed, as telling the whole story."[7] The thought process reflected here certainly conveys a contemporary message, for it remains a guiding principle of scholars attempting to defend the necessity of their own research.

Roosevelt's desire to write a more accurate and less biased history of the naval war fit into a broader late nineteenth-century trend. It had been spearheaded by the British naval historian John Knox Laughton, who had in 1875 published an article titled "The Scientific Study of Naval History." Of earlier writers on naval history, Laughton argued, "almost without exception, they have contented themselves with giving us a chronicle more or less faithful, of passing events . . . without attempting to trace the course of events to their origin, to distinguish the causes which have led to success or to failure, or to examine into the influences which have, at different periods, rendered different countries powerful by sea."[8] Though Roosevelt would fail to attain every one of Laughton's lofty aspirations, he certainly carried the study of the War of 1812 to new heights as he attempted to sort out the contradictions among the most serious historians of the naval war: William James, James Fenimore Cooper, and George Emmons.

James had written extensively on 1812. A contemporary to the events, he authored several studies of the conflict before writing a multivolume history of the British navy in the Revolutionary and Napoleonic Wars, *The Naval History of Great Britain from the Declaration of War by France in 1793 to the Accession of George IV.*[9] It should be noted that when writing *The Naval War of 1812* Roosevelt appears to have only consulted James' multivolume history, which contains only a condensed description of the War of 1812, leading Andrew Lambert to argue that Roosevelt's critiques would have been less critical if he had considered the full breadth of

James' scholarship. The work Roosevelt did examine lacked the analysis he would have found in James' studies specific to the war.[10]

Roosevelt found James' *Naval History* schizophrenic. On the one hand, the detail and conclusions dealing with the British were in Roosevelt's opinion "invaluable . . . written with fullness and care," making the work, on that side, one that "ought to be consulted by every student of naval affairs." In fact, he asserted, "James is an invaluable assistant, from the diligence and painstaking care he shows, and the thoroughness and minuteness with which he goes into details." Yet on the other hand, Roosevelt cautioned, "I have all along insisted on, that any of James' unsupported statements about the Americans, whether respecting the tonnage of the ships or the courage of the crews, are not worth the paper they are written on." James, according to Roosevelt, was "unfortunately afflicted with a hatred toward the Americans that amounts to a mono-mania." One cannot, in Roosevelt's opinion, forget that James wrote "a piece of special pleading by a bitter and not over-scrupulous partisan."[11]

If William James provided the best British perspective of the conflict, Fenimore Cooper and George Emmons had written the leading American ones. Roosevelt, however, described Cooper's history as "much less of an authority than James'" and as having been "written without great regard for exactness." He attempted to compensate for Cooper's flaws in writing his own narrative history by taking advantage of the statistical facts and figures in Emmons' *The Navy of the United States*.[12]

Roosevelt's book received generally positive reviews.[13] One near contemporary explained, "On the whole we may allow that Mr. Roosevelt is relatively fair,—more fair not only than his own countrymen, but than our own James."[14] Some have asserted, however, that Roosevelt's critiques of James and Cooper were unfairly harsh. William Dudley has noted, "It is as though he felt the necessity to denigrate his predecessor [Cooper] in order to promote his own accomplishment."[15] Andrew Lambert admits that Roosevelt wrote a more balanced account than previous American writers but also contends that he was unfairly critical to James. After all, Roosevelt had adopted metrics similar to those James employed to compare the relative force of British and American warships. Lambert concludes, "While well written and based on extensive research, Roosevelt's book was no more objective than James's."[16]

Roosevelt claimed to have written an unbiased account of the war, but one must understand what he considered bias to be. History "should be written impartially," he explained, "if only from the narrowest motives. Without abating a jot from one's devotion to his country and flag, I think a history can be made just enough to warrant its being received as an authority equally among to Americans and Englishmen." Roosevelt made his patriotism clear throughout the text. References to the "cool, gritty American Jack" and assertions that "the American seaman was very patriotic" were not in his opinion signs of bias, and neither was his going out of the way to argue that "the 44's were thus true frigates. . . . That they were better than any other frigates was highly creditable to our ingenuity and national skill."[17] His text is unabashedly pro-American, but Roosevelt did not believe that to reflect bias.

Roosevelt thought that he could develop a balanced assessment through his overtly patriotic lens. The result was a contradiction. On the one hand, he took pains to make such statements as "the rules cut both ways" and "no one pretends that either navy was invincible; the question is, which side averaged best?" On the other hand, consider several claims about the 1 June 1813 battle between HMS *Shannon* and the frigate *Chesapeake*. Though he described the American frigate as having been unprepared for the action, "There can be no doubt that the *Chesapeake* . . . would have been an overmatch for the *Guerriere, Macedonian,* or *Java*." Roosevelt believed that any of the three frigates the British lost in 1812 would have suffered defeat in an encounter with the *Chesapeake*. He also maintained that had the *Chesapeake* been at sea and the crew trained for seven weeks, it would probably have triumphed against the nearly seven years of operational experience the crew of the *Shannon* brought to the engagement. Likewise, one can detect clear disgust in his description of the 1813 action between the brig *Argus* and HMS *Pelican*, during which he clearly believed that the Americans had not fought to their limits. He points to comparable failings on the British side when HMS *Epervier* lost to the sloop of war *Peacock*, but not with a similar repugnance. Roosevelt, in sum, was not overtly anti-British but allowed his pro-American stance to be obvious. He even admitted, "Errors will probably be in favor of the American side."[18] Accepting British successes only grudgingly, he did all he could to explain results in the most positive light for the Americans.

The previous paragraphs have critiqued Roosevelt's bias through the lens of the early twenty-first century, not that of the late nineteenth. One recent authority has claimed that Roosevelt possessed both "intense American nationalism" and "a tempered Anglophilia." The result was "a substantial degree of objectivity toward the former enemy."[19] Contemporaries certainly noted Roosevelt's "fair-mindedness" and his "claims that he has endeavoured to make his history as impartial as possible."[20] One found it entirely acceptable that authors should revel in "the glories of one's own country"; "by all means," he thought, "let every man stand firm for his own people, and his father's house." The standards of the early 1880s were different, and certainly Roosevelt took greater pains than had Cooper and James to avoid unsubstantiated accusations.[21] Still, one relatively recent historian has described Roosevelt's writing as representing a standard "far from impartiality."[22]

Roosevelt found writing his naval history difficult, calling it "that favourite chateau-en-espagne of mine." It seemed like a lofty castle in a far-off land, or perhaps he even thought it an elusive aspiration. Elsewhere he lamented, "I have plenty of information now, but can't get it into words; I am afraid it is too big a task for me. I wonder if I won't find everything in life too big for my abilities."[23] Sorting through the contradictions among previous historians proved troublesome: "I have had to deal with a mass of confused and contradictory testimony, which it has sometimes been quite impossible to reconcile." Previous authors had not, in Roosevelt's opinion, done due diligence in their research, and he found it hard to disentangle their stories or even determine the validity of their individual arguments: "Often I have had simply to balance probabilities, and choose between two sets of figures, aware that, whichever I chose, much could be said against the choice."[24]

One way to avoid inaccuracies was to consult original sources. He gained access to the records of the U.S. Navy Department, including letters from officers, but, as he was aware, his documentation from the British side was weaker. He had the official dispatches printed in the *London Gazette* and the *Naval Chronicle*, but such archival material as reports from British commanders, court-martial records, ships' logs, and muster rolls proved elusive.[25]

Roosevelt continued to work on the manuscript while attending law school. In May 1881 he confided to his diary, "I spend most of my spare time in the Astor Library on my 'Naval History.'" Even at home, he had difficulty extracting himself from the project. One friend would recall, "He finished his *Naval History* . . . heedless of dinner engagements and the flight of time." In October 1881, Roosevelt claimed, "Am working fairly at my law, hard at politics, and hardest of all at my book ('Naval History') which I expect to publish this winter." Toward the end, Roosevelt burned the midnight oil to bring the book to completion. On 3 December 1881, he sent the finished manuscript to his publisher.[26]

By 1883, *Naval History* had entered its third edition and had even become a college text. One reviewer described it as "cool and impartial, and in some respects the most intrepid account that has yet appeared of the naval actions of the war of 1812." Yet this reviewer also found the text "calm almost to coldness."[27] This is, in some respects, true. Roosevelt often gave more space to assessing why the actual combats resulted as they did and determining relative forces of ships than to recounting the story of the engagements. Moreover, his youth betrayed him. He was, as some have contended, "combative."[28] He argued points with what amounts to the sheer brute force of massed detail. *The Naval War of 1812* is the product of an immature historian convinced of—and determined to prove—the justness of his argument.

Visceral denunciation of how previous historians had assessed the ship-on-ship battles drove his argument. This resulted in detailed assessments of those combats, with a particular emphasis on the 1812 duels between forty-four-gun American frigates and British thirty-eight-gun frigates: between the *Constitution* and HMS *Guerriere* in August, the *United States* and HMS *Macedonian* in October, and the *Constitution* and HMS *Java* in December. Of one of the American victors Roosevelt concluded, "It was not surprising that she should win, but it was surprising that she should win with ease and impunity." Or as he explained elsewhere in his description of the battle between the *Constitution* and *Guerriere,* "The disparity of force, 10 to 7, is not enough to account for the disparity of execution, 10 to 2." How could one explain this conundrum? Roosevelt claimed that previous American writers had focused on the superior skill and gunnery while British authors had pointed to the size of the American warships. Neither of these factors alone, according to Roosevelt, was sufficient to account for the outcome: the cumulative effects of both explain the result.[29]

The emphasis placed upon the individual ship-on-ship actions had implications for the structure of the book. Rather than a flowing narrative, it often seems episodic, comprising a series of vignettes detailing each major action. Though the entire book cannot be so characterized, lengthy expositions certainly fracture the narrative, particularly describing oceanic operations. Roosevelt is not unique in this approach. It follows the footsteps of such previous historians as Cooper and, particularly, James. Roosevelt, it could be argued, brought this methodology to its pinnacle.

The Royal Navy from the Earliest Times to the Present

A bit more than a decade after the publication of *The Naval War of 1812,* Roosevelt reengaged the subject. The work that resulted is less often consulted than the original but demonstrates far greater maturity. Not a vehicle for significant new research, the second publication is a distillation of the first. It constitutes one long chapter in the sixth volume of *The Royal Navy: A History from the Earliest Times to the Present,* edited by William Laird Clowes.[30] In *The Naval War of 1812,* Clowes explained editorially, "Theodore Roosevelt dealt with the struggle from the exclusively American point of view." In the new volume, Clowes contended, "He has now attacked the subject from the more purely critical side; and I do not hesitate to say that he has produced a piece of work which, while fair-minded and generous to a degree, is as remarkable for its analytical insight as for its impartial plain speaking."[31] Gone are the patriotic claims, the statistics piled on statistics. Roosevelt's critiques of William James all but disappear: the latter's name appears once in the actual text, and only one footnote contains what borders on a disparaging comment.[32] Most mentions in the notes are citations, and this time he had consulted one of James' specific accounts of 1812 in addition to his multivolume history.[33]

Prior to publication, some apprehension existed about an American contributing to a history of the Royal Navy.[34] Reviews were, however, quite positive. One called it a "condensation" of the first book, "mainly accomplished by the omission of nearly all the controversial matter and by eliminating unimportant details." This reviewer asserted, "In many places, the phraseology is identical and the narrative has actually become more readable by compression."[35] Another reviewer found that the new chapter "shows a much firmer grasp of the points at issue, a clearer insight into the whole business, than his former work[;] . . . he writes from the standpoint of scientific neutrality which conveys no hint of his nationality."[36]

In Clowes' volume, Roosevelt came closer to narrating the naval war, a shift that some reviewers ascribed to Alfred Thayer Mahan's influence.[37] By this time, Roosevelt had discussed naval issues with Mahan and had written reviews of *The Influence of Sea Power upon History* and *The Influence of Sea Power upon the French Revolution and Empire*.[38] Roosevelt's contribution to Clowes echoed one of Mahan's principal theses: "It was the Navy of Britain, it was the British sea power, which threw the deciding weight into the contest."[39] Though it is always difficult to determine the influence of one author on another, it is clear that this time Roosevelt addressed naval power more strategically. If that quality was not a direct inheritance from Mahan, it was a benefit of Mahan's overall influence on the field of naval affairs.

One minor critique of the work dealt with the hurried prose in its latter part.[40] This is unsurprising, for when Roosevelt wrote it, he was under a rising political star. Clowes invited Roosevelt to write the history when he was president of the Board of Police Commissioners of New York; he completed most of the first draft during this period. He submitted the chapter after becoming Assistant Secretary of the Navy.[41] Perhaps these responsibilities left him too little room for revision. Another reviewer claimed, "The work is repetitious to a degree almost vexatious."[42] Roosevelt does repeat variations of several arguments; however, these seem to have been intended. This contributed chapter signaled agendas and underscored lessons more overtly than his earlier book. He was no longer a student in his early twenties: he now had years of public service behind him. His latest appointment as Assistant Secretary of the Navy brought relevance to his argument. As Roosevelt pointed out about his new paper, "It contains a pretty strong plea for a powerful navy, and the ability of handling that navy effectively when necessary."[43]

The Agenda: Naval Preparedness

Roosevelt wrote with a purpose beyond mere narration of the history of 1812. He wished to influence the naval, and even the national, policy of the United States.[44] Many years later, he claimed, "I have always taken the interest in the navy which every good American ought to take."[45] As Mark Shulman writes, "He did not pretend that he was writing history for any other age than his own, and consequently made quite explicit what he expected his readers to learn."[46] Roosevelt did not aim at instilling mere soothing patriotic thoughts; rather, he asked his countrymen to do some soul-searching. He asserted, "There are always men who consider it unpatriotic to tell the truth, if the truth is not very flattering; but, aside from the morality of the case, we never can learn how to produce a certain effect unless we know rightly what the causes were that produced a similar effect in past times."[47] He used the War of 1812 to project contemporary lessons.

To understand the thrust of his lessons, let us consider one of Roosevelt's stillborn projects: a companion to his naval history on War of 1812 land operations. The reason he decided against it is telling: "A short examination showed that these operations were hardly worth serious study. They teach nothing new." The land war only offered the age-old story of what occurs when a government refuses to spend adequate funds to prepare for hostilities. Men are not trained, and weapons are not procured, series of military reverses results, and then years of making good at great cost in blood and treasure what a government should have done beforehand. Even so, Roosevelt in the early 1880s admitted, "This might be a lesson worth dwelling on did it have any practical bearing on the issues of the present day; but it has none, as far as the army is concerned." The land war failed to provide meaningful contemporary lessons. Continental land threats had all but disappeared; Native American power had been broken; the empire of Spain had given way to the weaker state of Mexico; and the British in Canada posed less of a threat than they once had. Roosevelt concluded, "There is now no cause for our keeping up a large army; while, on the contrary, the necessity for an efficient navy is so evident that only our almost incredible short-sightedness prevents our at once preparing one."[48]

That impassioned plea for preparation guided *The Naval War of 1812*. In the aftermath of the Civil War, the U.S. Navy had atrophied toward uselessness, as old vessels wore out and new ones were unable to defeat modern opponents.[49] Roosevelt maintained, "The subject merits a closer scrutiny than it has received." Analysis of American naval power during the War of 1812 pointed to the source of failure of the United States of the early 1880s: "I am not alluding to the personnel, which still remains excellent; but, whereas we now have a large number of worthless vessels, standing very low down in their respective classes, we then possessed a few vessels, each unsurpassed by any foreign ship of her class." He went so far as to suggest that the United States scrap its entire navy and in its place build half a dozen state-of-the-art warships.[50]

Roosevelt only had to cite the gunboats procured during the Jefferson administration to provide a telling contrast with the oceanic navy of the War of 1812: "The failure of the gun-boats ought to have taught the lesson (though it did not) that too great an economy in providing the means of defence may prove very expensive in the end, and that good officers and men are powerless when embarked in worthless vessels." Roosevelt entreated Americans of the 1880s to avoid repeating Jefferson's gunboat navy, and instead, the United States should build an oceanic navy similar to the one in which ships like the *Constitution, United States*, and *Wasp* demonstrated their superiority. Roosevelt argued for "a small but highly effective force, the ships well built, manned by thoroughly trained men, and commanded by able and experienced officers."[51]

The most important lesson presented by Roosevelt in *The Naval War of 1812* entailed "the value of efficient ships and, above all, of efficient men in them. Had we only possessed the miserable gunboats, our men could have done nothing; had we not possessed good men, the heavy frigate would have availed us little. Poor ships and impotent artillery had lost the Dutch almost their entire Navy; fine ships and heavy cannons had not saved the French and Spanish from the like fate. We owed our success to putting sailors even better than the Dutch on ships even finer than those built by the two Latin seaboard powers."[52] The War of 1812 demonstrated that even a small navy, state of the art and well trained, can produce outsized strategic effects.

This conclusion became a recurring message in Roosevelt's writings. His 1888 biography of the early American statesman Gouverneur Morris held that "he never showed greater wisdom than in his views about our navy; and his party, the federalists, started to give us one; but it had hardly been begun before the Jeffersonians came into power, and, with singular foolishness, stopped the work."[53] Roosevelt admonished Thomas Jefferson and James Madison for failing to nurture the U.S. Navy, leaving the country unprepared for war in 1812. Almost a decade later, Roosevelt, as Assistant Secretary of the Navy, could translate his beliefs on naval preparedness into action. He did not forget the second war between Britain and America: "The war of 1812 showed clearly the vital benefits conferred upon the nation by the little Navy which it possessed, and the terrible loss and damage caused by the fact that in size this Navy was but a small fraction of what it should have been."[54] The War of 1812 offered a dual lesson: what a well-trained navy could accomplish and the folly of not providing it with adequate resources.

It was at about this time that Roosevelt revisited the topic in Clowes' multivolume history of the Royal Navy. Roosevelt became even more outspoken. In the War of 1812 he saw conundrums similar to those he faced daily as assistant secretary. Contemporary naval affairs allowed him to appreciate that a warship is "so delicate and complicated that ample opportunity must be given, not merely to produce it, but to learn to use it right. This was true in the days of the American and French Revolutions; it is infinitely truer now." However, he asserted, "It is a very old truth, though one which many legislatures seem slow to learn, that no courage and skill on the part of sea-officers can atone for insufficiency in the number, and inefficiency in the quality, of ships." The Jefferson and Madison administrations had failed to procure an adequate fleet at a time when, Roosevelt believed, "there was but one possible way by which to gain and keep the respect of either France or Britain: that was by the possession of power, and the readiness to use it if necessary; and power in this case meant a formidable fighting navy." He even claimed, "Had America possessed a fleet of twenty ships of the line, her sailors could have plied their trade unmolested; and the three years of war, with the loss of blood and money, would have been avoided."[55] One cannot help but think that Roosevelt pondered how a fleet of twenty American battleships at the dawn of the twentieth century could have influenced hemispheric and even global affairs.

The War of 1812 left an indelible mark on Roosevelt. Even after his presidency, he continued to reflect on it, lamenting, "I suppose the United States will always be unready for war, and in consequence will always be exposed to great expense, and the possibility of the gravest calamity, when the Nation goes to war. This is not a new thing. Americans learn only from catastrophes and not from experience."[56]

Who deserved fault for failure to prepare for war in 1812? Roosevelt's first book often avoided assigning guilt, but when Roosevelt did issue blame, he aimed it at Jefferson and Madison. A decade later he continued to fault those who had been in the highest positions.[57] However, he also blamed the American people: "Had Jefferson and the other leaders of popular opinion been wiser and firmer men, they could have led the people to make better preparations, but the people themselves did not desire wiser or better leadership." Roosevelt developed contemporary analogies: "Men who get discouraged by the attitude of latter-day politicians may draw some hope and comfort from the reflection that the nation actually lived through the experiment of trying Jefferson's ideas." He then added to his critique of the American people, "It is the fashion to speak of the people as misrepresented by the politicians, but in this case certainly the people deserved just the government they had." Again, he linked his argument to the present: "There are plenty of philanthropists and politicians in

America of today who show the same timid, short-sighted folly, and supine indifference to national honour."[58]

In his contribution to Clowes' volume, Roosevelt still wrote for the United States, but for a very different America. It appeared after the United States had defeated Spain in 1898, and the U.S. Navy was no longer a collection of obsolete and useless warships. Yet Roosevelt did not wish the American people to become complacent. In the American victories in ship-on-ship battles during 1812 and early 1813 Roosevelt noted the following lesson: "The British government had paid dearly for its contemptuous disregard of the power of the United States at sea. It was utterly unprepared for the skill and energy shown by the Americans." Elsewhere he added, "The successes of the American cruisers show that no power can afford to lull itself to sleep by the dream of invincibility." Though he now used Britain as the example, his argument remained the same: "A nation should see that its ships are the best, and that the men are trained to the highest point of efficiency."[59]

Proper and adequate preparation is an imperative that leaders regardless of country must learn: "This is much like telling a prize-fighter that he needs to not train because he has such an excellent constitution that he may draw on it to make good defects in his preparation for the ring." Roosevelt then brought the reader back to naval affairs: "The truth seems to be that, in naval matters especially, nothing can supply the lack of adequate preparation and training before the outbreak of war. The lead which is lost at the beginning cannot be regained save by superhuman effort, and after enormous waste of strength."[60] Years later, after his presidency, he critiqued the American side of the war along the same lines: "My criticism of the United States in 1812 is heavy but not because she went to war with England; it is because she did not prepare effectively in advance for war and wage it effectively."[61]

The Lessons

"Something more than bravery," Roosevelt argued, "is needed before a leader can be really called great." He contrasted Capt. James Lawrence's decisions in command of the *Chesapeake* in its 1 June 1813 battle against the *Shannon* with Commo. Isaac Chauncey's actions leading the American squadron on Lake Ontario: "A little less rashness would have saved Lawrence's life and his frigate, while a little more audacity on one occasion would have made Commodore Chauncey famous for ever." Or as Roosevelt asked rhetorically, "Did Chauncey use his force to the best advantage? And it cannot be said that he did."[62] Unlike previous American historians of the War of 1812, Roosevelt critiqued American leaders on their individual merits. He blamed Lawrence's poor decisions for the loss of the *Chesapeake*. He refused to make excuses, because to do so would prevent future leaders from fully understanding what could be learned. Leaders needed to be more than courageous: they needed the knowledge of principles guiding naval warfare if they were to employ their forces most effectively.

Roosevelt drew different lessons from the operations on the open ocean and those on the freshwater lakes between the United States and British Canada. On the ocean, the two countries employed warships they had possessed at the start of hostilities. Both sides went into the war with navies, and each had to determine how to employ its forces to the best effect. On the lakes, neither side possessed an adequate fleet at the outset: warfare there became "a work as much of creating as of using a navy."[63] Accordingly, there were fundamental differences between the two theaters. On the lakes, the two sides vied for superiority: the result of a battle "might, and did, determine the success or failure of military operations the outcome of which would have great weight upon the result of the war; whereas, on the ocean, no success which the American warships could win could possibly have any other than a moral effect."[64] That contrast allowed Roosevelt greater breadth in developing lessons. On the lakes, he could write about a traditional naval campaign involving two similar naval forces: this was a symmetrical fight. On the oceans, Roosevelt could assess the possibilities of a qualitatively adept navy fighting a quantitatively superior foe.

First the lakes: Roosevelt saw the conflict there as a naval war in microcosm. First came preparation, then operations that had decisive bearing on the outcome. In his earlier, book-length work, Roosevelt asserted that "command of the lakes" was the critical factor.[65] His use of the term in 1882 prefigured significant discussion among turn-of-the-century naval commentators about "command of the sea."[66] Like Mahan, who used "command of the sea" and "control of the sea" interchangeably, Roosevelt meant by "control of the lake" the same as "command of the lake."[67] Though Roosevelt never defined the latter, the implication was clear: the side that could attain command would garner significant strategic advantage by what command allowed the side possessing it to accomplish. For Britian's part, Roosevelt assessed, "The failure of the British to obtain control of the lakes rendered it impossible to expect any decisive triumph of British arms. Indeed, in the War of 1812, the control of the lakes was the determining factor in the situation on the Canadian border."[68]

Roosevelt realized, however, that command of the lakes was not an end in itself but a necessary prerequisite for success in the theater. Roosevelt explained that "the real purpose was to enable Canada to be successfully invaded, or to assist in repelling an invasion of the United States." That is, the naval campaign was not the main effort but a necessary component of the land campaign, and its role "was not, except incidentally, 'the destruction of the enemy's fleet.'" Instead, it was

> getting the control of the lake, by which invaluable assistance could be rendered to the Army. The most thorough way of accomplishing this, of course, was by destroying the enemy's squadron; but it could also be done by building ships too powerful for him to face, or by beating him in some engagement which, although not destroying his fleet, would force him to go into port. If one side was stronger, then the weaker party by skilful manœuvring might baffle the foe, and rest satisfied by keeping the sovereignty of the lake disputed; for, as long as one squadron was not undisputed master it could not be of much assistance in transporting troops, attacking forts, or otherwise helping the military.[69]

This quote finds Roosevelt at his theoretical best. By outlining possible courses of action on the lakes, he prefigured critical arguments put forward by the naval theorists of the next two or even three decades, including Alfred T. Mahan, Julian S. Corbett, and Philip H. Colomb. For example, the ideas he expressed about a weaker fleet maneuvering to dispute command of the lakes clearly align with later arguments about "a fleet in being" put forward by several commentators, including Mahan and Corbett.[70] Roosevelt's statements detailing the relationship between maritime and land operations as well as the conundrums of bringing an enemy to battle presuppose similar arguments in Corbett's 1911 masterpiece, *Some Principles of Maritime Strategy*. Roosevelt's assessment of the war on the lakes demonstrates a theoretical understanding of naval warfare far in advance of what might be expected of authors in their early twenties.

If Roosevelt's arguments on naval operations on the lakes are forward-looking and detailed, those on British joint operations along America's eastern seaboard demonstrate incomplete understanding. In his book, Roosevelt showed little interest in their effects, because in his mind "they had very little to do with our navy."[71] This point underscores his agenda in that work: that there was little need to address efforts in which, or against which, the U.S. Navy did not play an integral role. Roosevelt had trouble seeing past the brutality with which the British conducted these operations to assess their strategic effects. In his contribution to Clowes' volume, Roosevelt's views moderated. There he could recognize, "So long as the British possessed absolute control of the sea, they could take the offensive whenever and wherever they wished and could choose their own point of attack, while the American government never knew what point to defend." That is, the initiative lay with the British, albeit "there is room for question as to whether the comparatively trifling loss inflicted on the Americans did much beyond irritating them. It certainly failed to cow them, though equally certainly it failed to rouse them to effective resistance."[72] Even so, and with the exception of the New Orleans campaign, Roosevelt considered joint operations along the American oceanic frontier only hastily, because the lessons arising there were not central to his overall argument.

Turning to oceanic operations, Roosevelt focused in *The Naval War of 1812* on the contest between the U.S. Navy and Britain's Royal Navy while privateers received a fraction of the attention. This emphasis fit into a broader discussion about the future of the U.S. Navy: Should its offensive function in war be to attack commerce or to engage an enemy battle fleet?[73] Roosevelt argued for the latter, and as a result, privateers drift into the background. He acknowledged that "the privateers were of incalculable benefit to us, and inflicted enormous damage on the foe." He, however, failed to provide sufficient evidence in support of the previous statement. Instead, he demonstrated "in fighting they suffered under the same disadvantages as other irregular forces; they were utterly unreliable. A really brilliant victory would be followed by a most extraordinary defeat."[74] Several years later, he labeled irregular forces "that weakest of all weak reeds," contrasting them sharply with regular forces, including the U.S. Navy in the War of 1812.[75]

In the years between Roosevelt's two publications on 1812, commerce raiding remained a divisive topic. Some considered it a potentially decisive means of war, while others denied that such operations could by themselves produce war-winning results. Roosevelt remained wedded to the latter camp, with the proviso that "their history does teach that very much can be accomplished by commerce destroying, if more directly efficient methods cannot be used." Though Roosevelt continued to stress the superiority of regular fleets, he saw the value privateers had in their absence: "Commerce destroying was annoying and vexatious, and it might prove sufficiently serious to incline an already disheartened combatant to peace; but no amount of destruction of commerce could cripple a thoroughly resolute antagonist, nor, giving heart to the nation which inflicted the loss, make it thrill with that warlike pride and determination to conquer which do so much toward winning victory."[76]

Roosevelt believed that possession of a powerful fighting fleet would have improved America's strategic position in the years before 1812 and perhaps even averted the war. He pondered America's strategic position at the dawn of the twentieth century in similar terms: "The substitution of the government commerce destroyers for the privateer would have done some good, but it could not have accomplished anything decisive. What was needed was the substitution of all these commerce destroyers with a great fighting fleet."[77]

In *The Naval War of 1812*, Roosevelt claimed an overall American victory in terms of "the comparative honor gained": "The British navy, numbering at the outset a thousand cruisers, had accomplished less than the Americans, which numbered but a dozen."[78] Roosevelt saw the war in purely maritime terms, asserting that "the wrongs inflicted on our seafaring countrymen by their impressment into foreign ships formed the main cause of the war." To Roosevelt, then, this was a naval war. Though admittedly the maritime questions upon which the Americans declared war were not settled in their favor, "or even alluded to, in the treaty of peace, the immense increase of reputation that the navy acquired during the war practically decided both points [i.e., impressment and neutral rights] in our favor." He explained, "The victories kept up the spirits of the people, cast down by the defeats on land; practically decided in favor of the Americans the chief question in dispute—Great Britain's right of search and impressment—and gave the navy, and thereby the country, a world-wide reputation."[79] The War of 1812, then, was a moral victory for the United States. History books not only document the past but become time capsules reflecting the mood of the ages in which they are written. In 1882, Roosevelt sought to sell the projected revival of the U.S. Navy to his domestic audience by showcasing just what it had accomplished against daunting odds.

Over time Roosevelt's audience evolved, and his arguments altered accordingly. The moral victory he espoused in *The Naval War of 1812* no longer matched his agenda by the late 1890s. Roosevelt now declared, "This navy was too small to do anything except win glory. It lacked the power to harm anything but British pride." If moral victory was enough in 1882, it was not sufficient by the turn of the century. Roosevelt remained focused on America, the question before him was no longer of reviving the U.S. Navy but of the type of navy the United States should possess. Roosevelt made it clear that "the lesson [history] teaches must not be misread. . . . The commerce-destroyers of America did their part toward making the war of 1812 a draw; but the great fighting fleets of England came near making the war a disastrous defeat for the United States."[80]

Conclusion

By the turn of the twentieth century, Roosevelt had developed a complex understanding of the utility of war—that "the two prime objects to be attained in successful warfare are to cripple the antagonist and to give heart and confidence to one's own side." The Americans succeeded at the latter but only by virtue of superior skill and instruments of war. They had been "powerless to inflict appreciable damage to the colossal sea might of England."[81] The Americans had chosen to meet raw British power but had prepared poorly. One does not have to read far between the lines to see that Roosevelt was commending this lesson to the Americans of his own day.

Roosevelt used the War of 1812 to advocate expansion of the U.S. Navy. For more than thirty years, his basic message from that war remained constant: the United States had prepared poorly. More effective naval preparation could very well have averted hostilities, and it would have entailed small cost in comparison to the blood and treasure expended between 1812 and 1815. If war had still proved unavoidable, a larger, better prepared navy would have enabled the United States to weather hostilities more effectively. Preparation remained for him a relevant lesson and guiding agenda for the future. As a young student in his early twenties, he voiced its importance. The specifics evolved over the following decades, but preparedness remained essential. In the opening days of World War I, well before America's entry, he reiterated, "Utter and complete lack of preparation on our part did not prevent our entering into war with Great Britain in 1812. . . . It merely exposed us to humiliation and disaster."[82] Roosevelt's impassioned argument, however, was not blind; he based his contentions on a deep understanding of naval warfare, one that was very much in line with leading turn-of-the-century naval authorities, some of whose conceptual frameworks he had actually anticipated. No mere chronicler of the past, Roosevelt attempted to apply his knowledge to political life. His work on the War of 1812 prepared him particularly well to argue for a modern, expanded U.S. Navy.

Notes

1. Theodore Roosevelt, *An Autobiography* (New York: Macmillan, 1913), 27.
2. Ferdinand C. Iglehart, *Theodore Roosevelt: The Man as I Knew Him* (New York: Christian Herald, 1919), 121–22. See also Henry J. Hendrix, "Roosevelt's Naval Thinking before Mahan," in *Theodore Roosevelt, the U.S. Navy, and the Spanish-American War*, ed. Edward J. Marolda (New York: Palgrave, 2001), 50–51.

3. Roosevelt, *Autobiography*, 15–16.

4. Theodore Roosevelt, *The Naval War of 1812*, 3rd ed. (New York: G. P. Putnam's Sons, 1882; repr. Knickerbocker, 1920), vii. Roosevelt also thanked Adolf Mensing, a German naval officer who had recently married a New Yorker.

5. Iglehart, *Theodore Roosevelt*, 122.

6. Richard W. Turk, *The Ambiguous Relationship: Theodore Roosevelt and Alfred Thayer Mahan* (New York: Greenwood, 1987), 13. There is also a question about the relationship of this work to Roosevelt's thesis. Henry J. Hendrix claims that Roosevelt "bypassed traditional subjects (and the chance for 'distinction') and instead addressed the subject that had fascinated him since childhood: the sea and its impact on national power" [*Theodore Roosevelt's Naval Diplomacy: The U.S. Navy and the Birth of the American Century* (Annapolis, Md.: Naval Institute Press, 2009), 4]. William S. Dudley asserts that Roosevelt never wrote a thesis ["Naval Historians and the War of 1812," *Naval History* (Spring 1990), 54]. Conversely, Edmund Morris has it that Roosevelt titled his thesis "Practicability of Giving Man and Woman Equal Rights" [*The Rise of Theodore Roosevelt* (New York: Coward, McCann and Geoghegan, 1979), 128].

7. Roosevelt, *Naval War of 1812*, iii, iv.

8. John Knox Laughton, "The Scientific Study of Naval History," *Royal United Service Institution* 18 (1875): 509. Laughton had first presented a paper on this subject in 1874.

9. In 1816, James published a pamphlet titled *An Inquiry into the Merits of the Principal Actions between Great Britain and the United States*. He expanded the pamphlet into a book, *Naval Occurrences of the War of 1812: A Full and Correct Account of the Naval War between Great Britain and the United States of America, 1812–1815*. He then developed a yet broader study of the war, *A Full and Correct Account of the Military Occurrences of the Late War between Great Britain and the United States of America*. Later, he wrote the six-volume *The Naval History of Great Britain from the Declaration of War by France in 1793 to the Accession of George IV* (repr. London: Macmillan, 1902).

10. Andrew Lambert, introduction to William James, *Naval Occurrences of the War of 1812* (repr. London: Conway Maritime, 2004), v.

11. Roosevelt, *Naval War of 1812*, iv, 14, 333.

12. J. Fenimore Cooper, *History of the Navy of the United States of America*, 3rd ed., 2 vols. (Cooperstown, N.Y.: H. & E. Phinny, 1847); George E. Emmons, *The Navy of the United States, from the Commencement, 1775 to 1853* (Washington, D.C.: Gideon, 1850); Roosevelt, *Naval War of 1812*, iv.

13. The several examples include *Journal of the Military Service Institution of the United States* 6 (December 1885): 410; *Westminster Review* 62 (July–October 1882): 563; and *Harper's New Monthly Magazine* 65 (1882): 964.

14. "An American Historian of the British Navy," *Macmillan's Magazine* 78 (May 1898): 15.

15. Dudley, "Naval Historians," 54.

16. Lambert, introduction to James, *Naval Occurrences*, v.

17. Roosevelt, *Naval War of 1812*, v, 32–33, 57.

18. Roosevelt, *Naval War of 1812*, v, 190–93, 208–10, 212, 310, 314–15.

19. Michael J. Crawford, "The Lasting Influence of Theodore Roosevelt's War of 1812," *International Journal of Naval History* 1 (April 2002).

20. Reviews in *Journal of the Military Service Institution of the United States* 6 (December 1885): 410, and *Westminster Review* 62 (July–October 1882): 563.

21. "American Historian of the British Navy," 14. Roosevelt notes this himself; see *Naval War of 1812*, 437.

22. Mark R. Shulman, "The Emergence of American Sea Power: Politics and the Creation of a U.S. Naval Strategy, 1882–1893" (Ph.D. diss., University of California at Berkeley, 1990), 12.

23. TR to Anna Roosevelt, 21 August 1881, in *The Letters of Theodore Roosevelt*, ed. Elting E. Morison (Cambridge, Mass.: Harvard University Press, 1951–1954), 1:50.

24. Roosevelt, *Naval War of 1812*, 520.

25. TR to Anna Roosevelt, 21 August 1881, *Letters of Theodore Roosevelt*, 1:50; Roosevelt, *Naval War of 1812*, vi.

26. Diary, 2 May, 17 October, 3 December 1881, Theodore Roosevelt Papers, Library of Congress, Washington, D.C., reel 430, series 8, vol. 4; Owen Wister, *Roosevelt: Story of a Friendship, 1880–1919* (New York: Macmillan, 1930), 24.

27. Book review, *Harper's New Monthly Magazine* 65 (1882): 964.

28. Dudley, "Naval Historians," 54; Turk, *Ambiguous Relationship*, 64.

29. Roosevelt, *Naval War of 1812*, 58, 60, 96, 114.

30. Theodore Roosevelt, "The War with the United States, 1812–15," in *The Royal Navy: A History from the Earliest Times to the Present*, ed. William Laird Clowes (London: Sampson Low, Marston, 1901), 6:1–180.

31. Clowes, editorial note in *Royal Navy*, 6:vi.

32. Roosevelt, "War with the United States," 6:25n, 166.

33. Roosevelt's citations indicate that he consulted two books by James: *Naval Occurrences of the War of 1812* and the multivolume *Naval History of Great Britain*.

34. "American Historian of the British Navy" and "A Letter to the Editor," *Macmillan's Magazine* 78 (May and July 1898): 13–14, 240.

35. Edward Cruikshank, review of Roosevelt's chapter in Clowes in *Review of Historical Publications Relating to Canada*, ed. George Wrong and H. H. Langton (Toronto: University of Toronto, 1902), 6:54.

36. Review of Clowes, in *The Athenaeum*, no. 3870 (28 December 1901): 863.

37. Review of Clowes, in *The Athenaeum*; Cruikshank, review, 54.

38. Roosevelt's review of *The Influence of Sea Power upon History*, in *Atlantic Monthly* 66 (October 1890): 563–67; Roosevelt's review of *The Influence of Sea Power upon History* and *The Influence of Sea Power upon the French Revolution and Empire*, in *Political Science Quarterly* 9 (March 1894): 171–73.

39. Roosevelt, "War with the United States," 6:3. This is essentially the thesis of Mahan's *The Influence of Sea Power upon the French Revolution and Empire, 1793–1812*.

40. Cruikshank, review, 55.

41. TR to Lodge, 17 March 1897, in *Selections from the Correspondence of Theodore Roosevelt and Henry Cabot Lodge, 1884–1918* (New York: Charles Scribner's Sons, 1925), 1:255; Clowes, editorial note in *Royal Navy*, 6:vi. Roosevelt's chapter was published after he became president of the United States.

42. Wallace Rick, "Navies, British and American," review of Roosevelt's chapter in Clowes, in *The Dial*, 1 May 1904, 292.

43. TR to Lodge, 17 March 1897, *Correspondence of Roosevelt and Lodge*, 1:255.

44. Hendrix, *Theodore Roosevelt's Naval Diplomacy*, 4, 7–8; Turk, *Ambiguous Relationship*, 63–64.

45. Roosevelt, *Autobiography*, 224.

46. Shulman, "Emergence of American Sea Power," 13.

47. Roosevelt, *Naval War of 1812*, 274–75.

48. Roosevelt, *Naval War of 1812*, ix, xxv.

49. Roosevelt, *Autobiography*, 224.

50. Roosevelt, *Naval War of 1812*, v, 135–36.

51. Roosevelt, *Naval War of 1812*, 10, 219.

52. Roosevelt, *Naval War of 1812*, 25.

53. Roosevelt, *Gouverneur Morris* (Boston: Houghton, Mifflin, 1888), 292.

54. Roosevelt, introduction to *American Naval Policy as Outlined in Messages of the Presidents of the United Statesw from 1790 to the Present Day* (Washington, D.C.: Government Printing Office, 1897), 4.

55. Roosevelt, "War with the United States," 6:6, 66, 108–9.

56. Roosevelt, *Autobiography*, 223.

57. Roosevelt, *Naval War of 1812*, ix, xxiv, 455–56; Roosevelt, "War with the United States," 6:6; TR to William Peterfield Trent, 20 April 1897, *Letters of Theodore Roosevelt*, 1:600.

58. Roosevelt, "War with the United States," 6:7, 23, 25, 66.

59. Roosevelt, "War with the United States," 6:56, 177.

60. Roosevelt, "War with the United States," 6:66.

61. TR to Hugo Münsterberg, 3 October 1914, *Letters of Theodore Roosevelt*, 8:823.

62. Roosevelt, *Naval War of 1812*, 193, 249, 271.

63. Roosevelt, *Naval War of 1812*, 140.

64. Roosevelt, "War with the United States," 6:109.

65. Roosevelt, *Naval War of 1812*, 140. Roosevelt also used this term in *Naval War of 1812*, 155, 221, 227, 242, 282, 360, and in "War with the United States," 132.

66. Cyprian Bridge, *Sea-Power and Other Studies* (London: Smith, Elder, 1910), 73; Philip H. Colomb, *Naval Warfare: Its Ruling Principles and Practice Historically Treated*, 3rd ed. (London: W. H. Allen, 1899), 25–79, 107–202; Julian S. Corbett,

Some Principles of Maritime Strategy (London: Longmans, Green, 1911; repr. Annapolis, Md.: Naval Institute Press, 1988), 91–106; Spenser Wilkinson, *The Command of the Sea* (Westminster, U.K.: Archibald, Constable, 1894).

67. For example, Mahan used both terms to mean the same thing in a single sentence in *Sea Power in Its Relations to the War of 1812* (Boston: Little, Brown, 1905), 1:86. Roosevelt used "control of the lake" in *Naval War of 1812*, 228, 253, and in "War with the United States," 6:109, 117, 141.

68. Roosevelt, "War with the United States," 6:141.

69. Roosevelt, *Naval War of 1812*, 228, 365.

70. John B. Hattendorf, "The Idea of a Fleet in Being in Historical Perspective," *Naval War College Review* 67 (Winter 2018): 43–60; Alfred T. Mahan, *Lessons of the War with Spain and Other Articles* (Boston: Little, Brown, 1899), 76–77; Corbett, *Some Principles of Maritime Strategy*, 209–27.

71. Roosevelt, *Naval War of 1812*, 321.

72. Roosevelt, "War with the United States," 6:71, 142.

73. Robert Seager II, "Ten Years before Mahan: The Unofficial Case for the New Navy, 1880–1890," *Mississippi Valley Historical Review* 40 (December 1953): 498–99.

74. Roosevelt, *Naval War of 1812*, 416–17.

75. Roosevelt, *Gouverneur Morris*, 349.

76. Roosevelt, "War with the United States," 6:58, 73.

77. Roosevelt, "War with the United States," 6:74.

78. Roosevelt, *Naval War of 1812*, 444. Roosevelt is incorrect about a thousand British warships; the Royal Navy in 1812 possessed about half that number of operational warships. See Ships in Sea Service, 1 July 1812, ADM 8/100, The National Archives, Kew, United Kingdom.

79. Roosevelt, *Naval War of 1812*, 3, 6, 442.

80. Roosevelt, "War with the United States," 6:65, 158.

81. Roosevelt, "War with the United States," 6:58.

82. Theodore Roosevelt, *America and the World War* (New York: Charles Scribner's Sons, 1915), 180.

3

A TEMPEST IN THE
NAVY DEPARTMENT

Theodore Roosevelt as Assistant Secretary of the Navy

Edward J. Marolda

On 26 February 1898, Secretary of the Navy John D. Long recorded in his journal that the day before "the very devil seemed to possess" thirty-nine-year-old Assistant Secretary of the Navy Theodore Roosevelt. During Long's temporary absence from the office on the 25th, Roosevelt had issued preemptory orders "distributing ships; ordering ammunition . . . sending messages to Congress for immediate legislation, authorizing the enlistment of an unlimited number of seamen; and ordering guns from the Navy Yard at Washington to New York, with a view to arming auxiliary cruisers which are now in peaceful commercial pursuit." In short, Roosevelt had "gone at things like a bull in a china shop."[1] Of greater significance, the acting secretary had telegraphed Commo. George Dewey, commander of the Asiatic Squadron, to concentrate his naval forces at the British colony of Hong Kong and to keep sufficient coal supplies on hand. Roosevelt also emphasized that "in event of declaration of war [with] Spain, your duty will be to see that the Spanish Squadron does not leave the Asiatic Coast and then [take] offensive operations in [the] Philippine Islands."[2]

Long, then enduring sleepless nights and anxious because a war with Spain seemed unavoidable, heatedly expressed his disapproval of Roosevelt's actions, which the secretary considered "very near causing more of an explosion than happened to the *Maine*."[3] Long suggested that Roosevelt's initiative had had something to do with the fact that "his wife is very ill and his little boy is just recovering from a long and dangerous illness; so his natural nervousness is so much accentuated that I really think he is hardly fit to be entrusted with the responsibility of the Department at this critical time." Just the day before, Long had confided to his journal that he lacked "confidence in [Roosevelt's] good judgement and discretion" since "he goes off very impulsively."[4] Later in Roosevelt's tenure, Long recorded a further impression of his assistant's demeanor. When a visitor asked the secretary and his deputy for support in passing legislation, Long suggested, the episode revealed "one of Roosevelt's lacks. He shouts at the top of his voice, and wanders all over creation. The harangue fails to [get to] the point. His forte is his push. He lacks serenity of discussion."[5]

These sentiments, however, reflected the heat of the moment and Long's concern that observers would think Roosevelt, not he, ran the Navy Department. Indeed, historian John Hattendorf and his coauthors have observed that Roosevelt's action in Long's absence reflected a strong belief on the part of Roosevelt, Alfred Thayer Mahan, and the Naval War College faculty in "advance planning, detailed preparation, and rational consideration coupled with rapid execution in the event of war. . . . It was, in fact, the type of preparation that had long been advocated by a significant group of naval officers."[6] Ronald Spector agrees that rather than an act of rashness, Roosevelt's "sending of the cable was in line with the department's long-standing plans and preparations for war with Spain. Long neither disapproved the telegram nor made any attempt to rescind it."[7]

Roosevelt's bold action occurred little less than a year after he had made it known that he wanted to serve in the administration of President-elect William McKinley as Assistant Secretary of the Navy. Roosevelt did not personally petition McKinley for the job, declaring loftily, "I am not a supplicant."[8] As H. W. Brands has tellingly observed, however, "he simply deemed it prudent to leave the direct pleading on his behalf to others."[9]

Indeed, several especially prominent men, understanding Roosevelt's value as an advocate of sea power, were not reticent on his behalf. Senator

Henry Cabot Lodge of Massachusetts had long advocated a greater role for the United States on the global stage and the development of a more powerful and modern navy. The senator was Roosevelt's closest friend and confidant, and he worked hard to persuade McKinley that Roosevelt was the right man for the position. When Lodge conferred with McKinley before the new administration took power, the senator admitted he had "no right to ask a personal favor of you, but I do ask for Roosevelt" to be the Navy's assistant secretary. Lodge also helped Roosevelt's chances by dropping his support for a particular candidate for Secretary of the Navy when McKinley made it clear that he wanted Long in that position. Lodge and Long were on friendly terms, and that affinity helped Roosevelt's case.[10] Moreover, at the time Long was of the opinion that Roosevelt was the "best man" for the job.[11] Senator Redfield Proctor, Mayor W. L. Strong, and social reformist Jacob Riis, prominent leaders from New York, and men in powerful positions in Congress shared this appraisal.

It was not an easy sell. McKinley had a perception of Roosevelt as "always getting into rows with everybody," and he was "afraid [Roosevelt] is too pugnacious."[12] Roosevelt's reputation for warlike behavior and his association with noted American expansionists must also have given McKinley pause. In his inaugural address, McKinley promised to avoid "wars of conquest" and "the temptation of territorial aggression." He emphasized his belief that "peace is preferable to war in almost every contingency."[13]

Roosevelt expressed surprise, feigned or real, that McKinley had selected him to be assistant secretary: "I was astonished at the appointment; for I had come to look upon it as very improbable." Roosevelt credited Lodge's "untiring energy and devotion which put me in." He added, in a bit of overstatement, "Long really wanted me."[14] Later that month, Roosevelt remarked that "my chief, Secretary Long, is a perfect dear."[15] He went as far as to declare that Long "is one of the most high-minded, honorable and upright gentlemen I have ever had the good fortune to serve under."[16]

Soon after his appointment, Roosevelt assured Capt. Bowman McCalla, an already distinguished naval officer, "I have always taken a great interest in the Navy, and I sincerely hope that my connection with the service will be as beneficial to it as it will certainly be to me."[17] Indeed, that Roosevelt was the "best man" for the Navy Department position was amply supported by his many years of intellectual and emotional development. He came into office armed with a deep understanding of sea power and a passion for the history of the U.S. Navy. As Nathan Miller has concluded, "If any job had been made to order for Theodore, it was Assistant Secretary of the Navy."[18]

Rear Adm. Stephen B. Luce, founder of the Naval War College at Newport, Rhode Island, was especially taken with Roosevelt's *The Naval War of 1812*.[19] He made the book required reading for his students. Moreover, copies of the book were provided to every large ship in the fleet. Historian George Baer avers that the War of 1812 soon became "the determining event for sea-power navalists."[20] Luce also had a political agenda. He wrote Roosevelt that "the study you have given to the early history of the Navy will lead you to take some interest in a naval institution now struggling through the ills of infancy."[21] Brands has observed that "even more than most historians, Roosevelt went hunting in the past for trophies that would impress the present."[22]

Among the arguments for the necessity of the Naval War College were the war games held there. These evolutions impressed not only civilian and military leaders but the public as well as an innovative and progressive approach to understanding naval warfare. Later, Assistant Secretary of the Navy Roosevelt planned his visits to Newport "so as to see one of your big strategic games." Observers would later credit much of the Navy's success in the Spanish-American War to the war games, plans, and charts developed at the college during the previous decade.[23]

At Luce's invitation, Roosevelt visited the Naval War College, where he lectured on *The Naval War of 1812* and met Mahan, with whom he established a lifelong intellectual bond. Richard Turk has aptly remarked that "it was the common interest in naval history . . . that brought the two men together in 1888."[24] Kenneth Hagan has observed that "the Roosevelt-Mahan axis, around which would pivot so much of the history of the American battleship navy, had been formed."[25] Commenting on

Mahan's seminal *The Influence of Sea Power upon History*, published in 1890, Roosevelt with uncharacteristic modesty praised the author's understanding of naval history and its connection to overall history as being of a level "such as no one else has shown."[26] Indeed, Baer observed that Mahan advocated offensive sea control because it was based on "rationality" and "historical fact." Hence, "past and present experience permitted reliable forecasting." Mahan argued that "history was a better guide to strategy and operations than unpredictable, always-changing technology.... History yielded principles of war."[27] Shortly after Mahan's death in 1914, Roosevelt wrote that with regard to educating the public about a "true understanding of naval needs, Mahan stood alone. There was no one else in his class, or anywhere near it." He thought Mahan the "only great naval writer who also possessed in international matters the mind of a statesman of the first class."[28]

Before Mahan's ascent to international fame, however, Roosevelt himself had already developed a clear-eyed appreciation of the connection between the U.S. Navy's history and America's global maritime potential. John Gable is on the mark in his observation that "it seems accurate to speak of them as part of the same naval tradition, and to say that together they gave the U.S. Navy an intellectual dimension that has been crucial in shaping the character of successive generations of naval officers."[29] Spector finds that "Theodore Roosevelt and Henry Cabot Lodge seized every possible occasion to enlighten their fellow citizens on the mysteries of naval strategy" but that "it was Mahan's lectures and writings, with their literary polish, their air of historical scholarship and scientific exactitude, which made the 'science of naval warfare' credible to the public.... It was for this reason that Mahan's name was endlessly invoked even by those who had come earlier to the same conclusions."[30]

Roosevelt took action as Assistant Secretary of the Navy to ensure the Naval War College's continued existence as a center of strategic analysis and war planning. In the late summer of 1897, Capt. Francis W. Dickens, acting head of the Navy's Bureau of Navigation (to which the college reported), suggested that the college's staff be moved to Washington and combined with the Office of Naval Intelligence. He called the proposal a matter of efficiency, but in actuality he believed that naval officers should gain insight through operational experience at sea, not shore-bound study and analysis. With Roosevelt's strong encouragement, the college's president, Capt. Caspar Goodrich, published an article in which he compared the effort against the Naval War College to the earlier unsuccessful campaign to prevent the establishment of the Naval Academy: "There is nothing new under the sun [alluding to Dickens' proposal]. . . . Such things may be expected." He added, tongue in cheek, that a colleague "once knew a man to speak disrespectfully of the equator." Roosevelt and Goodrich effectively quashed Dickens' proposal.[31]

The Secretary of the Navy and his assistant had a complicated and occasionally rocky relationship. Long recognized that he needed Roosevelt's expertise on the U.S. Navy. Long was a Boston lawyer who had served in the early 1880s as the governor of Massachusetts and in Congress. He knew little of naval or military matters. The Navy secretary—who was derided by some historians as beyond his prime as a leader, in ill health, and somnolent but praised by others as a reasonably proficient administrator—gladly deferred to Roosevelt with regard to the nuts and bolts of running the service. Indeed, the secretary complained that Roosevelt "bores me with his plans of naval and military movement, and the necessity of having some scheme of attack arranged for instant execution in case of an emergency." Long quipped of Roosevelt that in an excess of enthusiasm "by tomorrow morning, he will have got half a dozen heads of [Navy] bureaus together and have spoiled twenty pages of good writing paper, and lain awake half the night."[32] Historian Anna Nelson's observation that Roosevelt "learned more about the inner workings of the U.S. Navy in one week than Long would learn throughout his entire term in office" is overstated but relevant.[33]

By the end of Roosevelt's time in the Navy Department, Long admitted that his assistant had "been of great use" and was a "man of unbounded energy and force, and thoroughly honest, which is the main thing."[34] While on occasion put off by Roosevelt's high-energy advocacy of matters beyond the scope of his responsibilities as assistant secretary, Long gave the younger man great latitude in the execution of his duties and adopted an indulgent, fatherly attitude toward him. The Navy secretary, who, one historian writes, "made no pretense of knowing the difference between a bowline from a bollard," did not see the necessity of such understanding given that "I have right at hand a man possessed with more knowledge than I could acquire."[35] He often acknowledged that Roosevelt possessed unique qualities of leadership and was destined for greatness.

A month after his fulsome praise for the secretary soon after taking up his Navy Department post, Roosevelt regretted that Long was inclined to "stop building up the Navy until our finances are better."[36] By June Roosevelt was expressing to Mahan his "most profound concern" that Long was "only lukewarm about building up our Navy. . . . He is against adding to our battleships." He urged Mahan to write to Long and explain to him "the vital need of more battleships now, and the vital need of continuity in our naval policy." Roosevelt wanted Mahan to argue that the matter was "a measure of peace and not of war."[37]

Nonetheless, Roosevelt seems to have continued genuinely to respect his boss and even expressed affection for him. At the end of his term in office, Roosevelt wrote to Long that he considered the secretary "a chief whose whole conduct in office . . . has been guided solely by resolute disinterestedness and single-minded devotion to the public interest. . . . I deeply appreciate, and am deeply touched by, the confidence you have put in me. [You are] one of the most high-minded and upright public servants it has ever been my good fortune to meet."[38]

One of Roosevelt's first acts as Assistant Secretary of the Navy, after "rooting about in a basement storage room of the State, War, and Navy Building" (now called the Eisenhower Executive Office Building, next to the White House), was to locate and appropriate for his own office the desk used during the Civil War by Gustavus V. Fox, the first Assistant Secretary of the Navy.[39]

Roosevelt, however, already had a much broader view of his responsibilities in government than helping administer the Navy Department. Two weeks after he took up his post, Roosevelt transmitted in a "personal and private" letter to Mahan his vision for the future of American foreign policy.[40] As many times before and after, he called for the outright annexation of Hawaii or the establishment of a protectorate over the islands. Anticipating the U.S. construction of a canal across Nicaragua to link the Atlantic and Pacific Oceans, Roosevelt pressed for American dominance of the Caribbean and ejection of Spanish influence from the region. He specifically advocated ending Spain's sovereignty over the island of Cuba and other Caribbean islands, the existence of which he saw as a continuing menace to American interests. He admitted to Mahan that "if I had my way we would annex those islands tomorrow."[41] Representative Thomas S. Butler, a member of the House Naval Affairs Committee, later remembered that "Roosevelt came down here . . . looking for war. He did not care whom we fought as long as there was a scrap."[42] Indeed, years later Roosevelt observed that soon after he became assistant secretary he "became convinced that the war would come."[43] At another time, Roosevelt affirmed, "I hope to see the Spanish flag and the English flag gone from the map of North America before I'm sixty!"[44] Both he and Lodge even gave thought to the acquisition of Canada.[45]

Roosevelt "established himself as the leader of a coterie of like-minded imperialists: senators, congressmen, ranking military officers (both active and retired), writers, and prominent citizens." These men of influence who shared Roosevelt's "large view" of U.S. foreign policy included Lodge, John Hay, and Brooks Adams. They and similarly inclined men often gathered for lunch at the Metropolitan Club, Roosevelt's favorite haunt, right across 17th Street NW from his office.[46] Roosevelt found a kindred spirit in Adams, whom some nicknamed "Herodotus . . . for the sweep of his historical vision."[47] Roosevelt and his colleagues did not have an economic agenda for American expansion overseas. Rather, they wanted to embellish America's power and international standing. Roosevelt wrote, "I wish to see the United States the dominant power on the Pacific Ocean. . . . Our people are neither craven nor weaklings and we face the future high of heart and confident of soul eager to do the great work of a great power."[48]

In a letter to Mahan, Roosevelt expressed his determination to accomplish a goal long desired by himself and by Navy secretaries Benjamin F. Tracy and Hilary Herbert, Mahan himself, Lodge, U.S. Naval Academy professor James B. Soley, and naval officers Luce and Henry Taylor, and other "navalists." They envisioned a powerful fleet of big-gun battleships that would catapult the United States to world-power status alongside Great Britain, France, and Germany.[49]

On 2 June 1897, Roosevelt delivered at the Naval War College an address that clearly expressed one of his core beliefs—that peace was to be maintained through military strength. The concept was later simplified and popularized as "Speak softly but carry a big stick."[50] At the college Roosevelt alluded to George Washington, who, he suggested, believed that "to prepare for war is the most effectual means to promote peace." Roosevelt belittled the search for peace through arbitration or negotiation. He opined that national leaders "will be wise if they place reliance upon a first-class fleet of battleships rather than on any arbitration treaty. . . . Peace is a goddess only when she comes with sword girt on thigh." He concluded his address with the observation that "no triumph of peace is quite so great as the supreme triumphs of war. . . . It may be that at some time in the dim future of the race the need for war will vanish; but that time is yet ages distant. As yet no nation can hold its place in the world, or can do any work really worth doing, unless it stands ready to guard its rights with an armed hand."[51]

The McKinley administration at that point was stressing the settlement of many foreign policy concerns through diplomacy, so the Navy secretary was not pleased with his deputy's bellicose views expressed so publicly. But Long refrained from chastising Roosevelt. McKinley too registered no displeasure with Roosevelt's remarks. He told an aide, "I suspect Roosevelt is right [and] the only difference between him and me is the greater responsibility"; the president had to preserve peace.[52]

In mid-1897, McKinley asked the Senate to ratify a treaty annexing the Hawaiian Islands. Japan immediately protested that such an action would imperil the interests of the 25,000 Japanese immigrants who then lived and worked there. On 22 April, Roosevelt sent the president a long letter in which he suggested U.S. naval vessels might be deployed to Hawaii to counter the presence there of the Japanese cruiser *Naniwa Kan.* Roosevelt considered a war with Japan for domination of the Pacific Ocean as probable. The assistant secretary noted that even though the Japanese navy "is an efficient fighting navy," sending the battleship *Oregon* and other major combatants there would put Tokyo at a decided disadvantage.[53]

Writing to Captain Goodrich about a potential conflict with Japan over Hawaii, Roosevelt revealed his clear understanding of the concept of sea control. He observed that it did not matter if the Japanese invaded Hawaii with ground troops, since "if we smash the Japanese Navy, definitely and thoroughly, then the presence of a Japanese army corps in Hawaii would merely mean the establishment of Hawaii as a half-way post for that army corps on its way to our prisons." He stressed that the "determining factor in any war with Japan would be the control of the sea."[54]

Touring naval bases in the Great Lakes region, Roosevelt gave a speech in which he stated that "the United States is not in a position which requires her to ask Japan, or any other foreign power, what territory it shall or shall not acquire." To Roosevelt's surprise, McKinley approved of the statement.[55] Not so Long, who this time could not contain his anger at his subordinate once again venturing into the foreign policy arena. Roosevelt later admitted to Lodge that the "headlines and comment [about his remarks] nearly threw the Secretary into a fit." Roosevelt told Lodge that Long "gave me as heavy a wigging as his invariable courtesy and kindness would permit."[56] Roosevelt apologized to Long and promised not to speak out of turn in future. Soon afterward, Long departed Washington for a month-long vacation in Hingham Harbor, Massachusetts. During the summer, Roosevelt reassured Long that in his absence he, Roosevelt, would take no action that he thought the secretary would disapprove.

At the same time, Roosevelt intimated to a friend that "the Secretary is away, and I am having immense fun running the Navy."[57] Roosevelt later confided to Lodge that "my chief usefulness has arisen from the fact that when I was Acting Secretary I did not hesitate to take responsibilities." He added that he had "continually meddled with what was not my business, because I was willing to jeopardize my position in a way that a naval officer could not."[58]

Outside observers made note of Roosevelt's frenetic activity. The *New York Sun* reported that "the liveliest spot in Washington at present is the Navy Department. . . . The decks are cleared for action. Acting Secretary Roosevelt, in the absence of Governor Long, has the whole Navy bordering on a war footing. It remains only to sand down the decks and pipe to quarters for action."[59]

Roosevelt later admitted that "whenever I was left as Acting Secretary I did everything in my power to put us in readiness." He felt compelled to act because he was by then convinced that "like the people, the Government was for a long time unwilling to prepare for war, because so many honest but misguided men believed that the preparation itself tended to bring on war."[60] Roosevelt, however, feared there would be trouble "if we drift into the war butt end foremost, and go at it higgledy-piggledy fashion."[61]

Roosevelt regularly informed Long about the measures he was taking in the administration of the Navy. At one point in June 1897, Roosevelt itemized his actions: establishing the process for the selection of the best torpedo boats for the fleet; identifying a need to limit reporting requirements; and dealing with complaints about uniforms from naval officers, some of whom "apparently [liked] the cap, but object much to the amount of gold lace on the sleeves." Against the opposition of a captain, Roosevelt had recommended assigning one of the service's best-qualified officers to a training group. Finally, Roosevelt reported that instead of dismissing an officer from the Navy for some transgression, he "gave him a wigging." He ended with the wishful observation that "there isn't the slightest necessity of your returning."[62] In September, Roosevelt observed to Lodge that Long "has wanted me to act entirely independently while he was away, and to decide all these things myself, even where I have written him that I was going to decide them in a way that I doubted whether he would altogether like."[63]

Long did recognize how well Roosevelt was taking care of their business. Writing in 1903, the then-former Navy secretary remembered that Roosevelt was "heart and soul in his work." Long related that his assistant "was especially helpful in the purchasing of ships and in every line where he could push on the work of preparation for war." Long added that Roosevelt "was especially stimulating to the younger officers who gathered about him and made his office as busy as a bee hive."[64]

In addition to inspecting naval bases on the East Coast and in the Midwest, in September 1897 Roosevelt visited the fleet in the Atlantic. He reveled at the opportunity, even though he predicted he would get seasick. He had a firsthand look at how naval combatants operated on the ocean and how the large guns on board the battleship *Iowa* tracked targets. Indeed, his visit enabled him "to satisfy myself definitely of the great superiority of the battleship as a gun platform." He observed, "I never enjoyed or profited by anything more than I did my three days with the fleet."[65]

That fall, Roosevelt chaired a board that looked at eliminating the distinction between line and engineering officers; the retirement of unfit officers; and an increase in the salaries of line officers. The board's recommendations were incorporated into a bill that Congress passed in 1899. Roosevelt also pushed the concept that merit rather than seniority should determine promotion.[66]

It is a reflection of Roosevelt's determination to strengthen the Navy that he was open to the adoption of new methods of warfare and command organization. In a March 1898 letter to Long, Roosevelt expressed interest in Professor Samuel P. Langley's so-called flying machine, which "has worked." He recommended the establishment of a board of Army and Navy officers to examine the flying machine and "inform us whether or not they think it could be duplicated on a large scale . . . to be of use in the event of war."[67] Almost a century later, John F. Lehman, President Ronald Reagan's Secretary of the Navy and a man who idolized Roosevelt and drew inspiration from his style of leadership, bemoaned the fact that "Roosevelt's prophetic recommendation had been dismissed with contempt by a board of admirals soon after he left [office]. They said that the flying machine could possibly be of interest to the army but had no applicability at all to the navy."[68]

Roosevelt also supported a new look at the direction of fleet operations. Two leaders at the Naval War College, Henry C. Taylor and Luce, credited Germany's success against Austria and France in the wars of that era to the effectiveness of its general staff. They recommended that the U.S. Navy adopt a similar system; Roosevelt replied to Taylor, "I entirely agree with you." Long was not impressed, considering the concept "militaristic," and after Roosevelt left office killed it.[69] Nonetheless, by 1899 Long had had second thoughts. He directed Taylor, then head of the Navy's personnel bureau, to inform him as to "what concrete things should be done at present in the development of a General Staff."[70] Despite Long's turnaround and Roosevelt's earlier support, nothing came of the concept until the early twentieth century.

One reason why Roosevelt was not distressed that Long had disapproved of his outspokenness over Hawaii and other issues was Roosevelt's awareness that he himself enjoyed the favor of the president. In the fall, during a carriage ride to which he had invited Roosevelt, McKinley acknowledged that Roosevelt's views had been correct on Japan's reaction to the annexation of Hawaii.[71]

Long's absences from Washington in the summer and early fall of 1897 were frequent, and on several occasions Roosevelt personally met with McKinley. McKinley was no stranger to war, having served in combat during the Civil War. He once related, "I have been through one war. I have seen the dead piled up, and I do not want to see another."[72] McKinley nevertheless had to contend with the possibility of wars with not only Japan but Germany, Spain, even Great Britain. During this period, "the Naval War College staff was no longer convinced that war with Spain was certain. . . . Great Britain and Japan also appeared as threats. . . . Theodore Roosevelt directed the War College to consider as a 'special' problem a possible clash with Japan."[73] While McKinley hoped for a peaceful resolution of the serious differences that existed with Madrid, he was not blind to the possibility of a U.S.-Spanish war. Moreover, McKinley appreciated Roosevelt's public bellicosity, because it made him seem a peacemaker by comparison; Brands has concluded that McKinley wanted to appear the "good cop to Roosevelt's bad cop."[74] Moreover, McKinley applauded Roosevelt's concerted effort to ready the Navy for battle. In mid-September, Roosevelt told Lodge that during the carriage ride McKinley had "expressed great satisfaction" with Roosevelt's management of the department during the previous months.[75]

Roosevelt was invited to White House dinners and another carriage ride, during which he boldly presented to the president a strategic plan developed by the Navy Department. It incorporated the work of the Naval War College and the Office of Naval Intelligence with regard to a war against Spain. The plan anticipated a main battle fleet, based at Key West, Florida, establishing a naval blockade of Cuba. Another U.S. naval force would operate along the coast of Spain to divert enemy attention, and the Asiatic Squadron would blockade or destroy the Spanish squadron in the Philippines. The document also provided for the landing of U.S. troops in Cuba. Optimistically, the plan anticipated a victory over Spain in six weeks.[76]

To command the Asiatic Squadron the assistant secretary soon focused on a naval officer he considered a bold and innovative leader, Commodore Dewey. Roosevelt later observed that Dewey, a combat veteran of the Union Navy, fellow member of the Metropolitan Club, and frequent companion on horse rides through Washington's Rock Creek Park, "was a man who could be relied upon to prepare in advance, and to act promptly, fearlessly, and on his own responsibility when the emergency arose." He added, "In a crisis, the man worth his salt is the man who meets the needs of the situation in whatever way is necessary."[77] Roosevelt was confident that in the event of war Dewey would execute the core tenet of Mahan's sea-control theory, the destruction of the enemy fleet—in this case the Spanish squadron based in the Philippines. Roosevelt enlisted the help of his ally Senator Proctor, who proved instrumental in persuading President McKinley to give Dewey the Asiatic Squadron command.

Dewey was not Secretary Long's first choice, although in his *The New American Navy*, published in 1903, he contended that it was he who convinced McKinley to appoint Dewey. Initially, however, he wanted for the billet Commo. John A. Howell, an officer Roosevelt considered unfit for the role he expected the Asiatic Squadron to play in the coming war with Spain. The assistant secretary observed in a letter to Senator William E. Chandler, "I have rarely met one who strikes me as less fit for a responsible position. . . . I hardly know of a man of high rank in the Navy whom I would be more reluctant to see entrusted with a squadron or a fleet. . . . He is irresolute and he is extremely afraid of responsibility."[78]

In a fit of pique, Long did not promote Dewey to acting rear admiral, which had been customary for Asiatic Squadron commanders. According to Spector, Long might have been justified in his grievance, since Dewey's record to that point had been mediocre at best. "He had had no sea duty in eight years and only four years at sea in the last twenty years. . . . His role in the development of the new navy had been distinctly minor." Spector concluded that "Dewey owed his appointment to efforts of influential political friends like Senator Proctor and Theodore Roosevelt and to nothing else."[79] This assertion was in marked contrast to Long's, that "political or personal influence had nothing to do with his selection, which was entirely my own."[80]

In January 1898, Roosevelt pressed Long to take immediate measures to ready the Navy for a war with Spain. He insisted that "certain things should be done at once if there is any reasonable chance of trouble with Spain during the next six months. . . . If we do not prepare in advance, and suddenly have to go into hostilities without taking the necessary steps beforehand, we may have to encounter one or two bitter humiliations."[81] Roosevelt also complained to Adams of the "unwisdom of Congress" that he felt had left the Navy "lamentably weak in some particulars." At the same time, "our Navy is in much better shape than it was a year ago." He also recognized the connection between the sailors of 1898 and their historical legacy: "Our men have in them the stuff of those who fought in 1812, and in 1861, and they handle their ships and their guns as American seamen should."[82]

Adding to the pressures Roosevelt faced to prepare the Navy for war in early 1898 were, as Long had recognized, a life-threatening illness affecting his wife Edith and persistent headaches troubling his son Theodore Jr. The father admitted to Mahan that he had "been under a great strain this winter owing to the long and critical sickness of both my wife and my eldest son."[83] Adding to his concern was the rebellious nature of his fourteen-year-old daughter Alice, who was "running the streets uncontrolled with every boy in town."[84]

Whether the sinking of battleship *Maine* in Havana harbor on 15 February 1898 was the result of an internal explosion or Spanish perfidy mattered not in the least to Roosevelt. Having long advocated the expulsion of Spanish influence from the hemisphere, he saw in the sinking of the *Maine* and the death of 266 of her sailors powerful impetus to renew his call for war. In the short term, however, in a letter to a friend he attributed his passion to the "blood of the Cubans, the blood of women and children who have perished by the hundred thousand in hideous misery [in addition to] the blood of the murdered men of the *Maine*."[85]

Roosevelt observed, with false modesty, "I am of course merely a minor official in the administration," so he could not openly press for war. But in the same communication he admitted urging the president to take that action. At one point, McKinley kiddingly asked Leonard Wood, one of his White House physicians and a close friend and confidant of Roosevelt's, "Have you and Theodore declared war yet?" Wood, a Medal of Honor recipient who had helped track down the Apache chief Geronimo, replied, "No, Mr. President, but we think you should."[86] Nonetheless, soon afterward the "minor official" in the Navy Department declared openly at a Gridiron dinner that "we will have this war for the freedom of Cuba."[87] Brands' speculation that for most of his years "Roosevelt's fundamental outlook on life had been pointing toward war" and that "part of him harbored a death wish" seems overstated. Nonetheless, the historian was on the mark that during this period "Roosevelt certainly banged the drums of war."[88]

Long was unnerved by the *Maine* disaster.[89] On 16 February, he recorded in his journal that "in the old days, vessels could be peppered all day long, with comparatively little damage to ship or crew. Now, a battleship, with five hundred men on board . . . will probably go to the bottom and every life be lost." Clearly with his assistant in mind, he added that "this reflection ought to have weight with those who talk lightly of going to war."[90] On 24 February, Long expressed concern that the battleships promoted by

Roosevelt and Mahan might share fates similar to that of the *Maine*. In his journal, he observed that "our great battleships are experiments which have never yet been tried and in the friction of a fight have almost as much to fear from some disarrangement of their own delicate machinery or some explosion of their own tremendous administration as from the foe." He feared that the "horrors and costs and miseries of war are incalculable."[91]

Roosevelt harbored no such concerns. He wrote to Long that "it seems to me, Sir, that it would be well to take all possible precautions. If over . . . this destruction of the *Maine*, war should suddenly arise, the navy department would have to bear the full brunt of the displeasure of Congress and the country if it were not ready. . . . Until the department takes the lead, Congress will not only refuse to [increase the size of the Navy] but will hold itself justified in its refusal." He suggested to Long that if they failed to push for a more capable fleet, "it may be held against us for all time to come, not merely by the men of to-day, but by those who read history in the future."[92] In case Long needed specific recommendations, three days later Roosevelt pleaded with the secretary: "I earnestly wish you could see your way clear now, without waiting a day," to send Congress a message calling for not one but two more battleships, "or better still four battleships."[93]

Recognizing the need to bolster the readiness of the Navy, Long established a Naval War Board in March composed of Rear Adm. Montgomery Sicard, the chair, Roosevelt, and Mahan. The board had no executive authority but exerted considerable influence on strategy and operations, because the advice of its distinguished members was highly regarded.[94]

Rear Adm. William T. Sampson, commander of the naval force gathered at Key West, Florida, proposed that once war was declared against Spain, his battleships immediately proceed to Cuba and bombard the forts defending Havana. He suggested that that action would compel the Spanish authorities to surrender the city rather than allow its destruction and might even bring a quick end to the war.

Roosevelt and Mahan strongly opposed employing America's battleships in a risky gunfight with shore batteries in Cuba until the fleet had destroyed the squadron they knew Spain would dispatch to the island.[95] The concept of sea control that Roosevelt and Mahan had long preached would admit of nothing less. Roosevelt led the opposition to Sampson's proposal. Roosevelt became concerned that because Spanish naval strength was increasing at an alarming pace, the U.S. Navy could ill afford ships damaged or sunk in an exchange with coastal artillery. He drew Long's attention to "the steady way in which the Spanish force grows relatively to our own." He concluded on the basis of intelligence that following the loss of the *Maine*, Spain could put to sea six armored ships to meet America's seven comparable combatants. He feared that "month by month the Spanish navy has been put into a better condition to meet us."[96] On 6 April Secretary Long, with Roosevelt's encouragement, ended consideration of Sampson's plan. Instead of bombarding forts in Cuba, Long directed, Sampson was to focus on a blockade of the island.[97]

Meanwhile, McKinley was genuinely seeking a peaceful way out of the confrontation with Spain, at which Roosevelt was apoplectic. He observed to a friend, "Do you know what that white-faced cur up there [in the White House] has done? He has prepared two messages, one for war and one for peace, and he doesn't know which one to send in!"[98] On another occasion, Roosevelt observed to his brother-in-law that McKinley "had no more backbone than a chocolate éclair."[99]

Finally, faced with overwhelming pressure not only from Roosevelt but from an enraged citizenry and a bellicose press, on 7 March McKinley asked Congress to appropriate $50 million "for the National defense and for each and every purpose connected therewith to be expended at the discretion of the President."[100] Congress quickly passed the bill, and McKinley signed it on 9 March. The Navy Department then laid out $30 million of that fund to buy two new steel cruisers, a gunboat, a torpedo boat from Great Britain, a vessel from Brazil capable of firing "dynamite bombs," and a hundred merchant vessels from American sources. The Navy Department also added to its stores of ammunition, coal, and equipment and enlisted thousands more sailors. In short, "by mid-April the Navy was ready for action, its ships massed at strategic points and fully manned and supplied." In contrast, the Army spent its $20 million of the appropriation to strengthen its forts along the American coast.[101]

On 11 April McKinley asked Congress for authorization to employ armed force to settle the issue over Cuba. On the 19th, Congress approved a joint resolution that amounted to a declaration of war against Spain; the Senate supplied a formal declaration on the 21st.[102]

Even as he feverishly prepared the Navy for war, Roosevelt was planning to jump ship. During several meetings with McKinley, Roosevelt revealed that in the event of war he meant to resign his position and join the Army so he could take part in the actual fighting. Roosevelt had consistently stressed the virtues of war and bravery in battle and clearly wanted to prove to himself and everyone else that he had not just been bloviating. But there was a practical aspect as well. He wrote to a friend that "if I am to be any use in politics it is because I am supposed to be a man who does not preach what he fears to practice." He added that "for the last year I have preached war with Spain. I should feel distinctly ashamed . . . if I now failed to practice what I have preached." The president said he would help Roosevelt achieve his goal to serve in combat.[103]

Even having promised to accommodate Roosevelt, however, McKinley pleaded with him to rethink that decision, as did Long, many of his associates, and his family. In his journal, Long questioned Roosevelt's state of mind: "He has lost his head to this unutterable folly of deserting the post and . . . running off to ride a horse and, probably, brush mosquitoes from his neck on the Florida sands. . . . He is acting like a fool." But even then Long had an inkling that his extraordinary assistant was following a path to glory. Long mused prophetically about "how absurd all this will sound if, by some turn of fortune he should accomplish some great thing and strike a very high mark!" Several years later Long appended a note in the margin of his journal: "Roosevelt was right and we his friends were wrong. His going into the Army led straight to the Presidency."[104]

For the Navy, Roosevelt's hard work to prepare it for war during his year-long stint as assistant secretary paid huge dividends on the outbreak of the Spanish-American War. Nelson's remark is true that Roosevelt's "real contribution to the Spanish-American War went far beyond his celebrated career with the Rough Riders."[105] Roosevelt later observed that "when the Spanish War broke out the navy really was largely on a war footing.... The admirals, captains, and lieutenants were continually practicing their profession in almost precisely the way that it has to be practiced in time of war."[106]

The most creditable sources on the Spanish-American War, including those emphasizing the Army's operations, stress that the U.S. Navy was much better prepared than the American ground forces for the conflict. With little sympathy, Roosevelt later recalled that "as regards finding out what the plans of the War Department [for war with Spain] were, the task was simple. They had no plans. Even during the final months before the outbreak of hostilities very little was done in the way of efficient preparation."[107] Once the conflict began, Long informed Secretary of War Russell A. Alger that the Navy was prepared to transport as many as fifty thousand Army troops to Cuba. According to Long, Alger replied to the effect that "the War Department will take care of itself without any interference from the Navy." Long caustically observed that for two months Alger "has been saying that he would have his army ready in ten days.... In fact, not a volunteer has left his state, and in my judgement there has been a striking lack of preparation and promptness."[108] Even after Congress made money available in March, Alger ruled out measures anticipating a ground invasion of Cuba. As the historian Graham Cosmas has observed, "the joint war plan that President McKinley adopted at the outbreak of hostilities was a unilateral Navy plan with Army operations added on. Its main features came from a series of contingency plans drawn up by the Naval War College" and the Navy Department.[109]

Alerted by Roosevelt long before the outbreak of the war, Dewey's Asiatic Squadron was ready for action when it received orders on 27 April to destroy Spanish naval forces under Rear Adm. Patricio Montojo y Pasaron in the Philippines. On 1 May Dewey's six steel-hulled combatants pounced on Admiral Montojo's seven unarmored ships, the largest of which was wooden. The Americans, without losing a ship or a sailor, utterly destroyed the Spanish squadron, which was arranged passively along the shore in Manila Bay. On 7 May, after the Navy Department deciphered Dewey's coded report from the Far East, a beaming Roosevelt announced the great victory to a room of newspaper reporters.

The national reaction was rapturous. That same day, Roosevelt sent a telegram to Dewey assuring him that "every American is in your debt."[110]

The U.S. Navy's reputation was further burnished on 3 July. On that date, the Spanish cruiser squadron of Adm. Pascual Cervera y Topete made a desperate attempt to escape from the port of Santiago, Cuba, where it had been blockaded by the U.S. fleet since 29 May. As Cervera's ships steamed north along the coast, *Oregon* and three other American battleships, the armored cruiser *Brooklyn*, and a pair of armed yachts paralleled it, destroying one ship after another.[111]

Roosevelt's unequaled work as Assistant Secretary of the Navy done, in late spring 1898, he donned his Army uniform, tailor-made by Brooks Brothers of New York, and went off to the war for which he had so ardently pushed. Theodore Roosevelt's brief service as assistant secretary had demonstrated that he—historian, strategic thinker, and advocate of sea power—possessed the skill and determination to put his theories into practice. He had worked tirelessly and successfully to persuade President McKinley, Secretary Long, Congress, and ultimately the public that America's global interests demanded a modern, professional, and battleship-ready Navy. Unquestionably, his greatest achievement as assistant secretary was to put the Navy on a solid footing before a war began that would herald the United States as a truly global power. He helped ensure that the officers and sailors of the fleet were armed with a coherent strategy and concept of operations, advanced warships, and sufficient stores of ammunition, coal, equipment, and supplies—all the prerequisites of victory. Roosevelt's accomplishments as a "minor official" in the Navy Department made clear that when he entered the office of the president of the United States three years later, the nation and its Navy would be in especially capable hands.

Notes

1. Quoted in Margaret Long, ed., *The Journal of John D. Long* (Rindge, N.H.: Richard R. Smith, 1956), 216–17. Enervated after more than a week of tense, high-level meetings over the crisis with Spain over Cuba, Long needed a break and left Roosevelt in charge of the department. See also Nathan Miller, *Theodore Roosevelt: A Life* (New York: William Morrow, 1992), 267; and Lawrence Shaw Mayo, ed., *America of Yesterday: As Reflected in the Journal of John Davis*

Long, *Governor of Massachusetts and Secretary of the Navy* (Boston: Atlantic Monthly, 1924), 169–70. That same day Lodge wrote to Secretary Long and urged him to have "every ship we own made ready immediately and put into commission"; quoted in John A. Garraty, *Henry Cabot Lodge: A Biography* (New York: Alfred A. Knopf, 1953), 185–86.

2. Quoted in Ronald Spector, *Admiral of the New Empire: The Life and Career of George Dewey* (Baton Rouge: Louisiana State University Press, 1974), 43–44. There is little evidence to support the contention, as expressed in Ephraim K. Smith's "William McKinley's Enduring Legacy," in *Crucible of Empire: The Spanish-American War & Its Aftermath*, ed. James C. Bradford (Annapolis, Md.: Naval Institute Press, 1993), 213, that Roosevelt was part of an "expansionist cabal to seize the Philippines." Equally questionable is Howard K. Beale's conclusion in *Theodore Roosevelt and the Rise of America to World Power* (Baltimore: Johns Hopkins University Press, 1984), 63, that Roosevelt was intent on "grabbing the Philippines without a decision to do so by either Congress or the President, or least of all the people."

3. Quoted in Long, *Journal of John D. Long*, 216–17. An explosion had sunk the battleship *Maine* in Havana Harbor, Cuba, on 15 February 1898.

4. Quoted in Mayo, *America of Yesterday*, 168–69. See also Long, *Journal of John D. Long*, 216–17.

5. Quoted in Mayo, 188.

6. John Hattendorf, B. Mitchell Simpson III, and John R. Wadleigh, *Sailors and Scholars: The Centennial History of the Naval War College* (Newport, R.I.: Naval War College Press, 1984), 47.

7. Spector, *Admiral of the New Empire*, 44.

8. Roosevelt quoted in H. W. Brands, *T.R.: The Last Romantic* (New York: Basic Books, 1997), 303.

9. Brands, 303.

10. Quoted in Garraty, *Henry Cabot Lodge*, 177–79. See also Miller, *Theodore Roosevelt*, 246; Gardner Weld Allen, ed., *Papers of John Davis Long, 1897–1904* (Peabody: Massachusetts Historical Society, 1939), 10; Nathan Miller, *The Roosevelt Chronicles* (New York: Doubleday, 1979), 212; Beale, *Theodore Roosevelt and the Rise of America to World Power*, 55–56; William C. Widenor, *Henry Cabot Lodge and the Search for an American Foreign Policy* (Berkeley: University of California Press, 1980).

11. Quoted in Mayo, *America of Yesterday*, 147. See also William Henry Harbaugh, *Power and Responsibility: The Life and Times of Theodore Roosevelt* (New York: Farrar, Straus, and Cudahy, 1961), 92, 95; Brands, *T.R.*, 305. TR to A. R. Cowles, 11 April 1897, and TR to Board of Governors, Metropolitan Club, Washington, D.C., 16 June 1897, in *The Letters of Theodore Roosevelt*, ed. Elting E. Morison (Cambridge, Mass.: Harvard University Press, 1951–1954), 1:593, 626. See also Henry F. Pringle, *Theodore Roosevelt: A Biography* (New York: Harcourt, Brace, 1932), 168; Edmund Morris, *The Rise of Theodore Roosevelt* (New York: Coward, McGann, and Geoghegan, 1979).

12. Quoted in Miller, *Theodore Roosevelt*, 246.
13. Quoted in Graham Allison, *Destined for War: Can America and China Escape Thucydides's Trap?* (Boston: Houghton Mifflin, 2017), 95.
14. TR to Mrs. Cowles, 11 April 1897, Morison, *Letters of Theodore Roosevelt*, 1:593.
15. TR to Cecil Arthur Spring Rice, 28 April 1897, Morison, 1:604.
16. TR to Alfred Thayer Mahan, 3 May 1897, Morison, 1:608.
17. TR to Bowman McCalla, 19 April 1897, Morison, 1:599.
18. Miller, *Roosevelt Chronicles*, 213.
19. Ronald Spector, *Professors of War: The Naval War College and the Development of the Naval Professions* (Newport, R.I.: Naval War College Press, 1977), 54.
20. George W. Baer, *One Hundred Years of Sea Power: The U.S. Navy, 1890–1990* (Stanford, Calif.: Stanford University Press, 1993), 13.
21. Quoted in Spector, *Professors of War*, 55.
22. Brands, *T.R.*, 302. See also Richard W. Turk, *The Ambiguous Relationship: Theodore Roosevelt and Alfred Thayer Mahan* (New York: Greenwood, 1987), 11–13.
23. Quoted in Spector, *Professors of War*, 74, also 97.
24. Turk, *Ambiguous Relationship*, 7, also 20.
25. Kenneth J. Hagan, *This People's Navy: The Making of American Sea Power* (New York: Free Press, 1991), 189.
26. Quoted in Henry J. Hendrix II, "Roosevelt's Naval Thinking before Mahan," in *Theodore Roosevelt, the U.S. Navy, and the Spanish-American War*, ed. Edward J. Marolda (New York: Palgrave, 2001), 58. See also John A. Gable, "Theodore Roosevelt and the Heritage of the U.S. Navy," in Marolda, 42; TR to Brooks Adams, early 1898, Morison, *Letters of Theodore Roosevelt*, 1:798; Turk, *Ambiguous Relationship*, 16–17.
27. Baer, *One Hundred Years of Sea Power*, 20, 24.
28. Quoted in Turk, *Ambiguous Relationship*, 2.
29. Gable, "Theodore Roosevelt and the Heritage of the U.S. Navy," 42.
30. Spector, *Professors of War*, 49.
31. Quoted in Hattendorf, Simpson, and Wadleigh, *Sailors and Scholars*, 50.
32. Quoted in Miller, *Theodore Roosevelt*, 262. See also Morison, *Letters of Theodore Roosevelt*, 1:603n.
33. Anna K. Nelson, "Theodore Roosevelt, the Navy, and the War with Spain," in Marolda, *Theodore Roosevelt, the U.S. Navy, and the Spanish-American War*, 2. See also Harbaugh, *Power and Responsibility*, 94.
34. Quoted in Long, *Journal of John D. Long*, 223–24, also 209, 213, 225. A friction developed between them in the early years of the twentieth century. Long, according to one biographer, complained that President Roosevelt had meddled in the affairs of the Navy Department. For his part, Roosevelt bridled at Long's suggestion in a 1903 publication that Roosevelt had dispatched U.S. warships

against the Spanish fleet "while we were yet at peace with Spain." Quoted in Allen, *Papers of John Davis Long*, 433–38. See also John D. Long, *The New American Navy* (New York: Outlook, 1903), 174; Edmund Morris, *Theodore Rex* (New York: Random House), 275–76. Long was also incensed when Roosevelt did not support William Howard Taft's presidential candidacy in the election of 1912; see Long, *Journal of John D. Long*, 261, 325–26.

35. Quoted in Miller, *Theodore Roosevelt*, 251–52.
36. TR to Alfred Thayer Mahan, 3 May 1897, Morison, *Letters of Theodore Roosevelt*, 1:608.
37. TR to Mahan, 9 June 1897, Morison, 1:622–23.
38. TR to Long, 6 May 1898, Allen, *Papers of John Davis Long*, 115.
39. Miller, *Theodore Roosevelt*, 250.
40. TR to Alfred Thayer Mahan, 3 May 1897, Morison, *Letters of Theodore Roosevelt*, 1:607–8. See also Miller, *Theodore Roosevelt*, 251.
41. TR to Alfred Thayer Mahan, 3 May 1897; TR to A. S. Hartwell, 7 June 1897, Morison, *Letters of Theodore Roosevelt*, 1:607–8, 622. See also Miller, *Theodore Roosevelt*, 251; Pringle, *Theodore Roosevelt*, 167; Brands, *T.R.*, 309; Turk, *Ambiguous Relationship*, 26–27, 102.
42. Quoted in Pringle, *Theodore Roosevelt*, 171.
43. Theodore Roosevelt, *An Autobiography* (New York: Macmillan, 1913), 227.
44. Quoted in Miller, *Theodore Roosevelt*, 264.
45. Harbaugh, *Power and Responsibility*, 93; Garraty, *Henry Cabot Lodge*, 185.
46. Miller, *Theodore Roosevelt*, 253.
47. Brands, *T.R.*, 308.
48. Quoted in Nelson, "Theodore Roosevelt, the Navy, and the War with Spain," 2.
49. Garraty, *Henry Cabot Lodge*, 180, 181; Miller, *Theodore Roosevelt*, 251, 253; Nelson, "Theodore Roosevelt, the Navy, and the War with Spain," 3; Harbaugh, *Power and Responsibility*, 98; Baer, *One Hundred Years of Sea Power*, 11.
50. Roosevelt, *Autobiography*, 224.
51. Quoted in Miller, *Theodore Roosevelt*, 254–55. See also Roosevelt, *Autobiography*, 226.
52. Quoted in Miller, 255. See also TR to Mahan, 9 June 1897, Morison, *Letters of Theodore Roosevelt*, 1:623.
53. TR to McKinley, 22 April 1897, Morison, 1:601–602. See also Spector, *Professors of War*, 95; Nelson, "Theodore Roosevelt, the Navy, and the War with Spain," 4; Raymond A. Esthus, *Theodore Roosevelt and Japan* (Seattle: University of Washington Press, 1967).
54. TR to Goodrich, 16 June 1897, Morison, *Letters of Theodore Roosevelt*, 1:626.
55. Quoted in Miller, *Theodore Roosevelt*, 257. See also Brands, *T.R.*, 314.
56. Quoted in Miller, *Theodore Roosevelt*, 257.
57. Quoted in Miller, 257. See also Harbaugh, *Power and Responsibility*, 95.

58. Quoted in Harbaugh, 95.

59. Quoted in Miller, *Theodore Roosevelt*, 258.

60. Roosevelt, *Autobiography*, 233, also 234; Brands, *T.R.*, 317.

61. Quoted in Beale, *Theodore Roosevelt and the Rise of America to World Power*, 61.

62. TR to Long, 22 June 1897, Morison, *Letters of Theodore Roosevelt*, 1:630.

63. Quoted in Brands, *T.R.*, 313.

64. Long, *New American Navy*, 174–75.

65. Quoted in Brands, *T.R.*, 320, 21. Roosevelt brought two reporters with him from newspapers that he figured would not print "fake stories" about the Navy.

66. Harbaugh, *Power and Responsibility*, 94–95. See also Donald Chisholm, *Waiting for Dead Men's Shoes: Origins and Development of the U.S. Navy's Officer Personnel System, 1793–1941* (Stanford, Calif.: Stanford University Press, 2001).

67. TR to Long, 25 March 1898, Morison, *Letters of Theodore Roosevelt*, 1:799.

68. John F. Lehman Jr., *Command of the Seas* (New York: Charles Scribner's Sons, 1988), 419.

69. TR to Taylor, 24 May 1897, Morison, *Letters of Theodore Roosevelt*, 1:617. See also Spector, *Admiral of the New Empire*, 125.

70. Quoted in Spector, *Professors of War*, 136.

71. Quoted in Miller, *Theodore Roosevelt*, 259. See also TR to Long, 18 June 1897, Morison, *Letters of Theodore Roosevelt*, 1:628.

72. Quoted in Miller, 266. See also Brands, *T.R.*, 313.

73. Hattendorf, Simpson, and Wadleigh, *Sailors and Scholars*, 47. See also Spector, *Professors of War*, 96, 103; Harold D. Langley, "Winfield S. Schley and Santiago," in Bradford, *Crucible of Empire*, 72.

74. Brands, *T.R.*, 314.

75. Quoted in Miller, *Theodore Roosevelt*, 259.

76. Spector, *Admiral of the New Empire*, 35–36; Miller, *Theodore Roosevelt*, 260; Hattendorf, Simpson, and Wadleigh, *Sailors and Scholars*, 45; Spector, *Professors of War*, 94–95; Brands, *T.R.*, 315; Turk, *Ambiguous Relationship*, 29–35.

77. Roosevelt, *Autobiography*, 231 and see also 230; Spector, *Admiral of the New Empire*, 36–37.

78. Quoted in Spector, *Admiral of the New Empire*, 37, also 38; Long, *Journal of John D. Long*, 225.

79. Spector, *Admiral of the New Empire*, 39. See also Hagan, *This People's Navy*, 312.

80. Quoted in Long, *Journal of John D. Long*, 225, also 224.

81. Quoted in Miller, *Theodore Roosevelt*, 262.

82. TR to B. Adams, early 1898, Morison, *Letters of Theodore Roosevelt*, 1:798.

83. TR to Mahan, 24 March 1898, Morison, 1:799.

84. Quoted in Miller, *Theodore Roosevelt*, 263, also 266, 268–69.

85. Quoted in Miller, 270. See also Roosevelt, *Autobiography*, 227–28; TR to Long, 15 October 1903, Allen, *Papers of John Davis Long*, 437; Garraty, *Henry Cabot Lodge*, 184–85; Beale, *Theodore Roosevelt and the Rise of America to World Power*, 59.

86. Quoted in Miller, *Theodore Roosevelt*, 270.

87. Quoted in Miller, 271.

88. Brands, *T.R.*, 316.

89. Hagan, *This People's Navy*, 209, relates that Long "avoided military duty in the Civil War" and "loathed war."

90. Long, *Journal of John D. Long*, 16 February 1898, 215.

91. Quoted in Mayo, *America of Yesterday*, 168.

92. TR to Long, 16 February 1898, Allen, *Papers of John Davis Long*, 53–55.

93. TR to Long, 19 February 1898, Allen, 58.

94. Michael J. Crawford, Mark L. Hayes, and Michael D. Sessions, *The Spanish-American War: Historical Overview and Select Bibliography* (Washington, D.C.: Naval Historical Center, 1998), 9; Graham A. Cosmas, *An Army for Empire: The United States Army in the Spanish-American War* (College Station: Texas A&M University Press, 1998), 74.

95. Langley, "Winfield S. Schley and Santiago," 71.

96. Quoted in Diane E. Cooper, "George L. Dyer, Naval Attaché," in Bradford, *Crucible of Empire*, 14.

97. Cosmas, *Army for Empire*, 105–6, 122; Hagan, *This People's Navy*, 208, 217–18, 223.

98. Quoted in Miller, *Theodore Roosevelt*, 271.

99. Quoted in Allison, *Destined for War*, 95.

100. Quoted in Cosmas, *Army for Empire*, 73, also 74.

101. Cosmas, *Army for Empire*, 83. See also Graham A. Cosmas, "Joint Operations in the Spanish-American War," in Bradford, *Crucible of Empire*, 107.

102. Harbaugh, *Power and Responsibility*, 101–2.

103. Quoted in Miller, *Theodore Roosevelt*, 273–74. See also Harbaugh, *Power and Responsibility*, 102–103; Brands, *T.R.*, 315.

104. Quoted in Mayo, *America of Yesterday*, 186–87. See also Long, *Journal of John D. Long*, 224; Long, *New American Navy*, 175; Miller, *Theodore Roosevelt*, 273.

105. Nelson, "Theodore Roosevelt, the Navy, and the War with Spain," 1.

106. Roosevelt, *Autobiography*, 242.

107. Roosevelt, 240, also 242.

108. Quoted in Mayo, *America of Yesterday*, 188.

109. Cosmas, "Joint Operations in the Spanish-American War," 106. See also Cosmas, *Army for Empire*, 87.

110. Quoted in Spector, *Admiral of the New Empire*, 65. See also Crawford, Hayes, and Sessions, *Spanish-American War*, 12–13.

111. Crawford, Hayes, and Sessions, 15–17.

4

FROM KNOWLEDGE, SEA POWER

Theodore Roosevelt, Naval Education, and the New Navy

William P. Leeman

Watching his inaugural parade on 4 March 1905, President Theodore Roosevelt caught sight of U.S. Military Academy cadets and U.S. Naval Academy midshipmen marching toward him. "Those are the boys," he announced enthusiastically. "They're superb."[1] To Roosevelt, the young men wearing cadet gray and navy blue represented the future of the American military, a future that the commander in chief hoped would see the United States take its place among the world's preeminent powers. Roosevelt had a lifelong obsession with the military, particularly the U.S. Navy. This passion for naval affairs included a personal interest in the inner workings of the Naval Academy in Annapolis, Maryland, and the Naval War College in Newport, Rhode Island. Expansion and modernization were the hallmarks of Roosevelt's vision for the Navy during his time as Assistant Secretary of the Navy and as president. An ardent proponent of technological innovation, Roosevelt understood that the most technologically advanced ships were useless without a well-educated and highly trained officer corps, which meant that the education provided by the Naval Academy and the Naval War College was critical to achieving his vision for the Navy. Beyond their educational missions, both institutions served broader purposes for Roosevelt by attracting the public's interest in the country's naval history and by helping to gain public support for America's development into one of the world's leading naval powers.

The New Naval Academy: Theodore Roosevelt and Annapolis

By the turn of the twentieth century, Annapolis had become the cultural center of the American naval profession, providing the Navy with an educational standard for its officers as well as a historic campus, known as "The Yard," featuring monuments to the great naval battles and heroes of the past. The Naval Academy's establishment by Secretary of the Navy George Bancroft in 1845 was a foundational event in the Navy's professional development. By the late nineteenth century, the Naval Academy staff had become an important base of operations for a navalist reform agenda, and Annapolis graduates held a virtual monopoly on the Navy's officer positions.[2] The Navy's dramatic victories in the Spanish-American War, the first American war in which Naval Academy graduates such as George Dewey and William T. Sampson held the top leadership positions, captured the imagination of political leaders and the public. Renewed interest and pride in the Navy as well as the increasing size of the fleet during the 1890s created a favorable environment for expansion and reform at Annapolis. The Naval Academy was too small to meet the officer needs of the growing fleet, and that prompted Congress and the Navy to begin a major construction project that would provide the academy with a larger, modern campus built on a grand scale befitting the Navy's newfound stature.[3]

Theodore Roosevelt's concept of naval leadership emphasized modernization in naval technology and institutions while also reflecting a more personal, traditional, and even Victorian approach that emphasized character and honor. His personal and professional interest in the Naval Academy reflected this somewhat contradictory aspect of his leadership. The public's recent fascination with the Navy, the Naval Academy's impressive new campus, and Roosevelt's entry into the White House made the start of the twentieth century a "golden age" at Annapolis. Roosevelt had endorsed New York architect Ernest Flagg's elaborate Beaux-Arts

design for the Naval Academy's new campus while Assistant Secretary
of the Navy, and it was during his presidency that the architectural plan
came to fruition. Dahlgren Hall (the armory) and Macdonough Hall
(originally a boathouse) opened in 1903; the latter was converted to
a gymnasium in 1906. Construction on the midshipmen's dormitory,
Bancroft Hall, began in 1901, the first wing opening in 1904 and the
remaining original wings in 1906. Admiral Dewey laid the cornerstone of
the new chapel in 1904; the first religious service was held there in 1908.
The superintendent's quarters (later named Buchanan House, after the
academy's first superintendent, Franklin Buchanan) opened in 1906, while
the academic buildings (Mahan, Sampson, and Maury Halls) and the
administration building opened in 1907. Roosevelt was a frequent visitor
to The Yard and took a personal interest in the operation of the academy.
It was during the Roosevelt years that the future admirals who would
lead American forces to victory in World War II learned their profession
at Annapolis, among them Ernest J. King (who received his diploma
from then–vice president Roosevelt in 1901), William F. Halsey (Class
of 1904), Chester W. Nimitz (Class of 1905), and Raymond A. Spruance
(Class of 1907). Although Roosevelt's top priority was the expansion of
the battleship fleet, he saw the professional development of naval officers
as a critical component of his efforts to build a navy that was second only
to Britain's Royal Navy.[4]

The main purpose of the nation's military academies was to initiate
young men from civilian life into the military profession through a program
of strict discipline, a regimented daily schedule, athletics, military training,
and military history.[5] The thoroughly military and masculine environment
of the academies appealed to Roosevelt, who viewed the U.S. Military
Academy at West Point, New York, and the Naval Academy at Annapolis
as uniquely American institutions that reflected the greatness of the entire
nation and of American manhood. In remarks at the Military Academy's
centennial celebration at West Point on 11 June 1902, Roosevelt stated,

> of all the institutions in the country, none is more absolutely Ameri-
> can; none in the proper sense of the word, more absolutely democratic
> than this. Here we care nothing for the boy's birthplace, nor his

creed, nor his social standing. . . . Here you represent, with almost mathematical exactness, all the country geographically. You are drawn from every walk of life by a method of choice made to insure . . . that heed shall be paid to nothing save the boy's aptitude for the profession into which he seeks entrance. Here you come together as representatives of America in a higher and more peculiar sense than can possibly be true of any other institution in the land, save your sister college [the Naval Academy].[6]

Roosevelt continued this theme in an August 1902 speech in Haverhill, Massachusetts. By way of emphasizing the need for military preparedness as the best way to ensure peace and arguing that the education of naval officers was a vital component of preparedness, Roosevelt pointed out that the officers who had commanded America's ships during the Spanish-American War had been products of many years of training. He continued, "Annapolis is, with the sole exception of its sister academy at West Point, the most typically democratic and American school of learning and preparation that there is in the entire country. Men go there from every state, from every walk of life, professing every creed—the chance of entry being open to all who perfect themselves in the necessary studies and who possess the necessary moral and physical qualities. There each man enters on his merits, stands on his merits, and graduates into a service where only his merit will enable him to be of value." Emphasizing the connection between shipbuilding and officer development, the president warned, "It is impossible after the outbreak of war to improvise either the ships or the men of a navy."[7]

The course at Annapolis had always been a balance between training (defined as instruction and practice to develop specific technical skills) and education (defined as instruction and individual study designed to develop one's intellect and analytical skills).[8] The academy's curriculum during Roosevelt's presidency featured mathematics, chemistry, physics, engineering, the liberal arts (including English, foreign languages, American naval history, and American government), and naval and military science (including seamanship, infantry and artillery drill, naval tactics, gunnery, and navigation). After completing four years of study and professional training at Annapolis, midshipmen would go to sea for an additional two years of practical, on-the-job training. At the end of this two-year period, the midshipmen would undergo an examination and, if they passed, would receive their commissions as ensigns in the Navy.[9]

During his time as assistant secretary, Roosevelt had been directly involved in a major change in the structure of the curriculum at Annapolis. During the nineteenth century, the Naval Academy had offered two separate educational tracks: one for midshipmen who intended to become line officers and one for those who aspired to be engineers. This separation reflected the sharp division between line officers and engineers in the existing fleet. The advent of steam power meant that engineers had an important role to play, that of powering the ship. Despite their critical responsibilities, engineers felt underappreciated by line officers, who tended to look down upon engineers as little more than mechanics. Roosevelt himself chaired a Navy board that recommended merging line officers and engineers. The Personnel Act of 1899 required that all officers be proficient engineers.[10] Roosevelt explained, "Every officer on a modern war-vessel in reality has to be an engineer, whether he wants to or not." It was no longer efficient to categorize some duties as for engineers, some for line officers: "The line officer has to understand the operation, the repair, upkeep, care and limitations of all machinery on board ship in order to fight them efficiently in battle." With the amalgamation of the line officers and engineers, the Naval Academy began educating all midshipmen according to the same curriculum, eliminating the separate tracks for line officers and engineers.[11]

Despite his own academic and scholarly accomplishments, Roosevelt's vision for the academy's curriculum tended to be more practical, seeing no need for the course of studies to resemble the curriculum at a civilian college. Although he was a strong supporter of the nation's military academies, Roosevelt's romantic notion of military leadership emphasized such character traits as courage, honor, aggressiveness, and the ability to inspire one's men far more than classroom learning. After all, one of the transformational moments of Roosevelt's own life had been his service as a Rough Rider in the Spanish-American War without benefit of a West Point education. Referring to West Point and Annapolis, Roosevelt declared, "We do not need to have these schools made more scholastic.

On the contrary, we should never lose sight of the fact that the aim of each school is to turn out a man who shall be above everything else a fighting man."[12] The president repeated this theme in his annual message a year later when he quoted from the Naval Academy Board of Visitors report that stated, "The Naval Academy is not a university but a school, the primary object of which is to educate boys to be efficient naval officers. Changes in curriculum, therefore, should be in the direction of making the course of instruction less theoretical and more practical." The Board of Visitors went so far as to recommend that the academy not require the midshipmen to purchase so many textbooks.[13]

Roosevelt's annual messages to Congress reflected his special interest in the Naval Academy. In his first message, the new president called for a "large addition to the classes at Annapolis" in an effort to increase the size of the naval officer corps. He also waded into a controversy about what the academy's students should be called. At this time, the students held the rank of "naval cadet," which was unpopular within naval circles. Roosevelt made it clear which side he was on: "The pretentious and unmeaning title of 'naval cadet' should be abolished; the title of 'midshipman,' full of historic association, should be restored."[14] Roosevelt used his annual message to endorse commissioning graduates of the Naval Academy as ensigns immediately, instead of requiring them to spend an additional two years at sea as midshipmen. The president declared that with the existing system, "we do not now get the full benefit from our excellent naval school at Annapolis. It is absurd not to graduate the midshipmen as ensigns; to keep them for two years in such an anomalous position as at present the law requires is detrimental to them and to the service." Roosevelt argued that requiring additional leadership experience while at the academy would prepare graduates to enter the line as ensigns immediately upon graduation.[15] Over the course of his presidency, Roosevelt achieved a substantial increase in the size of the student body at Annapolis, from 280 in 1899 to 879 in 1906. In recognition of this growth, the "battalion" of midshipmen was reorganized as a "brigade" in 1903, the term still in use today. On 1 July 1902, Congress abolished the term "naval cadet" and permanently reinstated the rank of "midshipman" for the academy's students. Roosevelt was unable, however, to see midshipmen graduate as ensigns. That reform would finally take place with the Class of 1912, putting Annapolis graduates on a level of equality with West Point graduates, who received commissions as second lieutenants in the Army on graduation day.[16]

In both his personal life and his political life, Roosevelt lived the "doctrine of the strenuous life." The strenuous man was strong in mind and body, aggressive, courageous, honorable, and willing to sacrifice for a noble cause. Such men participated in athletics, particularly "manly" sports like football, boxing, and hunting.[17] Roosevelt's keen interest in physical training and athletics at the Naval Academy reflected his devotion to the strenuous life. He believed that increased physical fitness of officers, as measured by tests, would enhance the military's effectiveness and ensure that manly virtues defined the officer corps. West Point and Annapolis began to put greater emphasis on athletics around the turn of the century, seeing competitive sports as a crucial component of physical development. Participation in competitive athletics also fostered teamwork and leadership skills, often serving as a metaphor for combat.[18]

Roosevelt's interest in Navy athletics went back to his time as assistant secretary, when he pressed for resumption of the annual Army-Navy football game, which had been suspended by President Grover Cleveland in 1893 because of excessive rowdiness among the spectators and disruption of the academy routine. In a letter to Secretary of War Russell A. Alger, Roosevelt argued that disorder within the academy's routines previously associated with the football game could be avoided by not allowing any cadet to participate who was unsatisfactory in his academic performance or conduct. Furthermore, Roosevelt stated, no classes or military drills should be eliminated in favor of football practice. The McKinley administration approved the reinstatement of the Army-Navy game in 1899, and Roosevelt, as president, attended the game in 1901. By the time of Roosevelt's presidency, the midshipmen fielded intercollegiate teams in football, baseball, fencing, rowing, and track.[19]

Despite such emphasis on the physical development of the midshipmen, Roosevelt was not satisfied. After hearing that the academy administration was eliminating some martial arts instruction, Roosevelt complained to Secretary of the Navy Charles J. Bonaparte, "I am not satisfied about the giving up of the judo or jujitsu at the Naval Academy. It is not physical exercise so much as it is an extraordinarily successful means of self-defense and training in dexterity and decision." Roosevelt ordered that the martial arts instruction, which he deemed of great use to military men, be retained in the academy's physical education curriculum.[20]

Roosevelt also became involved in one of the most controversial aspects of Naval Academy life at the time: the practice of hazing. The years of Roosevelt's presidency witnessed an outbreak at Annapolis of hazing, which had all but disappeared by the end of the nineteenth century, when Congress had outlawed it under penalty of court-martial and dismissal for the guilty. Naval Academy graduate and author Park Benjamin attributed the resurgence of hazing to the major increase in the number of midshipmen, the increasing age of midshipmen, the disorder on campus resulting from construction of the new buildings, the practice of giving the first classmen (seniors) more disciplinary authority over the younger midshipmen, and the disruption to the midshipmen's routine caused by athletics "to such an inordinate degree that the question may well be asked whether we are paying to educate naval officers or football players." The annual reports of the Naval Academy superintendent acknowledged incidents of hazing in 1903 and 1904, three midshipmen being dismissed from the academy in 1904. In 1905, however, the superintendent reported that no incidents of hazing, that "unmanly practice," had occurred in the past year.[21]

The superintendent's optimism was premature: 1906 brought further controversy surrounding hazing, even the personal intervention of the commander in chief. In a letter to Congressman George E. Foss, the chairman of the House Naval Affairs Committee, Roosevelt explained why he had issued a pardon to Midn. John Paul Miller, who had been convicted of hazing and subsequently dismissed from the academy. Roosevelt saw as unjust the law that required midshipmen accused of hazing to be tried by court-martial and, if found guilty, dismissed. Roosevelt did not condone hazing and wished to see the practice "thoroughly eradicated," but he did not agree that dismissal was always a just punishment for the act, which often amounted to "nothing more than exhibitions of boyish mischief attended with no consequence of any moment to those hazed, and indicating on the part of the hazers only some exuberance of animal spirits." Taking a "boys will be boys" approach to the issue, Roosevelt believed it was a serious injustice to deny a career to a young man who made a youthful mistake. Furthermore, such a "disproportionate punishment of what may be a trivial offense may result in depriving the Government of a promising officer on whose education it has already expended several thousands of dollars." In cases of hazing involving brutality and cruelty toward younger midshipmen, however, Roosevelt favored some punishment even more severe than dismissal, presumably imprisonment. He concluded by expressing hope that Congress would correct the hazing law. In April 1906, Congress passed and Roosevelt signed an act that allowed for more flexibility in hazing cases and did not require court-martial for those charged with hazing and dismissal for those found guilty of it. Roosevelt's personal involvement provoked criticism from Park Benjamin, who blamed the president's leniency for the continuation of hazing at Annapolis.[22]

The American Nelson:
Reimagining John Paul Jones in the Age of Theodore Roosevelt

There was nothing Theodore Roosevelt liked more than an elaborate military ceremony. Fortunately for him, a major archaeological discovery abroad combined with the completion of the Naval Academy's impressive new campus provided him with the opportunity to put on a monumental display of American naval pageantry. At the center of the episode was John Paul Jones, the great naval hero of the Revolutionary War, a daring and at times volatile officer who had given the new United States its first victories at sea. Jones's dream of becoming America's first admiral, in command of a powerful American fleet, had disappeared when the last Continental Navy ships were sold off at the end of the war. Disillusioned with the Continental Congress's lack of interest in naval power, Jones had left the United States in search of naval glory elsewhere. After a brief tour of duty as a rear admiral in the Russian navy of Catherine the

Great, Jones took up residence in Paris, where he died bitter and alone in 1792. With little fanfare, his remains were interred in a small Protestant cemetery on the outskirts of the city.[23]

Over the course of the next hundred years, the cemetery was forgotten, becoming a cesspool and a burial ground for dead animals. By the twentieth century, the cemetery had been paved over and covered by a laundry business. Over the years, the U.S. government had made no effort to recover Jones's remains and bring them to the United States for a more dignified burial. That changed when the Navy became the pride and joy of the American people after the Spanish-American War. In June 1899, an attempt to find Jones's grave began under the direction of Horace Porter, the American ambassador to France. Porter, a West Point graduate and Civil War veteran who had served on the staff of Gen. Ulysses S. Grant, was an admirer of Jones and on his own authority began the project with personal funds. Through an extensive archival search in Paris, Porter and his research team found documentary evidence of the possible location of Jones's grave. Realizing the public relations potential associated with finding Jones, Roosevelt soon took great interest in Porter's project.[24]

By February 1905, Porter had found the cemetery and begun excavating. Believing he was close to finding Jones's remains, he requested that Roosevelt secure government appropriations to fund a full-scale archaeological excavation. Roosevelt duly sent a message to Congress reporting Porter's progress and requesting an appropriation of $35,000. Roosevelt explained, "The great interest which our people feel in the story of Paul Jones's life, the national sense of gratitude for the great service done by him toward the achievement of independence, and the sentiment of mingled distress and regret felt because the body of one of our greatest heroes lies forgotten and unmarked in foreign soil, lead me to approve the ambassador's suggestion" that Congress appropriate the funds in order "to do proper honor to the memory of Paul Jones."[25] Finally, on 14 April 1905, Porter informed Secretary of State John Hay by telegram that Jones's remains had been found and positively identified. An autopsy conducted by two distinguished anthropologists at a Paris medical school had confirmed that the remains were Jones'.[26]

There was no question but that the body would be brought back to the United States. The question that remained was the Revolutionary War hero's final resting place. The Navy originally planned to bury Jones in Arlington National Cemetery, but Roosevelt had another idea. In Roosevelt's mind, there was only one appropriate location for Jones: the Naval Academy in Annapolis. Fittingly, Flagg had designed its new chapel with the intention of making it the "Pantheon or Westminster Abbey of the Navy," incorporating catacombs for America's naval heroes of the past and a crypt reserved for the greatest hero, John Paul Jones. Ambassador Porter agreed with Roosevelt's decision, writing, "The sight of his monument there will be an inspiration to every graduate of that admirable institution."[27]

On 6 July (Jones' birthday), Jones' coffin proceeded down the Champs-Élysées in a grand procession of five hundred American sailors, French military personnel, American and French government officials, and two companies of U.S. Marines, as well as delegations from the Chamber of Commerce, the Society of the Cincinnati, the Sons of the American Revolution, and the Navy League of the United States. The coffin then traveled by train from Paris to Cherbourg to meet a U.S. Navy cruiser squadron for the voyage home. Jones' coffin was loaded on board the cruiser *Brooklyn*, flagship of the newly designated John Paul Jones Squadron, under the command of Rear Adm. Charles D. Sigsbee. The Jones Squadron set sail for America on 8 July. As the squadron approached the New England coast, it was joined by seven battleships. The enlarged fleet steamed southward to the Virginia Capes and then up the Chesapeake Bay. Four of the battleships broke off from the fleet, each firing a salute to the *Brooklyn* as it moved away. The rest of the ships continued on to Annapolis, anchoring off the Naval Academy on 23 July. The next day, as rows of midshipmen stood at attention along the academy's seawall, the naval tug *Standish*, one of the academy's practice ships, carried Jones' coffin ashore. A solemn procession through The Yard followed, the Naval Academy band playing the funeral march by Chopin. The coffin was placed in a temporary brick mausoleum across from the chapel as Marines fired a salute and a Navy bugler played "Taps."[28]

For Roosevelt, the discovery of John Paul Jones' remains and their reburial on the grounds of the Naval Academy was the perfect occasion to gain public support for his goal of expanding and strengthening the Navy with powerful battleships manned by a highly trained officer corps. Jones could serve as a professional role model for the midshipmen who would one day command those warships. Jones could also symbolize American naval power, given that Roosevelt's naval policy was the fulfillment of Jones' own grand vision for the American navy in the post–revolutionary war era.[29] However, this portrayal of Jones as a paragon of naval professionalism would require a reimagining of Jones' character as well as a reinterpretation of his historical legacy.

Depictions of Jones during the early nineteenth century had produced an image of him as a swashbuckling man of action. The Navy acknowledged his success as a Revolutionary War combat leader but did not consider him an ideal role model because of his prickly personality, sexual promiscuity, violent temper, and touchy sense of honor. Early American naval officers had questioned Jones' devotion to America, seeing him as more a naval mercenary than the prototypical professional officer. Roosevelt, an accomplished naval historian in his own right, had at one time shared this appraisal, dismissing Jones as little more than a "daring corsair."[30] The turn of the twentieth century brought a significant shift in Jones' reputation as a historical figure, away from the rough-around-the-edges naval adventurer and toward the highly professional naval officer. The popular biography *Paul Jones: Founder of the American Navy*, published by Augustus C. Buell in 1900, sparked this change in Jones' reputation, despite the fact that Buell had combined fact with fiction, fabricating documentary "evidence" to fit his main theme of Jones as the professional father of the American navy.[31] Roosevelt was not deterred by Buell's derelictions and expanded on this reinterpretation of Jones by making the revolutionary hero "the Navy's new patron saint." By the time of his presidency, Roosevelt viewed Jones as a valuable public-relations tool for gaining the public's support for a large battleship Navy commanded by professional officers. Jones became a professional and heroic role model of the type of officer Roosevelt wanted the Naval Academy to produce.[32]

For Roosevelt, military celebrations and ceremonies "gave him a forum for spreading his message about a vigorous military policy. Such ceremonies allowed him to invoke the nation's martial past to arouse support for modern-day forces."[33] Jones' reburial at Annapolis gave Roosevelt a perfect opportunity to energize the public about the Navy's glorious past and its aspirational future. With a strong sense of the theatrical, Roosevelt ordered a majestic ceremony in commemoration of Jones to be held at the Naval Academy on 24 April 1906, the anniversary of Jones' 1778 defeat of HMS *Drake* in the Irish Sea while in command of the sloop *Ranger* during the Revolutionary War. Roosevelt micromanaged the Annapolis ceremony from start to finish, ensuring maximum press coverage. In addition to furthering the public's interest in Jones' life and career, the ceremony also served to show off the Naval Academy's magnificent new campus.[34]

Approximately seven thousand people attended the three-hour ceremony in the academy's armory (Dahlgren Hall). Always fascinated with the trappings of naval officership—uniforms, medals, swords, and (in the Europe of his day) coats of arms—Jones would have reveled in the ceremony held in his honor. An American flag covered Jones' casket; a wreath and the gold sword presented to Jones by King Louis XVI lay on top. Among the distinguished speakers on the dais were President Roosevelt, French ambassador to the United States Jean Jules Jusserand, Horace Porter, Secretary of the Navy Bonaparte, and Maryland governor Edwin Warfield.[35] Describing the festivities in a letter to his father, Midn. Alfred K. Schanze expressed surprise at the number of people in Annapolis that day, far more than he had ever seen there previously. Many people had traveled to the Naval Academy by train from Washington, D.C., or by water. Annapolis Harbor bustled with naval ships as well as private yachts and steamers. The midshipman declared, "The whole ceremony was about the most impressive I have ever witnessed and I shall remember it for years to come."[36]

In his thirty-minute address, Roosevelt stated that he had received letters from representatives of municipalities all over the United States requesting that their cities be Jones's final resting place. But only in Annapolis, at the

Naval Academy, Roosevelt declared, would Jones "be a living force," an inspiration to future generations of naval officers: "The future naval officers, who live within these walls, will find in the career of the man whose life we this day celebrate, not merely a subject for admiration and respect, but an object lesson to be taken into their innermost hearts. Every officer in our Navy should know by heart the deeds of John Paul Jones. Every officer in our Navy should feel in each fiber of his being an eager desire to emulate the energy, the professional capacity, the indomitable determination and dauntless scorn of death which marked John Paul Jones above all his fellows."[37] Roosevelt connected Jones with the naval heroes that had come after him, including Oliver Hazard Perry and Thomas Macdonough of the War of 1812, David Farragut of the Civil War, and, most recently, Dewey of the Spanish-American War (who was in attendance at the ceremony and received "hearty" applause from the audience). Roosevelt's depiction of Jones represented his model of what he hoped Annapolis would produce: officers who were courageous men of action as well as true professionals who recognized the importance of efficiency, thorough preparation, careful training, and the proper maintenance of ships.[38]

The president concluded his remarks by imploring his fellow Americans, particularly political leaders, to "study the history of our nation, not merely for the purpose of national self-gratification, but with the desire to learn the lessons that history teaches." For Roosevelt, history was not merely an academic discipline; it was a valuable guide for policy making. Pointing to the poor condition of the U.S. Navy at the start of the War of 1812, a topic on which he was an expert, and blaming the foolishness and parsimony of the Jefferson administration for that regrettable situation, the president challenged the political leaders of his own time not to repeat the same mistakes and instead support policies that would maintain a strong American navy.[39]

After the commemoration ceremony, a funeral dirge was played as Jones' casket was transferred to Bancroft Hall, where it was placed underneath the main staircase. The casket remained in this somewhat undignified location for seven years before Congress finally appropriated the funds for a permanent resting place in the crypt beneath the chapel dome. On 26 January 1913, Jones' remains were entombed in a twenty-one-ton sarcophagus in the crypt in a manner reminiscent of the burial of Britain's greatest naval hero, Lord Nelson, at St. Paul's Cathedral in London. Comparisons between Nelson and Jones abounded, since both men were small in stature, assertive, vain, insecure, in love with military trappings, and brave to the point of recklessness.[40]

By choosing Annapolis as Jones' final resting place, Roosevelt solidified the Naval Academy's status as the professional and cultural center of the U.S. Navy, which, by Roosevelt's presidency, was quickly becoming the modern, powerful, and professional fleet that Jones had hoped to command in the years after the American Revolution. Through his reimagining of John Paul Jones' life and legacy, his use of military pomp and ceremony, and the grandeur of the Naval Academy's new campus, Roosevelt effectively enlisted Jones in his quest for strengthening American naval power. As historian Lori Bogle has observed, "The mystery and majesty surrounding the Revolutionary War hero's life and death and the later discovery of his remains linked the twentieth-century navy to its past and enabled the president . . . to advance his vision for the navy as a professional, progressive service prepared for offensive fleet action."[41]

Studying the Art of War:
Theodore Roosevelt and the Naval War College

Mark Twain once wrote that Theodore Roosevelt was "clearly insane . . . and insanest upon war and its supreme glories."[42] Given this characterization, it surprised no one that Roosevelt showed personal interest in the Naval War College, a school dedicated to instruction in the art of war. By the late nineteenth century, a small group of forward-thinking officers recognized the need for theoretical and strategic studies in warfare to guide America's growing military power. These reformers saw the need to produce officers who were not merely technical experts but also strategic thinkers. War was no longer merely the act of fighting; it had become a true science, in which technological advancements in weaponry required the development of new tactics and logistical support systems. These developments necessitated a new approach to strategy in the modern era, which in turn demanded that officer education move beyond the mostly technical curriculum at the undergraduate academies.[43]

Progressive officers spoke of the need for two kinds of professional military education: first, scientific and technical instruction, and second, the theoretical analysis and critical thinking needed to devise strategy and policy. The scientific and technical education would take place at West Point and Annapolis, as well as at such postgraduate programs as the Army's specialized schools for infantry, cavalry, artillery, and engineers, or the Navy's torpedo school at Newport, Rhode Island, the naval architecture school at the Massachusetts Institute of Technology, or the postgraduate course in engineering and ordnance at the Naval Academy (which would eventually become the Naval Postgraduate School, originally at Annapolis). Established in 1881, the Army's Infantry and Cavalry School at Fort Leavenworth, Kansas, the forerunner of today's Command and General Staff College, by beginning to provide more theoretical instruction in warfare, served as the inspiration for Commo. Stephen B. Luce, whose goal was to establish a school for the Navy that would educate officers in the art of war.[44]

Appointed as a midshipman at the age of fourteen in 1841, Luce served tours of duty as an instructor and commandant of midshipmen at the Naval Academy during the Civil War and authored textbooks on gunnery and seamanship. He was the rare combination of an expert seaman and tactician who was also a well-read and scholarly naval reformer. Luce staunchly opposed a strictly technical approach to naval education. In his view, officers had to be more than just seamen, navigators, and engineers; they had to be able to think critically about war. In a letter to Secretary of the Navy Richard W. Thompson, Luce explained his vision for a postgraduate "course of instruction in the Art of War." Arguing that naval officers were not being taught the more advanced aspects of their profession, Luce declared that "with the recent revolution in naval warfare comes a demand for a higher order of talent in the conduct of naval operation." He continued, "The introduction of steam and the telegraph enabling military operations both on land and at sea to be conducted with great rapidity, and shortening to months great campaigns which had in times past consumed years, renders it absolutely necessary that to be a successful naval captain of the present day an officer must be a strategist as well as a tactician." Luce believed that the study of history was vital to forming the intellectual foundation needed to understand the principles of strategy. While emphasizing the importance of naval history, Luce also saw great value in studying the history of armies, convinced that the principles that governed military science on land could be applied to naval warfare.[45]

The Naval War College was established in 1884 on Coasters Harbor Island in Newport, Rhode Island, with the purpose of offering naval officers advanced studies in strategy, tactics, naval and military history, logistics, and international law. The course of instruction at the college would build upon the undergraduate liberal arts and technical education provided at the Naval Academy; Luce did not intend for the new college to compete with Annapolis, as some Naval Academy staff feared. In addition to its educational mission, Luce strove to use the college to elevate the importance of naval strategy in the eyes of the public. In this endeavor, he found an ally in Capt. Alfred Thayer Mahan.[46]

Mahan, born in 1840 at West Point, was the son of longtime Military Academy professor Dennis Hart Mahan. Going against his father's wishes, the younger Mahan attended the Naval Academy, graduating second in the Class of 1859. Something of a "Navy misfit," Mahan was "an aloof and solitary figure" who preferred study and writing on shore to sea duty. During the Civil War he served as an instructor in seamanship at the Naval Academy, where he first met Luce. At Luce's invitation, Mahan arrived at the Naval War College in 1885 as an instructor in naval history and strategy. Soon after, he succeeded Luce as the college's president. Mahan catapulted to worldwide fame in 1890 with the publication of his groundbreaking book *The Influence of Sea Power upon History, 1660–1783*, which began as a series of lectures at the college. It quickly became the standard work on sea power around the world, earning Mahan honorary degrees from such universities as Oxford, Cambridge, Harvard, Yale, Columbia, and McGill.[47] With the founding of the Naval War College and Mahan's rise to prominence, the study of naval history became a way to expand the Navy's intellectual pursuits beyond science and engineering. History provided a valuable, broader perspective for examining theoretical issues of naval organization and the nature of naval power.[48]

The first course of instruction at the college in 1885 was limited in its scope, but with Mahan's arrival later that year it expanded into the curriculum that Luce had originally intended. Students attended lectures on naval gunnery tactics, military strategy and tactics, military history, and international law, the centerpiece being Mahan's lectures on naval history and strategy. By the end of the nineteenth century, the Naval War College experience included several components: lectures and readings on professional subjects, a war problem requiring students to apply the material learned from the lectures and readings to a specific situation, the creation of war plans, and participation in war games. The main goal of the college curriculum was to develop inductive reasoning among its students, enabling them to take theoretical principles from their studies and apply them to specific military scenarios.[49]

Luce had known Roosevelt since the early 1880s when Roosevelt was a member of the New York State Assembly and the two men served together on the New York Board of Education. Always eager to cultivate relationships with political leaders and recognizing the young New York politician as a rising star in the Republican Party, Luce reached out to Roosevelt after rereading Roosevelt's *The Naval War of 1812*. Praising the work and informing Roosevelt that the book would be used as a textbook at the Naval War College, Luce invited him to give a lecture on the topic to the college's faculty and students. Roosevelt gladly accepted the invitation, and it was during this visit to Newport in 1888 that he met Mahan.[50]

Roosevelt and Mahan would form a mutually successful professional, if not quite personal, friendship; Roosevelt recognized that Mahan's naval theories supported his own quest to grow American naval power, and Mahan saw in Roosevelt a strong political patron. When in 1893 it was time for Mahan to leave Newport to return to sea duty, he wrote to Commo. Francis M. Ramsay, chief of the Bureau of Navigation, requesting to be excused from sea duty to continue his writing and teaching at the college. Ramsay, a staunch opponent of the new naval intellectualism of the era in general and of the Naval War College in particular, denied Mahan's

request, stating that "it is not the business of naval officers to write books."
Anticipating Ramsay's response, Mahan had already asked Roosevelt
to intervene on his behalf with the Navy Department, arguing that his
planned scholarly projects in naval strategy and history could be far more
useful to the Navy. He also pointed out that since he planned to retire
from the Navy in 1896, after almost forty years of service, an additional
period of command at sea was useless to his professional development as a
naval officer. Roosevelt discussed the matter with Assistant Secretary of
the Navy William McAdoo, who ultimately declined to overrule Ramsay.
Roosevelt lamented, "I fear all hope for the War College (which is nothing without you) has gone." He also vowed retribution against Ramsay,
whom Roosevelt described as a "blind, narrow, mean, jealous pedant; if
I can I ever do him a bad turn I most certainly will." Mahan accepted
his fate and went to sea as captain of the cruiser *Chicago.* It is unlikely
that Roosevelt ever followed through on his threat against Ramsay, who
retired from the Navy as a rear admiral shortly before Roosevelt took
office as Assistant Secretary of the Navy in April 1897.[51]

Roosevelt's appointment as assistant secretary put him in a position
to enhance the Naval War College's stature within the Navy and with
the public. Roosevelt signaled his support for the college by giving his
first major speech as assistant secretary in Newport on 2 June 1897. The
address was classic Roosevelt, a strong argument in favor of preparedness for war by building a modern and powerful American fleet, with
historical examples to support his main thesis. Declaring that "preparation for war is the surest guarantee of peace," Roosevelt stated that "the
great masterful races have been fighting races." Using America's lack of
preparedness for the War of 1812 as a warning to his fellow Americans
and directing particular blame at Thomas Jefferson's flawed leadership
as commander in chief, Roosevelt cautioned that the instruments of war
in contemporary times, both technological and human, were far more
complex and required more time to bring to bear against an enemy. For
the Navy, these instruments included the ships and guns needed to fight
but also the men who would command and operate them. The professional
development of naval officers through education was vital to America's

standing in the world: "They must have skill in handling the ships, skill in tactics, skill in strategy, for ignorant courage can not avail; but without courage, neither will skill avail."[52] The speech gained significant press coverage. The *New York Sun* praised it as "manly, patriotic, intelligent, and convincing." Even President Willaim McKinley admitted, "I suspect Roosevelt is right and the only difference between him and me is the greater responsibility [of the presidency]." One person who was not particularly pleased was Roosevelt's boss, Secretary of the Navy John D. Long, who believed that the address was too militaristic. In a letter to Mahan, Roosevelt commented, "[Long] didn't like the address I made to the War College at Newport the other day."[53]

By the mid-1890s, the Naval War College had become more than a Navy graduate school; it had also become a strategic planning organization, preparing war plans for file at the Office of Naval Intelligence in Washington, D.C. The war problems in 1896 and 1897 presciently envisioned a possible war with Spain. The mutual interest of the United States and Japan toward Hawaii prompted Roosevelt to order Capt. Caspar F. Goodrich, president of the college, to assign a special war problem on that potential military situation. Roosevelt also showed a special interest in the college's war games, telling Goodrich that he would like to time his next visit to Newport so that he could "see one of your big strategic games" in person. The addition of war gaming to the college curriculum gave the school a distinctive feature and attracted the attention of the public. The college's growing emphasis on strategic planning and preparation for future conflicts influenced Roosevelt's own thinking. On 25 February 1898, while Acting Secretary of the Navy in Long's absence, Roosevelt issued orders to prepare the Navy for war with Spain if hostilities broke out.[54]

In addition to promoting the scholarly and strategic work of the Naval War College, Roosevelt became its defender against elements within the Navy that sought to eliminate it. Despite the international influence of Mahan and the attention it brought, the college's existence remained precarious in its early years. Often merely tolerated by and sometimes openly attacked within the naval community, the college lacked a clearly defined relationship with the Navy. Some critics believed the college was too small to have any real impact on the Navy; after all, it had taught only around two hundred students in its first ten years of existence. Officers with more technical approaches to the naval profession questioned the relevance of the historical studies emphasized there. As a result, the college faced attempts to abolish it outright, absorb it into the Naval Academy as a postgraduate course, or relocate it to Washington as a planning staff attached to the Office of Naval Intelligence. Luce considered any attempt to remove the Naval War College from Newport as intended to abolish the school entirely. If it moved to Washington, it would lose its educational mission and become incorporated into the Navy Department's administrative structure. If it moved to Annapolis, it would lose its independence and distinctiveness. An 1897 effort to eliminate the college came when Commo. Francis W. Dickens, the acting chief of the Bureau of Navigation, recommended to Roosevelt the reassignment of the Naval War College staff to the Office of Naval Intelligence. To gain support for his idea, Dickens published an article in the *Army and Navy Register*. Roosevelt encouraged Caspar Goodrich, as the college's president, to publish an article defending the Naval War College as an independent educational institution. Goodrich did so in the November 1897 issue of the *Army and Navy Register*, effectively ending Dickens's assault on the college.[55]

Roosevelt's support for the Naval War College continued during his presidency. Acting on the advice of Cdr. William S. Sims, the president convened a conference on battleship design in Newport in July 1908. The purpose of the conference was to bring together ship designers and naval officers to examine defects in the battleship *North Dakota* and to make recommendations for future battleship construction. An article by Henry Reuterdahl, an editor of *Jane's Fighting Ships*, in January 1908 had sharply criticized the Navy's organization and its shipbuilding program. Roosevelt grew concerned that the negative attention produced by the article would undermine the favorable press the Navy was receiving for the cruise of the Great White Fleet. Traveling to Newport on the presidential yacht *Mayflower*, Roosevelt personally opened the conference on

22 July. The conference produced a report to Roosevelt that recommended modifications to the new battleships *North Dakota* and *Delaware* as well as changes in the design of the next class of battleships. Roosevelt approved the report and ordered that its recommendations be implemented by the Navy. In addition to the conference's importance to the Navy's shipbuilding program, the conference was significant as the first time an American president had become directly involved in the Naval War College and its planning activities, an involvement that furthered the institution's prestige within the Navy and with the public.[56]

Educating Officers for the New Navy: Annapolis and Newport at the Turn of the Century

One of Theodore Roosevelt's greatest legacies was his advocacy of the American navy, educating the public about the Navy's historical significance and its contemporary importance to the nation while also instilling pride in the fleet and its capabilities. Roosevelt "provided his country with the organization with which to build naval supremacy."[57] He knew that building modern battleships without having well-educated and highly trained officers to command them would ultimately lead to failure on the world stage. The Naval Academy and Naval War College played a critical educational role in the professional development of American naval officers, but the two institutions were also important components of Roosevelt's public relations campaign to glorify America's naval past and gain public support for American naval power. Whether it was the architectural grandeur of the Naval Academy's new campus, highlighted by the reburial of John Paul Jones at Annapolis, or the historical studies and strategic planning that took place in Newport, each institution made significant contributions to Roosevelt's overall naval mission. The leadership, faculty, and graduates of each school, most notably men like Luce and Mahan, provided Roosevelt with a crucial base of support for his navalist agenda. Through his personal interest in the Naval Academy and Naval War College, Roosevelt prepared the U.S. Navy for its future success in two world wars and beyond.

Notes

1. *New York Times*, 5 March 1905, 1.
2. William P. Leeman, *The Long Road to Annapolis: The Founding of the Naval Academy and the Emerging American Republic* (Chapel Hill: University of North Carolina Press, 2010), 234, 237–38; Carl Cavanagh Hodge, "The Global Strategist: The Navy as the Nation's Big Stick," in *A Companion to Theodore Roosevelt*, ed. Serge Ricard (Malden, Mass.: Wiley-Blackwell, 2011), 260; and Samuel P. Huntington, *The Soldier and the State: The Theory and Politics of Civil-Military Relations* (New York: Vintage Books, 1957), 244.
3. H. Michael Gelfand, *Sea Change at Annapolis: The United States Naval Academy, 1949–2000* (Chapel Hill: University of North Carolina Press, 2006), 3–4; Mardges Bacon, *Ernest Flagg: Beaux-Arts Architect and Urban Reformer* (New York and Cambridge, Mass.: Architectural History Association and MIT Press, 1986), 112–13; Jack Sweetman, *The U.S. Naval Academy: An Illustrated History*, 2nd ed. (Annapolis, Md.: Naval Institute Press, 1995), 138–39, 141.
4. Matthew Oyos, *In Command: Theodore Roosevelt and the American Military* (Lincoln: Potomac Books of the University of Nebraska Press, 2018), 10–11; Bacon, *Ernest Flagg*, 114–15; Sweetman, *U.S. Naval Academy*, 143–44, 149; James C. Bradford, *The Reincarnation of John Paul Jones: The Navy Discovers Its Professional Roots* (Washington, D.C.: Naval Historical Foundation, 1986), 8; Gordon Carpenter O'Gara, *Theodore Roosevelt and the Rise of the Modern Navy* (Princeton, N.J.: Princeton University Press, 1943; repr. New York: Greenwood, 1969), 94.
5. Morris Janowitz, *The Professional Soldier: A Social and Political Portrait* (New York: Free Press, 1960; repr. 1971), 127–31.
6. Quoted in Theodore J. Crackel, *West Point: A Bicentennial History* (Lawrence: University Press of Kansas, 2002), 166–67.
7. Theodore Roosevelt, "Speech at Haverhill, Massachusetts," 26 August 1902, in Theodore Roosevelt, *Addresses and Presidential Messages of Theodore Roosevelt, 1902–1904* (New York: G. P. Putnam's Sons, 1904), 29–30.
8. John W. Masland and Laurence I. Radway, *Soldiers and Scholars: Military Education and National Policy* (Princeton, N.J.: Princeton University Press, 1957), 50–51.
9. *Annual Register of the United States Naval Academy, Annapolis, Md., Fifty-Ninth Academic Year, 1903–1904* (Washington, D.C.: Government Printing Office, 1903), 123–26; Richard Wainwright, "The New Naval Academy," *World's Work* 4 (July 1902): 2284.
10. Oyos, *In Command*, 50–51, 53; O'Gara, *Theodore Roosevelt and the Rise of the Modern Navy*, 105–106.
11. Theodore Roosevelt, "The Genesis of the Personnel Bill," *North American Review* (December 1898), in *The Works of Theodore Roosevelt*, ed. Hermann Hagedorn (New York: Charles Scribner's Sons, 1926), 14:280–83; TR to Henry

Reuterdahl, 27 May 1916, in *The Letters of Theodore Roosevelt*, ed. Elting E. Morison (Cambridge, Mass.: Harvard University Press, 1951–1954), 8:1047.

12. Oyos, *In Command*, 75; Theodore Roosevelt, "Sixth Annual Message," 3 December 1906, in *A Compilation of the Messages and Papers of the Presidents*, ed. James D. Richardson (New York: Bureau of National Literature, 1918), 15:7068.

13. Theodore Roosevelt, "Seventh Annual Message," 3 December 1907, Richardson, *Messages and Papers of the Presidents*, 15:7117; "Report of the Board of Visitors to the United States Naval Academy," in *Annual Report of the Secretary of the Navy, 1907* (Washington, D.C.: Government Printing Office, 1908), 120–21.

14. Theodore Roosevelt, "First Annual Message," 3 December 1901, Richardson, *Messages and Papers of the Presidents*, 15:6667.

15. Theodore Roosevelt, "Eighth Annual Message," 8 December 1908, Richardson, 16:7238.

16. Charles Oscar Paullin, *Paullin's History of Naval Administration, 1775–1911* (Annapolis, Md.: U.S. Naval Institute, 1968), 465; Sweetman, *U.S. Naval Academy*, 149; Ralph Earle, *Life at the U.S. Naval Academy: The Making of the American Naval Officer* (New York: G. P. Putnam's Sons, 1917), 24–25. For a detailed discussion of the efforts to increase the number of midshipmen at the Naval Academy, see Donald Chisholm, *Waiting for Dead Men's Shoes: Origins and Development of the U.S. Navy's Officer Personnel System, 1793–1941* (Stanford, Calif.: Stanford University Press, 2001), 467–524.

17. Theodore Roosevelt, *The Strenuous Life: Essays and Addresses* (New York: Century, 1905), 1, 10–15.

18. Oyos, *In Command*, 311–16; Janowitz, *Professional Soldier*, 130.

19. TR to Russell Alexander Alger, 17 August 1897, in *Theodore Roosevelt: Letters and Speeches*, ed. Louis Auchincloss (New York: Library of America, 2004), 114–15; Sweetman, *U.S. Naval Academy*, 160; "Report of the Superintendent of the United States Naval Academy," in *Annual Report of the Secretary of the Navy, 1902* (Washington, D.C.: Government Printing Office, 1902), 424. Despite his love of the sport, Roosevelt threatened to ban college football by executive order if the colleges did not clean up the game and decrease the brutality on the field, which had resulted in the deaths of eighteen players during the 1905 season. The president wanted football to be rough but played fairly and according to rules. See Frederick Rudolph, *The American College and University: A History* (Athens: University of Georgia Press, 1990), 375–77.

20. H. W. Brands, *T.R.: The Last Romantic* (New York: Basic Books, 1997), 554; TR to Charles J. Bonaparte, 17 February 1906, Auchincloss, *Letters and Speeches*, 448–49.

21. Park Benjamin, "The Trouble at the Naval Academy," *Independent* 60 (18 January 1906): 154–56, quotation on 156; "Report of the Superintendent of the United States Naval Academy," in *Annual Report of the Secretary of the Navy, 1903* (Washington, D.C.: Government Printing Office, 1903), 581; "Report of the Superintendent of the United States Naval Academy," in *Annual Report*

of the Secretary of the Navy, 1904 (Washington, D.C.: Government Printing Office, 1904), 508; "Report of the Superintendent of the United States Naval Academy," in *Annual Report of the Secretary of the Navy, 1905* (Washington, D.C.: Government Printing Office, 1906), 445.

22. TR to George E. Foss, 1 February 1906, Morison, *Letters of Theodore Roosevelt,* 5:143–45; Benjamin, "Trouble at the Naval Academy," 156.

23. Leeman, *Long Road to Annapolis,* 231; Bradford, *Reincarnation of John Paul Jones,* 1.

24. Evan Thomas, *John Paul Jones: Sailor, Hero, Father of the American Navy* (New York: Simon & Schuster, 2003), 4; Lori Lyn Bogle, "The President and the Corpse: Theodore Roosevelt and the 1906 John Paul Jones Reinterment Ceremony," *Theodore Roosevelt Association Journal* 38 (Winter-Spring-Summer 2017): 62; Joseph Callo, *John Paul Jones: America's First Sea Warrior* (Annapolis, Md.: Naval Institute Press, 2006), 181–82; Horace Porter to TR, 20 October 1903, Theodore Roosevelt Papers, Library of Congress, Theodore Roosevelt Digital Library, Dickinson State University, http://www.theodorerooseveltcenter.org/Research/Digital-Library (accessed 10 August 2018).

25. TR to the Senate and House of Representatives, 13 February 1905, in *John Paul Jones: Commemoration at Annapolis, April 24, 1906,* comp. Charles W. Stewart (Washington, D.C.: Government Printing Office, 1907), 43–44.

26. Horace Porter to the Secretary of State [John Hay], 14 April 1905, Stewart, 44–45.

27. Bogle, "The President and the Corpse," 65; Bacon, *Ernest Flagg,* 130; Horace Porter to TR, 22 June 1905, Theodore Roosevelt Digital Library (accessed 10 August 2018). Ironically, after Jones's body was found, another architect finished the crypt beneath the chapel; by that point Flagg had alienated the Navy by initiating a lawsuit for additional fees for his architectural services and by claiming publicly that he deserved recognition as the first person to suggest a search for Jones's body in Paris.

28. Callo, *John Paul Jones,* 182–84; Thomas, *John Paul Jones,* 3; Samuel Eliot Morison, *John Paul Jones: A Sailor's Biography* (Boston: Little, Brown, 1959), 407–409.

29. Leeman, *Long Road to Annapolis,* 231–32.

30. Lori Lyn Bogle and Joel I. Holwitt, "The Best Quote Jones Never Wrote," *Naval History* 18 (April 2004): 19; Bradford, *Reincarnation of John Paul Jones,* 2–7; Bogle, "The President and the Corpse," 64.

31. Bradford, *Reincarnation of John Paul Jones,* 7–8; Thomas, *John Paul Jones,* 310.

32. Bogle and Holwitt, "Best Quote Jones Never Wrote," 19–20.

33. Oyos, *In Command,* 106–107.

34. Bogle, "The President and the Corpse," 65; Callo, *John Paul Jones,* 185.

35. *New York Times,* 25 April 1906, 8; Bogle, "The President and the Corpse," 65; Thomas, *John Paul Jones,* 4–5; Callo, *John Paul Jones,* 185.

36. Alfred K. Schanze to his father, 27 April 1906, in *Letters from Annapolis: Midshipmen Write Home, 1848–1969*, ed. Anne Marie Drew (Annapolis, Md.: Naval Institute Press, 1998), 94–97, quotation on 97.

37. "Address of President Roosevelt," Stewart, *Commemoration at Annapolis*, 16.

38. "Address of President Roosevelt," 17.

39. "Address of President Roosevelt," 17–18.

40. Callo, *John Paul Jones*, 187; Ernest Flagg, "New Buildings at the United States Naval Academy, Annapolis, Md.," *American Architect and Building News* 94 (1 July 1908): 6; Thomas, *John Paul Jones*, 309; Sweetman, *U.S. Naval Academy*, 149; Morison, *John Paul Jones*, 411.

41. Leeman, *Long Road to Annapolis*, Bogle, 234; "The President and the Corpse," 66.

42. Quoted in Kathleen Dalton, *Theodore Roosevelt: A Strenuous Life* (New York: Alfred A. Knopf, 2002), 9.

43. Huntington, *Soldier and the State*, 237, 256; Masland and Radway, *Soldiers and Scholars*, 76, 80–81.

44. John B. Hattendorf, B. Mitchell Simpson III, and John R. Wadleigh, *Sailors and Scholars: The Centennial History of the U.S. Naval War College* (Newport, R.I.: Naval War College Press, 1984), 6–7; Huntington, *Soldier and the State*, 239–41.

45. Ronald Spector, *Professors of War: The Naval War College and the Development of the Naval Profession* (Newport, R.I.: Naval War College Press, 1977), 11–12, 14, 17–18; Stephen B. Luce to Richard W. Thompson, 8 August 1877, in Albert Gleaves, *Life and Letters of Rear Admiral Stephen B. Luce* (New York: G. P. Putnam's Sons, 1925), 169; John B. Hattendorf, "Stephen B. Luce: Intellectual Leader of the New Navy," in *Admirals of the New Steel Navy: Makers of the American Naval Tradition, 1880–1930*, ed. James C. Bradford (Annapolis, Md.: Naval Institute Press, 1990), 3–4, 8, 13.

46. Leeman, *Long Road to Annapolis*, 238; Hattendorf, Simpson, and Wadleigh, *Sailors and Scholars*, 20–22; Peter Karsten, *The Naval Aristocracy: The Golden Age of Annapolis and the Emergence of Modern American Navalism* (New York: Free Press, 1972), 336.

47. Philip A. Crowl, "Alfred Thayer Mahan: The Naval Historian," in *Makers of Modern Strategy: From Machiavelli to the Nuclear Age*, ed. Peter Paret (Princeton, N.J.: Princeton University Press, 1986), 444–46, quotations on 445; Laurence Wood Bartlett III, "Not Merely for Defense: The Creation of the New American Navy, 1865–1914" (Ph.D. diss., Texas Christian University, 2011), 92; Alfred Thayer Mahan, *From Sail to Steam: Recollections of Naval Life* (New York: Harper & Brothers, 1907; repr. Da Capo, 1968), 313.

48. Hattendorf, Simpson, and Wadleigh, *Sailors and Scholars*, 7–8.

49. Hattendorf, Simpson, and Wadleigh, 22–24, 40–41; Spector, *Professors of War*, 32–34.

50. Hattendorf, Simpson, and Wadleigh, *Sailors and Scholars*, 28; Spector, *Professors of War*, 54–55.

51. Stephen Howarth, *To Shining Sea: A History of the United States Navy, 1775–1991* (New York: Random House, 1991), 236–37; Spector, *Professors of War*, 61–62; Alfred Thayer Mahan to TR, 1 March 1893, Alfred Thayer Mahan to Francis M. Ramsay, 17 March 1893, and Alfred Thayer Mahan to TR, 18 March 1893, in *Letters and Papers of Alfred Thayer Mahan*, ed. Robert Seager II and Doris D. Maguire (Annapolis, Md.: Naval Institute Press, 1975), 2:96–99; Ramsay quoted in Mahan, *Sail to Steam*, 311; TR to Alfred Thayer Mahan, 1 May 1893, Morison, *Letters of Theodore Roosevelt*, 1:315.

52. Theodore Roosevelt, *Address of Hon. Theodore Roosevelt, Assistant Secretary of the Navy, before the Naval War College, Newport, R.I., Wednesday, June 2, 1897* (Washington, D.C.: Government Printing Office, 1897), quotations on 4 and 17.

53. Henry J. Hendrix, *Theodore Roosevelt's Naval Diplomacy: The U.S. Navy and the Birth of the American Century* (Annapolis, Md.: Naval Institute Press, 2009), 13–14; Nathan Miller, *Theodore Roosevelt: A Life* (New York: William Morrow, 1992), 255; TR to Alfred Thayer Mahan, 9 June 1897, in *The Selected Letters of Theodore Roosevelt*, ed. H. W. Brands (New York: Cooper Square, 2001), 141.

54. Hattendorf, Simpson, and Wadleigh, *Sailors and Scholars*, 42, 45, 47; Spector, *Professors of War*, 74, 95; TR to Caspar F. Goodrich, 28 May, 16 June 1897, Morison, *Letters of Theodore Roosevelt*, 1:617–18, 626.

55. Masland and Radway, *Soldiers and Scholars*, 82–83; Hattendorf, Simpson, and Wadleigh, *Sailors and Scholars*, 38, 49–50; Spector, *Professors of War*, 53–55, 97–99.

56. Oyos, *In Command*, 288–90; Hattendorf, Simpson, and Wadleigh, *Sailors and Scholars*, 61–64; *Annual Report of the Secretary of the Navy, 1908* (Washington, D.C.: Government Printing Office, 1908), 15–16.

57. O'Gara, *Theodore Roosevelt and the Rise of the Modern Navy*, 111, quotation on 113.

5

"A HIGHER STANDARD OF PROFICIENCY"

Theodore Roosevelt and the U.S. Naval Officer Corps

Jon Scott Logel

At the end of 1897, Theodore Roosevelt, as the Assistant Secretary of the Navy, delivered the Roosevelt Board's recommendations to reform naval officer personnel policy. Specifically, Roosevelt sought to "remedy the evils of the present situation" by "amalgamating," or combining, the line officers and engineers into one single officer corps and by adopting a promotion policy based on merit rather than time in service. "It is absolutely essential," the *New York Times* quoted Roosevelt as declaring "that the best naval officer of the future shall be proficient in engineering." Roosevelt acknowledged that "this is an age of specialization; but there can be no specialization in command." The half-century practice of separating the engineers from the line officers had become inefficient, if not outright counterproductive in a fleet of modern steel battleships. A change in policy was long overdue. In his appointment as assistant secretary, Roosevelt sought to transform the U.S. Navy for the modern world he and other progressives saw emerging at the end of the nineteenth century. Fixing the naval officer system remained his goal as president; he told Congress, "History, modern and ancient has invariably shown that an efficient personnel is the greatest factor toward an effective navy."[1]

Indeed, the amalgamation of the line officers and engineers would be one of Roosevelt's enduring legacies for the modern U.S. Navy.

Proficient, efficient, effective—this was what Roosevelt really expected out of any government bureau, service, or enterprise. The Navy was no different from the New York City Police Department, which he had supervised as police commissioner for two years prior to his naval appointment. In 1897, the Navy was in many ways just another American institution, a bureaucracy suffering the trials and tribulations of modernization. In the decades following the Civil War, the Navy Department had stagnated and atrophied while the nation expanded westward and then ventured across the Pacific. The advent of new ship technologies and late nineteenth-century naval thinking revealed the department to be inefficiently organized, resourced, and managed, ill equipped to adapt to the new circumstances of a modern world. Roosevelt and his fellow progressives viewed this institutional resistance to change as the source of multiple evils and injustices that only reform could remedy.

From April 1897 through May 1898, Roosevelt applied his ideas of progressive reform to the Navy, expanding his campaign of reform from the New York City Police Department (and the U.S. Civil Service Commission before that) to the Navy Department in Washington, D.C., across naval bases and shipyards in the United States, and to American territories abroad. With Roosevelt as the Assistant Secretary of the Navy, the progressive moment, or "impulse," as many have called it, swelled from the local to the national level, from the domestic to the international scene. For historians today Roosevelt's personnel policies as assistant secretary and then as president present several questions for consideration. First, what was Roosevelt's role in shaping naval officer personnel policy, and how did Roosevelt's personnel policy decisions immediately affect the naval profession? A second, broader question is, how did progressive reform influence Roosevelt's tenure as assistant secretary and continue with respect to the naval officer corps when he assumed the presidency? After his initial campaign to correct the Navy's personnel problems, Roosevelt quickly proceeded to meet head-on the multitude of other challenges in the turn-of-the-century U.S. Navy. From 1897 through the end of his presidency in 1909, Roosevelt left his mark on the American military not only in personnel policies but also in the emergence of the new steel Navy, and the crafting of a strategy for that Navy.[2] Even when his responsibilities increased during his presidency, Roosevelt continued the progressive crusade that had begun when he was assistant secretary to reform the Navy personnel system.

The Roosevelt Board of 1897 serves as a case study of how Roosevelt's progressive vision influenced his decisions and actions as Assistant Secretary of the Navy, foreshadowing what aims he would pursue as commander in chief. Roosevelt's efforts were part of the "transformation of the Navy from a force of cruisers to one of battleships, from a defensive force to an offensive one."[3] Pragmatic, determined, tenacious—all apply to Roosevelt in this circumstance. Just as his presidency left a legacy for the nation as a whole, his terms as assistant secretary and then as commander in chief indelibly shaped the U.S. Navy officer corps in the twentieth century.

Roosevelt and Progressive Reform

"Progressive reform" and "Theodore Roosevelt" are almost synonymous in the history of the Progressive Era of the late nineteenth and early twentieth centuries. Richard Hofstadter's characterization is probably as definitive as any other. In *The Age of Reform* he wrote, "The generation that went Progressive was the generation that came of age in the nineties. Contemporaries had often noticed how large a portion of the leaders at any Populist convention were the silver-haired veterans of old monetary reform crusades; Progressivism, however, passed into the hands of the youth." Hofstadter points to William Allen White, the Kansas progressive and newspaper editor who described the reformers that followed the Populists as "young men in their twenties, thirties, and early forties" who recognized "the inequities, injustices, and fundamental wrongs of American society" and became inspired to reform. For Hofstadter, "[The] ascension of Theodore Roosevelt to the presidency . . . was no more than symbolic of the coming-of-age of a generation whose perspectives were sharply demarcated from those of their fathers and who felt the need for a new philosophy and new politics."[4]

Living in New York, Roosevelt dwelled and worked in the most modern, dynamic urban metropolis in the world. Contradiction, however, permeated New York City's emergence as the global city of the 1890s. Victorian Gotham brimmed with disorder and order, triumph and failure, extravagant wealth and abject poverty, corruption and reform, boom and bust. These circumstances spurred an ambitious Roosevelt to act and lead in the city—following in the footsteps of his father. The depression of 1893 forced city leaders to combat financial crises and budgetary waste. Addressing the First National Conference for Good City Government in 1894, Roosevelt said, "There are two gospels I want to preach to reformers.... The first is the gospel of morality; the next is the gospel of efficiency.... I don't think I have to tell you to be upright, but I do think I have to tell you to be practical and efficient." For Roosevelt, efficiency was a means to achieve better government at a reduced cost.[5] He believed that a better government, one that was reformed, could not only be efficient but also remedy the future ills that were likely to develop.

As president of the Police Commission, Roosevelt proved his mettle as the ever-pragmatic idealist. He entered the job writing, "I have the most important, and the most corrupt, department in New York on my hands. I shall speedily assail some of the ablest, shrewdest men in the city, who will be fighting for their lives, and I know well how hard the task ahead of me is."[6] To combat corruption, Roosevelt enlisted a cast of urban reformers and muckraking journalists, leveraging the newspapers and progressive allies as he went. For him, it was more a matter of imposing order over an organization failing to conform to rules and regulations than it was of creating a whole new organization. For the commissioners who came before the Progressive Era, reforming the city's police force was a task to be done within the existing system of government, political relationships, and perhaps most importantly, the self-interests of Gotham's leaders. Radical change came to the Police Department with TR and his accomplice Jacob Riis, the muckraking photographer. As Roosevelt and Riis exposed the squalid living conditions of the Lower East Side to the rest of New York, the Progressive Movement gained in support.

When Mayor William L. Strong, a businessman who represented the interests of merchants and professionals, demanded "honest, efficient, and businesslike" municipal government, he saw Commissioner Roosevelt as the man to bring it about.[7]

Roosevelt took a more militaristic approach to policing than his predecessors had done, and he used Riis' photographs of impoverished immigrants to generate public support. He thought that managing New York's police force required "many of the principles" that one could "obtain in the army."[8] Under Roosevelt, the New York City Police Department's purposes were to wage "[war] on dishonesty" and "increase efficacy."[9] He and fellow commissioner Avery Andrews changed the uniforms and reorganized the department along the lines of a military organization. Additionally, Roosevelt began the practice of publicly recognizing police officers for feats of heroism, rewarding them with promotions.[10] Granted, as president of the Police Commission he was more known for prowling the night streets with Riis than for any other aspect of the job, but his adaptation of military organization and personnel incentives had a lasting effect on Gotham's police.[11] Thus, the eventual progressive reform of the department occurred through the use of military-style practices as well as Roosevelt's stubborn will. He understood the value of winning public opinion to achieve his ends. Roosevelt also wanted greater responsibility, and William McKinley's victory in the presidential election of 1896 presented Roosevelt with that opportunity.

Through that winter and the early spring of 1897, Roosevelt's advocates lobbied Republican bosses Thomas Platt and Mark Hanna to get Roosevelt into the Navy Department. Having campaigned for McKinley in 1896, Roosevelt desperately wanted appointment as Assistant Secretary of the Navy. Roosevelt's transition from the municipal to national scene as a progressive looked, perhaps a bit ironically for a reformer, like the old-fashioned crony-party politics of the Gilded Age. Henry Cabot Lodge, accompanied by Ohio congressman Bellamy Storer and his wife, traveled to Canton, Ohio, shortly after the Republican victory to lobby McKinley on Roosevelt's behalf. Lodge and Storer were close Republican friends of

Roosevelt and recognized his leadership potential. McKinley's selection of Roosevelt depended on how New York's Thomas Platt, a reelected Republican senator, viewed the appointment. When Roosevelt withheld his endorsement of Platt's rival Thomas Choate for Senate majority leader, Platt realized that the pugnacious former police commissioner had switched his allegiance to him. After much speculation in the first three months of 1897, and only with Platt's intervention, McKinley offered Roosevelt the post of Assistant Secretary of the Navy.[12] Many in the city were more than ecstatic to see the progressive police commissioner move on; the cause of reform in New York would feel acutely the loss of Roosevelt and his animated style.[13]

Nevertheless, Roosevelt embraced his new opportunity and relished the chance to try his hand at the federal level, in the department of his dreams. He met with Alfred Thayer Mahan at Sagamore Hill, addressed the U.S. Naval Academy in January, and revised his book *The Naval War of 1812*.[14] Of course, Roosevelt and Mahan's interests immediately intersected in their shared study of the War of 1812 and naval warfare generally. Mahan's *The Influence of Sea Power upon History* earned Roosevelt's praise and respect and, more importantly, informed TR's continual promotion of sea power.[15] With respect to foreign policy, Mahan reinforced Roosevelt's opinion that America had to project its power into the Pacific, annex the Hawaiian Islands, and put its best admirals in the Asiatic Fleet if it was to keep the world's rising powers in check.[16] Roosevelt could advance these expansionist ideas as the Assistant Secretary of the Navy.

By April 1897, he was officially confirmed by the Senate and out of New York.[17] Despite his notoriety in the Empire state, Roosevelt was a bit of an unknown at the Navy Department. His new boss, Secretary of the Navy John D. Long, had heard the concerning rumors about his new underling but upon meeting Roosevelt thought him the "best man for the job," an "entirely loyal and subordinate" individual who would likely be an asset in the department by virtue of his naval knowledge and not challenge Long's authority.[18] However, as time would quickly prove, this was not quite the case. Roosevelt's effort to reform Navy personnel policy soon took shape and, when his new boss left Washington to summer in Boston, it would broaden into an agenda to energize the entire Navy Department into the future.

The Navy's Personnel Problem

Donald Chisholm's authoritative, exhaustive study *Waiting for Dead Men's Shoes* aptly characterizes the Navy's personnel dysfunction at the end of the nineteenth century.[19] The dysfunction emerged from two general situations—the fleet's transformation to steam engines and the stagnancy of promotion for officers. From the beginning of the American naval profession in the age of sail, the "line officers dominated the U.S. Navy." Sailing and fighting a ship required only physical strength and knowledge of navigating with wind power. Specialized corps of surgeons, paymasters, and naval constructors arose when the Navy organization demanded their expertise, but these staff officers would as a group be secondary to line officers and have no authority to command. At midcentury, the transition from sail to steam created the naval Engineer Officer Corps, which the line officers lumped with the other specialized staff officers. Naval engineers proved to be different from other specialist officers, however, because their expertise was vital to operating the ship. Over time, the naval engineers came to resent their second-class status and protested not being "commissioned officers" initially, as a matter of equity. By the 1890s, proponents in the Navy and in Congress had recognized that one could not operate a steel, steam-powered ship without understanding the machinery, and the naval engineers' cause became a matter of efficiency.[20]

As for promotion, the nineteenth-century naval officer could not advance in rank until someone senior either retired, which they normally did not do until they were in their sixties or died. Infrequent promotions dominated line officers' "grievances." Some were lieutenants for over twenty years. In 1898, there were lieutenants in their forties who had been commissioned during or soon after the Civil War. In the prime of their professional lives, these lieutenants languished, performing "trifling and routine tasks." By the time they reached command, they were old men, past their prime, on the verge of retirement. Moreover, their terms as captain, commodore, and admiral were necessarily too brief to allow them to accumulate the experience appropriate to the responsibilities associated with each command position.[21] Charles Paullin characterized the problem in this way: "The acute cause dated from the Civil War. Under a system of promotion by seniority, if at any time the movement from grade to grade is abnormally accelerated, then at some subsequent period it will be unduly retarded." This acceleration happened during the Civil War, after which came the stagnation.[22] By the time Roosevelt arrived at the Navy Department in April 1897, both the "evils of infrequent promotions" and the line officer/engineer controversy were coming to a head, and the main challenge for the progressive New Yorker was to take them head-on.[23]

Assistant Secretary Roosevelt's Pursuit of Efficiency

As he did with almost all endeavors, Roosevelt immersed himself completely in his work as Long's assistant secretary. He embraced every detail from ship design and construction to the management of coaling stations, from the development of war plans to the conduct of naval gunnery. What Roosevelt did not know, he studied, and he quickly learned what he needed in order to make decisions and meet his responsibilities in the Navy Department. Moreover, Long's frequent absences from Washington granted Roosevelt the time and space to take charge of the Navy bureaucracy.[24]

After taking office in 1897 Roosevelt became "the hot weather Secretary," running the Navy during the notoriously uncomfortable Washington summers, when Long was away in Boston, and President McKinley was out of town as well. In June, Roosevelt emerged as the leading expansionist in America after a speech at the Naval War College, in Newport, Rhode Island, arguing that preparation for war was the only way to guarantee peace. In July, he rebutted Japan's protest of the American annexation of the Hawaiian Islands. In these interludes, Roosevelt unapologetically ran the Navy Department as though he were the top appointee.[25] No task or detail was too small for him; he managed the Navy and its eight bureaus with his trademark vigor. With Secretary Long away, Roosevelt resolved a conflict between the Bureaus of Ordnance and Construction, evaluated production rates of the various Navy yards, wrote a draft plan to reform naval personnel, and removed Navy Department employees who had received subpar evaluations. Throughout, he corresponded with Secretary Long, sending reports designed to reassure his boss.[26]

Roosevelt was able to apply his beliefs on American power and the ills of bureaucracy. Specifically, he viewed himself as a reformer of arguably the most potent Navy in the world at the time, save Great Britain's. First and foremost, Roosevelt wanted competent and aggressive leaders in his Navy. In one of his first reports as assistant secretary, he wrote, "The business of a naval officer is one which, above all others, needs daring and decision, and if he must err on either side the nation can best afford to have him err on the side of too much daring rather than too much caution."[27] He understood the critical importance of putting only the best in command. Adm. David Farragut was for Roosevelt the quintessential naval commander, "an example, not only of patriotism, but of supreme skill and daring in his profession."[28] Given Roosevelt's study of naval history, Farragut's exploits in the War of 1812 and the Civil War were logical sources for Roosevelt's vision of an ideal naval leader. Writing about the frigate USS *Essex* in the War of 1812, Roosevelt observed that "among her youngest midshipmen was one by the of name David Glasgow Farragut then but thirteen years old who afterward became the first and greatest admiral of the United States."[29] During the Civil War Farragut proved "among the great sea-captains of all time," one who "was not only the greatest admiral since Nelson, but, with the sole exception of Nelson, he was as great an admiral as ever sailed the broad or narrow seas."[30] If Britain's Lord Nelson was the epitome of an admiral, then Farragut was a close second. Both were supreme naval leaders whose greatness resulted from merit and heroic action not nepotism and privilege. Based on Roosevelt's experience in the Civil Service Commission and the New York City Police Commission, promotion based on merit was necessary to ensure that only the best leaders, with Farragut-like qualities, would command in Roosevelt's beloved Navy.[31]

Merit-based promotion, however, required changes in policy and process, and those changes took time. Roosevelt, however, was a master at working existing political arrangements to get what he wanted. For example, in September 1897 he slow-rolled the appointment of Commo. John A. Howell to lead the Asiatic Fleet, thereby giving Commo. George Dewey, who was junior to Howell, time to lobby Senator William E. Chandler for the post. By 28 September, when Secretary Long returned to Washington, it was too late to reverse the orders, as Dewey had already assumed his new duties. This was but just one of the many examples of Roosevelt's "reforming" the seniority rule for promotion in the Navy's officer corps.[32]

Aside from bureaucratic chicanery, Roosevelt hoped to get a bill introduced to amalgamate the line and engineer officers. He asked Ira Nelson Hollis, a Harvard engineering professor who had served as an engineer in the Navy, "Have you seen Gideon Wells' [*sic*] report on the subject, I think in 1865? What he says is very interesting, and is really in line with what you say. We must amalgamate the two; then, later, let those who have a real bent for engineering differentiate themselves into an engineering corps. . . . If the Secretary will let me go ahead with that bill I shall try my luck."[33] Roosevelt found Gideon Welles, as a wartime Secretary of the Navy, the perfect example to emulate. Throughout the Civil War, Welles had adopted personnel policies that enabled the Navy to conduct the war on a par with the Union army. In the summer of 1862, Welles had pushed Congress to abolish the temporary "flag officer" rank and establish permanent ranks, from ensign through rear admiral. He also sought to restrict by departmental decree promotions from favoritism and politics, but by the end of the war, promotion still favored line officers.[34] In Secretary Welles, Roosevelt saw how a principled civilian official could force the stubborn naval profession to change and adapt to the new circumstances created by war—or, in Roosevelt's case, created by the demands of American expansionism.

During the McKinley administration, Secretary Long recognized that the promotion-stagnation problem and the line/engineer conflict were not getting any better. In the fall of 1897, he appointed Roosevelt to preside over a Naval Reorganization Board and recommend legislation to solve these issues. At its convening on 6 November 1897, Long charged the board, thereafter known as the "Roosevelt Board," to bring "harmony to the service."[35] For Roosevelt, here was precisely the vehicle to achieve reform befitting the Progressive Era. It was his preferred approach to finding a pragmatic solution.

A Pragmatic Approach

In a little less than a month, Roosevelt and his board of line and engineer officers produced an eight-thousand-page report. Using language as only Roosevelt could, the board recommended a bill that would "if enacted into law, be of literally incalculable good to the Navy, and would make our naval service the pioneer in the proper solution of problems, some of which are old, but some of which are so new that they have not yet been solved by any naval nation."[36] The board made three recommendations: two to address the officer problems and a third to provide equal pensions to enlisted men ashore and at sea. For the officers they proposed "(a) that the line officers and engineers be amalgamated; [and] (b) that when the number of officers to be promoted is so far in excess of the vacancies as to cause stagnation in the service, the requisite number of vacancies shall be caused by weeding out the men who are least fit to meet the heavy requirements of modern naval duty."[37] As Roosevelt explained in his letter to Secretary Long, "Every officer on a modern war vessel in reality has to be an engineer whether he wants to or not. Everything on such a vessel goes by machinery, and every officer, whether dealing with the turrets or the engine room, has to do engineer's work. . . . What we need is one homogenous body, all of whose members are trained for the efficient performance of the modern line officer." From Annapolis through initial sea duty, American naval officers would follow a system that integrated command and engineering expertise. Still, Roosevelt assured Long, "We are not making a revolution; we are merely recognizing and giving shape to an evolution, which has come slowly but surely and naturally, and we propose to reorganize the Navy along the lines indicated by the course of the evolution itself."[38] For progressives like Roosevelt, these changes were practical, as were the logical outcomes of any "good" reform.

Roosevelt finished his recommendation by characterizing a modern-day Farragut: "On the fighting ship the fighting man must stand supreme." Roosevelt continued, "[O]nly[,]he must know how to handle his tools, and must change as the ship changes."[39] His letter concluded, "In short, it is absolutely essential that the best naval officer of the future shall be proficient in engineering. . . . This is an age of specialization, but there can be no specialization of command."[40] In the age of steam and steel, Roosevelt realized, the skills mastered by American naval leaders had to meet the demands of the time.

On 26 January 1898, Senator Eugene Hale, a Republican from Maine, introduced the bill recommended by the Roosevelt Board to Congress. Events two weeks later in Havana Harbor forced the personnel bill to the back burner while the Navy, Congress, and the nation turned their attention to possible war with Spain. A year later, the bill was reintroduced and signed into law as the Personnel Act of 1899. In it many of the Roosevelt Board's proposals were adopted, including the amalgamation of line and engineer officers. However, Congress limited "selection-out" for ending officer stagnation to the ranks of captain and below, which meant that admirals could stay until they reached retirement.[41] The Navy's officer promotion stagnation problems would endure until the start of World War II.[42] For its part, the amalgamation mandated by the Personnel Act proved difficult to enforce, or at least to put into practice. Young line and engineer officers were supposed to be assigned "indiscriminately," but often they were not, and when they were, the young "seaman officers" did not take their engineering tasks seriously.[43]

Elting E. Morison's biography of William S. Sims describes the law's shortcomings. The law "eradicated one of the evils of the existing method of promotion, for in cutting out the deadwood of the service it relieved the Navy of the most undesirable officers and it increased the rapidity of advancement." However, the "fundamental defect" of the law was that it failed to provide "for the selection and rapid advance of the most efficient." Rather, "it encouraged the rule of the mediocre."[44] Roosevelt and the Navy were in the midst of radical change, a transformation that would not fully culminate until well into World War II. Even so, the

Roosevelt Board and the Personnel Act of 1899 were critical steps in naval personnel policy.

Getting beyond Efficiency:
Naval Personnel Reform and Aggressive Officers

After the Spanish-American War, the U.S. Navy had more change in store. Once Roosevelt became president, he spearheaded a transformation that would incorporate much of his reform ideal as well as instill his aggressive spirit into the naval officer corps. The United States now had territories in the Caribbean and the Pacific; Roosevelt accordingly sought a larger, more modern fleet and a reformed organization to manage that fleet. Ever the progressive, President Roosevelt pushed the modern battleship naval agenda further, upsetting such conservative members of Congress as Senator Hale, the chairman of the Senate Naval Affairs Committee. Hale had supported modernization and organizational reform of the fleet but strongly opposed using it to support a new era of "American imperialism."[45] Regardless, Roosevelt remained determined to reinforce American expansion through his campaign to improve the Navy.

Over the course of his administration Roosevelt went through six Navy secretaries, but most historians credit the naval advances of the turn-of-the-century Navy to the "insurgent officers" who led movements for its reform and growth.[46] Prior to 1900, Roosevelt had found like naval minds in Newport, in Mahan, Stephen B. Luce, and Henry Taylor. The next generation of naval officers urged significant reforms in armaments, administration, and personnel. Sims and Albert L. Key led that cohort. Key served as Roosevelt's naval aide from 1905 to 1907, and Sims from 1907 to 1909. Both Sims and Key had at times more influence than the secretaries and the previously all-powerful chiefs of the Bureau of Navigation. Sims and Key focused on three important reforms: "altering ship design processes, reorganizing naval administration, and promotion by selection." Their proposed solutions were unpopular, but they advanced them by publishing articles in *McClure's Magazine*, the *North American Review*, and the U.S. Naval Institute *Proceedings*. The Bureau of Navigation managed to remain the Navy's personnel authority, but there would be other progressive forces, specifically the General Board of the Navy, to push reform during Roosevelt's presidency.[47]

In 1900, at Secretary Long's insistence, the Navy formed the General Board, with Admiral Dewey, the hero of Manila Bay, as its president. The board was to advise the Secretary of the Navy on problems "related to ships, ordnance, strategy and tactics, and the personnel system."[48] Given the rising popularity of progressive reform in the United States at the end of the nineteenth century, the establishment of the General Board appeared a popular, if not logical development. For the Navy, the board reflected the professionalization of its officer corps and the general acceptance of military thinking and values by Americans. Its establishment also affirmed the idea that new organizations or bureaucracies could mend problems not solvable within the powers of existing, older institutions.[49] Like all the other established American institutions and agencies since the founding of the country, the Navy had its older bodies of governance—most importantly the eight fractious naval bureaus, among them Steam Engineering, Ordnance, and Construction and Repair. The bungled execution of naval operations during the Spanish-American War convinced both naval officers and civilians that the existing system of bureaus was far from adequate to run a modern navy. By design, the General Board was to be the new, responsive source of naval expertise for the Secretary of the Navy and the president, especially necessary given the Navy's role as the national instrument of power over the new American territories.

Additionally, naval modernization increased the Navy's personnel challenges; the advent of the first submarine, the torpedo boat destroyer, and new battleships exacerbated the shortage of experienced officers. Even more critically for future wars at sea, the Navy needed to address its serious shortcomings in naval gunnery. During the Spanish-American War, naval gunfire had been only 3 percent accurate. Updated naval gunfire practices devised by Sims and Bradley Fiske highlighted competence, not seniority, as the basis for promotion.[50] Roosevelt reinforced this view of officer competence when he convened a battleship design conference in 1908 at the Naval War College. There participants decided that line officers would have much more input, through the General Board, on battleship design and capabilities. Roosevelt and his naval reformers were expanding the expectations upon the officer corps beyond just operating ships. Now they desired expertise in the design and procurement of the modern steel warships. The Navy's separate bureaus continued to function and exist, but after Roosevelt their chiefs had to share their influence with the General Board.[51]

In the process of pursuing efficiency in the naval officer corps, Roosevelt also altered its purpose, with new guidance for the modern Navy. He wrote to Congress in 1908 that the U.S. battleship fleet must be "footloose," meaning that "we need always to remember that in time of war the navy is not to be used to defend harbors and sea-coast cities. . . . The only efficient use for the navy is for offense."[52] Just as he had connected department efficiency with officer effectiveness in the New York City Police Department, Roosevelt viewed an efficient naval officer corps as the key to a modern, offensive U.S. Navy of battleships, cruisers, and destroyers.

Roosevelt's Navy

By most accounts, Roosevelt's year in the Navy Department as assistant secretary was groundbreaking, for both him and the U.S. Navy. For Roosevelt, it honed his administrative acumen and obliged him to wrestle for the first time with the foreign policy implications of his decisions. For the Navy, Roosevelt set the officer personnel system on a course to keep up with the needs of the modern steel fleet that would enable the United States to become an international power—and all in the name of reform, efficiency, and pragmatism. In contrast to his supervisor, Secretary Long, Roosevelt possessed the energy, charisma, and panache to bring his progressive charge onto the national scene.[53] Roosevelt was an impetus for change—he served as a vehicle by which older officials could test and explore ideas of reform. Certainly this was the case in the Navy Department of 1897.

His impact on the naval officer corps as president had its limits. With the support and maturing staff capabilities of the General Board, the

U.S. Navy under Roosevelt modernized its ships, greatly improved the accuracy of its gunfire, and proved its potential with the voyage of the Great White Fleet. However, Roosevelt's opponents, led by Senator Hale, preserved the Navy's cumbersome bureau organization, resisted efforts to adopt fully promotion by merit, and made pay for officers more equitable but less incentivized.[54] The amalgamation of the line and engineer officers progressed throughout Roosevelt's tenure but endured growing pains and left gaps in necessary engineering expertise across the naval enterprise. For the century that followed, the Navy personnel system, one could argue, followed Roosevelt's prescription.[55] After Roosevelt left office, further shifts in Navy personnel practices and policy occurred, reacting to the needs of the wars of the twentieth century as well as the domestic social and cultural pressures in the times of peace that followed. Today's "unrestricted line" and "restricted line" naval officer designations can be traced directly to the actions of Assistant Secretary Theodore Roosevelt over a century ago.

Notes

1. Theodore Roosevelt, "Message to Congress," 17 December 1906, in *Theodore Roosevelt Cyclopedia*, ed. Albert Bushnell Hart and Herbert Ronald Ferleger (New York: Roosevelt Memorial Association, 1941), 372–73.
2. Matthew Oyos, *In Command: Theodore Roosevelt and the American Military* (Lincoln: Potomac Books of the University of Nebraska Press, 2018), 44.
3. George W. Baer, *One Hundred Years of Sea Power: The U.S. Navy, 1890–1990* (Stanford, Calif.: Stanford University Press, 1994), 11.
4. Richard Hofstadter, *The Age of Reform: From Bryan to F.D.R.* (New York: Vintage Books, 1955), 166–67.
5. Melvin G. Hollis, "Urban Reform," in *The Progressive Era*, ed. Lewis L. Gould (Syracuse, N.Y.: Syracuse University Press, 1974), 143–44.
6. H. Paul Jeffers, *Commissioner Roosevelt: The Story of Theodore Roosevelt and the New York City Police, 1895–1897* (New York: John Wiley & Sons, 1994), vii.
7. James F. Richardson, *The New York Police: Colonial Times to 1901* (New York: Oxford University Press, 1970), 264–65; Arthur S. Link and Richard L. McCormick, *Progressivism* (Wheeling, Ill.: Harlan Davidson, 1983), 39.
8. Jeffers, *Commissioner Roosevelt*, 117.
9. Theodore Roosevelt, *An Autobiography* (New York: Charles Scribner's Sons, 1922), 175.

10. Jeffers, *Commissioner Roosevelt*, 117, 177.
11. Richardson, *New York Police*, 265.
12. Edmund Morris, *The Rise of Theodore Roosevelt* (New York: Random House, 1979; repr. 2001), 576–81.
13. Edward P. Kohn, *Heir to the Empire City: New York and the Making of Theodore Roosevelt* (New York: Basic Books, 2014), 167–68.
14. Morris, *Rise of Theodore Roosevelt*, 581.
15. Richard W. Turk, *The Ambiguous Relationship: Theodore Roosevelt and Alfred Thayer Mahan* (New York: Greenwood, 1987), 15–16.
16. Turk, 116–17.
17. Morris, *Rise of Theodore Roosevelt*, 583–84.
18. Morris, 590.
19. Donald Chisholm, *Waiting for Dead Men's Shoes: Origins and Development of the U.S. Navy Officer Personnel System, 1793–1941* (Stanford, Calif.: Stanford University Press, 2001).
20. Chisholm, 435–36.
21. Charles Oscar Paullin, *Paullin's History of Naval Administration, 1775–1911* (Annapolis, Md.: U.S. Naval Institute, 1968), 457.
22. Paullin, 458.
23. Paullin.
24. Oyos, *In Command*, 45–46.
25. Morris, *Rise of Theodore Roosevelt*, 596, 598–605.
26. Morris, 606–607.
27. Report as Assistant Secretary of the Navy, May 1897, in *Theodore Roosevelt Cyclopedia*, 372.
28. Oyos, *In Command*, 50.
29. Theodore Roosevelt, *The Naval War of 1812*, 3rd ed. (New York: G. P. Putnam's Sons, 1882), 79–80.
30. Theodore Roosevelt, "Farragut at Mobile Bay," in *The Works of Theodore Roosevelt*, ed. Hermann Hagedorn (New York: Charles Scribner's Sons, 1926), 10:147.
31. Oyos, *In Command*, 50.
32. Morris, *Rise of Theodore Roosevelt*, 613–14.
33. TR to Ira Nelson Hollis, 24 September 1897, in *The Letters of Theodore Roosevelt*, ed. Elting E. Morison (Cambridge, Mass.: Harvard University Press, 1951–1954), 1:688.
34. John Niven, "Gideon Welles," in *American Secretaries of the Navy*, ed. Paolo E. Coletta (Annapolis, Md.: Naval Institute Press, 1980), 1:349.
35. Chisholm, *Waiting for Dead Men's Shoes*, 447.
36. TR to John Davis Long, 9 December 1897, Morison, *Letters of Theodore Roosevelt*, 1:726.
37. TR to John Davis Long, 1:726–27.

38. TR to John Davis Long, 1:728.
39. TR to John Davis Long, 1:729.
40. TR to John Davis Long, 1:730.
41. Chisholm, *Waiting for Dead Men's Shoes*, 455, 459, 465–66; Oyos, *In Command*, 53.
42. Chisholm, 809–11.
43. Paullin, *Paullin's History of Naval Administration*, 462–63.
44. Elting E. Morison, *Admiral Sims and the Modern American Navy* (Boston: Houghton Mifflin, 1942), 69.
45. Chisholm, *Waiting for Dead Men's Shoes*, 467–68; Morison, *Admiral Sims and the Modern American Navy*, 181.
46. Chisholm, 468.
47. Chisholm, 468–69.
48. Chisholm, 468.
49. John T. Kuehn, *America's First General Staff: A Short History of the Rise and Fall of the General Board of the Navy, 1900–1950* (Annapolis, Md.: Naval Institute Press, 2017), 9–10.
50. Chisholm, *Waiting for Dead Men's Shoes*, 469.
51. Kuehn, *America's First General Staff*, 4.
52. Gordon Carpenter O'Gara, *Theodore Roosevelt and the Rise of the Modern Navy* (Princeton, N.J.: Princeton University Press, 1943; repr. New York: Greenwood, 1969), 70–71; and Baer, *One Hundred Years of Sea Power*, 32.
53. Kohn, *Heir to the Empire City*, 169; John Milton Cooper Jr., *The Warrior and the Priest: Woodrow Wilson and Theodore Roosevelt* (Cambridge, Mass.: Belknap Press of Harvard University Press, 1983), 38.
54. Chisholm, *Waiting for Dead Men's Shoes*, 522–23.
55. Oyos, *In Command*, 53–55.

Assistant Secretary of the Navy Theodore Roosevelt, 1897–98
Naval History and Heritage Command

Assistant Secretary Theodore Roosevelt at the U.S. Naval War College,
Newport, Rhode Island, 1897
Naval War College Museum

Theodore Roosevelt welcomed on board the cruiser *Olympia*
by Adm. George Dewey, 1899
Naval History and Heritage Command

President Theodore Roosevelt inspecting the midshipmen at the U.S. Naval Academy, Annapolis, Maryland, accompanied by the Naval Academy's superintendent, Cdr. Richard Wainwright, 1902
Naval History and Heritage Command

President Theodore Roosevelt at the U.S. Naval Academy commencement exercises, Annapolis, Maryland, 1902
Library of Congress

President Theodore Roosevelt delivering a speech on U.S. naval preparedness, Haverhill, Massachusetts, 1902
Library of Congress

President Theodore Roosevelt on board the presidential yacht *Mayflower* reviewing a naval parade off Long Island, 1903
Library of Congress

The U.S. Navy submarine *Plunger* off Oyster Bay, Long Island, 1905
Library of Congress

President Theodore Roosevelt coming on board the battleship *Louisiana*
at Ponce, Puerto Rico, 1906
Naval History and Heritage Command

President and Mrs. Theodore Roosevelt with Rear Adm. Robley D. Evans and Cornelius Vanderbilt III on board the *Mayflower* during fleet maneuvers, 1906
Naval History and Heritage Command

President Theodore Roosevelt speaking at the John Paul Jones
Commemoration Ceremony, U.S. Naval Academy, Annapolis,
Maryland, 1906
Naval History and Heritage Command

President Roosevelt and the gun pointers of the battleship *Missouri*
From Theodore Roosevelt, An Autobiography *(New York: Macmillan, 1914), 573*

U.S. battleships of the Great White Fleet saluting the presidential yacht
Mayflower at the start of the fleet's world cruise, Hampton Roads, Virginia, 1907
Library of Congress

The battleship *North Dakota*, ca. 1912
Naval History and Heritage Command

President Roosevelt arriving at the Naval War College for the start of the battleship conference, 1908
Naval War College Museum

President Roosevelt addressing the officers and crew of the battleship *Connecticut* upon her return from the world cruise of the Great White Fleet, Hampton Roads, Virginia, 1909

Naval History and Heritage Command

"Welcome Home," an editorial cartoon by W. A. Rogers, 1909
Theodore Roosevelt Center, Dickinson State University

Assistant Secretary of the Navy Franklin D. Roosevelt, 1918
Naval History and Heritage Command

NAVY DAY · OCTOBER 27TH
Anniversary of Theodore Roosevelt's Birth

U. S. S. PENSACOLA
In The Panama Canal

334

"The best possible assurance against war is an adequate Navy." — — Theodore Roosevelt.

NRB—14291—10-2-31—18M

Navy Day poster commemorating Theodore Roosevelt's birth on October 27 and depicting the cruiser USS *Pensacola* passing through the Panama Canal, 1931
Naval History and Heritage Command

The *Nimitz*-class aircraft carrier USS *Theodore Roosevelt* (CVN 71), commissioned in 1986
Naval History and Heritage Command

6

FACILITATOR, MEDIATOR, DABBLER

Theodore Roosevelt and Technological Innovation in the U.S. Navy

Matthew Oyos

On 8 November 1906, the *Washington Post* announced "Roosevelt Starts for Panama This Afternoon."[1] That day, Theodore Roosevelt began a journey that would make him the first president to leave U.S. territory while in office. He was going to inspect the work on the Panama Canal. To Roosevelt, the construction of a path between the seas represented a great deed by his country and one of the chief accomplishments of his presidency. This trip would tie him more closely to a project that had been contemplated for centuries. His visit to Panama satisfied for Roosevelt more than his sense of destiny. He also indulged a fascination with technology. At the Canal Zone, he clambered over the machinery and pumped the workers for information. Steam shovels cutting into the earth made for a compelling sight, along with the vision of what the canal would look like upon completion. Although the canal was the purpose of Roosevelt's trip, his transportation there was equally enthralling, for he traveled on the symbol of American power, the battleship *Louisiana*. The president sought to learn about as many features of this newly commissioned vessel as possible. His investigation of the *Louisiana* was just one demonstration of the link that he drew between technological advances, military might, and world influence.

Roosevelt was fascinated with gadgets. Born in 1858, he had come of age during a time of accelerating industrial growth and rapid urbanization. Roosevelt was never fully at home with economic matters—he saw himself as man of action, politics, and letters—but he understood the benefits wrought by industrialization. A growing economy meant increased national wealth, and a fuller treasury brought greater standing in the world. However, to Roosevelt and others of his era, the products that flowed out of the nation's workshops represented something more than economic progress and political influence. They stood for the cultural vigor of the American republic. Simply put, mighty nations produced great works. This nexus between technology and cultural power stood clearest for Roosevelt in the U.S. Navy, particularly in the form of battleships. In an age of imperialism, he held fast to the idea that only the most capable nations could build and maintain the complex technology of a seagoing fleet. This belief combined with diplomatic, economic, and political imperatives to inspire Roosevelt's commitment to equip the U.S. Navy with the most modern technology possible. His knowledge of history further validated his drive to maintain a technological edge. The overall result would be Roosevelt's promotion of important technological advances throughout his years of public service.

Over the course of three decades, Roosevelt contributed to naval technological advancement. He praised the turn toward steel and steam in the 1880s, as the United States began a naval modernization program. As Assistant Secretary of the Navy in the late 1890s, he helped to oversee the physical and shipbuilding plant of the service. He spent only a year in this position, but in that time he gained familiarity with technical matters. Roosevelt would also make forays into the promotion of innovations that promised to take sea war into new dimensions, both in the air and under the waves. His presidency gave him the greatest opportunity to generate change. During his tenure, Roosevelt endorsed a major shift in battleship design, championed technology to improve American gunnery, and encouraged submarine development, among other things. He would also rise to the defense of naval technologies when charges of design errors threatened his program of fleet expansion. This active engagement in technological issues, both large and small, placed Roosevelt in special company among American presidents. Perhaps only Thomas Jefferson and Abraham Lincoln demonstrated more avid interest in inventions and technological developments.

Roosevelt's interest in naval technology began during his youth. His relationship to his uncle James Bulloch particularly sparked a fascination with naval matters. Bulloch's past in the U.S. Navy and his actions as a naval agent of the Confederacy captured the young Roosevelt's imagination. When Roosevelt worked on the senior thesis that became his first book, *The Naval War of 1812*, "Uncle Jimmy" assisted him.[2] *The Naval War of 1812* first appeared in 1882, and in it Roosevelt demonstrated a detailed knowledge of the warships of the time and an appreciation of the design and armament of American vessels. On page after page, he compared the relative power of American ships and their British counterparts, looking at the weight of cannon and variations within classes of ships.[3] He assessed that American frigates "were of better make and armament than any others."[4] Roosevelt exuded technological nationalism, and this statement was hardly the last in which he asserted the qualitative superiority of American vessels in the face of the crushing British numerical advantage during that war. Although Roosevelt would later preside in a period of greatly different naval technology, he derived from this study principles about ship size and armament that he would apply in his own time. For him, the essential element was a navy that was "blue water" in nature and centered on large vessels. He despised Jefferson's emphasis on small gunboats and made a point of condemning both Jefferson's and James Madison's military policies as "ludicrous and painful folly and stupidity."[5]

Roosevelt never researched another naval war to the same extent. He did, however, study the technology produced by later conflicts, principally the American Civil War. Roosevelt understood by the early 1880s that the technology that had helped produce a Union victory was now obsolete.[6] Ships akin to those of 1812 had in the 1860s patrolled the high seas and blockaded southern ports, while ironclad monitors had made their debut—a sign, along with steam power, that the world of the sailor was changing fast. Monitors had served their purpose in the Civil War, but they were not what navalists had in mind for making the United States into a great sea power. In fact, limited as they effectively were to enclosed waters, the low-freeboard monitors likely reminded Roosevelt of Jefferson's gunboats. The only time that they proved of utility after the Civil War, in his opinion, came in the confrontation with Spain in 1898—but for strictly political and not military purposes. After the battleship *Maine* blew up and war clouds darkened, Roosevelt, as assistant secretary, received appeals from members of Congress to provide protection from Spanish naval raids against East Coast cities. Ordered to do so, the Navy dispatched monitors such as the USS *Terror* and USS *Catskill* to patrol the harbors of New York and Boston. The *Terror*, completed in the 1870s, boasted double turrets, whereas the *Catskill* was a single turret affair that had served during the Civil War. Roosevelt recalled that sending a vintage monitor such as the *Catskill* was not "worth anything," because of the outdated smoothbore cannon and crew of naval militia. "It was a hazardous trip for the unfortunate naval militiamen but it was safely accomplished; and joy and peace descended upon the Senator and the Congressman, and upon the President whom they had jointly harassed."[7]

The year that Roosevelt spent as assistant secretary was the ideal school in which to learn about naval technology. During 1897–98, he handled various responsibilities, among them the administration of the Navy's shipyards, which brought him into close contact with the bureaus of Yards and Docks, Equipment, Navigation, Ordnance, Steam Engineering, and Construction and Repair. This work drew Roosevelt into detailed technological considerations. As assistant secretary, Roosevelt would discourse on armament and ship architecture, but he was not in a position to make a major impact on design. He did not have the technical background, nor was he in the post long enough. Nevertheless, in May 1897, having been in place not even a month, Roosevelt argued for major changes to the new battleships *Kearsarge* and *Kentucky*. Naval constructors had decided to put the secondary-battery guns on top of the main-battery turrets as a way to save weight. The configuration may have made structural sense, but the stacked arrangement prevented independent aiming of the primary and secondary batteries. Roosevelt declared, "I do not myself at all like the superimposed turrets," and he pressed his case with naval constructors in Newport News, Virginia, stating, "I hope that I may yet get them taken off." In this case there was nothing to be done, as both ships were already well under construction, and "it would be idle to try to make an alteration in them now." Rather, he was left to defend the design: "But the Department has decided the other way and I am bound to say that the man who is primarily responsible for them, Captain [William T.] Sampson, is one of the best officers in our service."[8] He had a greater chance to affect the design of the *Illinois*-class battleships. The first in the series had just been laid down, and Roosevelt felt that the secondary battery should consist of eight-inch and five-inch guns, not six-inch, as was British practice. He had no impact. "The constructors here do not agree with me, however, and in our last ships they have followed the English model."[9] Subsequent classes of ships would carry the six-inch secondary battery until the *Connecticut*, which was launched in 1904.

Roosevelt may have been overruled on the secondary guns, but he was on the right side of trends regarding overall ship design. With only slight exception, every successive class of battleship was bigger. The first American battleships, *Maine* and *Texas*, both commissioned in 1895, had displaced, respectively, 6,682 tons and 6,315 tons. The ships of the *Indiana* class ranged between 10,300 tons and nearly 11,700 tons. The *Kearsarge* and *Illinois* classes weighed in at over 11,500 tons.[10] Roosevelt welcomed such developments, for they would help keep the United States abreast of other navies. He felt that larger ships were also essential to an expansive foreign policy. In May 1897, he expressed to Capt. Alfred Thayer Mahan his wish for a dozen new battleships that would "have large coal capacity and a consequent increased radius of action."[11] He understood that larger ships could carry heavier ordnance and also had more range and endurance. His study of American frigates in 1812 bolstered the notion of bigger as better, given the power of those vessels over the standard for that type.[12]

Roosevelt enthused about grand strategy and the design of the biggest naval units. Yet his work as assistant secretary demanded that he learn about various technologies and absorb many details. No matter, for Roosevelt was a quick study, although he did have the unfortunate trait of acting as if he were the master of many topics once he had acquired a little knowledge of them. One naval constructor whom he met at Newport News, J. J. Woodward, observed, "I have been told that he considers himself an expert in many lines. Now I know he thinks he's an expert in naval architecture."[13] Woodward had hoped to win Roosevelt over to design changes to the *Kearsarge* but gave up after the assistant secretary lectured him for a half-hour. Roosevelt's intense curiosity and his desire to display new information inspired, in part, such behavior. His interest in simply seeing how gadgets worked also motivated him. He wanted, for example, to witness the operation of naval guns at sea in May 1897. He wrote Capt. Henry C. Taylor of the *Indiana* that "if I can get away for two or three days when you test your guns I shall do so. I shall be very seasick, but I won't mind that if I can see the guns in operation."[14] Nearly a month later Roosevelt was dealing with work on the boilers of the torpedo boat *Cushing* and reporting the latest information on torpedoes that the Japanese were deploying on new warships.[15]

Roosevelt was happiest when he could deal directly with the ships of the Navy. As assistant secretary, he took a special interest in torpedo boats. Although these sleek, small craft were hardly the battleships he wanted so badly, they were potential equalizers in a confrontation with a greater naval power. Speed was essential to their performance, and a controversy involving the Herreshoff Manufacturing Company, of Bristol, Rhode Island, drew in Roosevelt. The Herreshoff brothers had constructed the first all-steel American torpedo boat.[16] At issue was a charge from two Navy bureaus that defects had occurred in the construction of one of them, the *Porter.* Supported by line officers like Commo. George Dewey, Roosevelt sided with the Herreshoffs. He felt that they produced the best boats, as "the successful pioneers of torpedo-boat building in this country," and he wanted them to keep on building such craft "if only as a spur to the others, because we must get the best torpedo boats afloat."[17] As for torpedo craft built by the Navy Department, the assistant secretary felt "great dissatisfaction with the torpedo-boat work of the Construction Bureau."[18]

Tellingly, in accepting Dewey's judgment, Roosevelt had demonstrated more confidence in officers who operated ships than in bureau officers, whom he saw as having become hidebound in their staff positions.[19] His tendency was to favor individuals who fit his vision as men of action.

As assistant secretary and later as president, Roosevelt would also display a decided interest in naval guns and their use. His study of the War of 1812 persuaded him that the weight of guns (i.e., the size and aggregate weight of their projectiles) played a central role in the outcome of battles; *The Naval War of 1812* is replete with comparisons of American and British cannon.[20] Prior lessons about the weight of cannon had surfaced in 1897, as shown, in connection with the replacement of eight-inch intermediate batteries on battleships with six-inch guns. Roosevelt had informed the British journalist and naval historian William Laird Clowes in August 1897, "I personally rather regret that the 8-inch gun was taken off these battleships. It is to a certain extent an armor piercer, and the 6-inch gun is not."[21] This comment echoed Roosevelt's account of the 1813 battle between the frigate USS *Chesapeake* and HMS *Shannon*, in which "it may have been partly owing to their short weight that so many of the *Chesapeake*'s shot failed to penetrate the *Shannon*'s hull."[22] Such sentiments would be heard again when Roosevelt deliberated the merits of the all-big-gun battleship design during his presidency.

Stories of the past were important, but Roosevelt lived in an age of rapid technological change. He saw himself as part of a new, post–Civil War generation rising to prominence, and he wanted to be someone who promoted technological innovation. As assistant secretary he would have at least fleeting involvement with two technologies that would profoundly affect warfare in the twentieth century.[23] First, he took an interest in Irish immigrant John Holland's work on submarines. In November 1897 Roosevelt wrote to Lt. Cdr. William Kimball about plans regarding a "submarine boat" and in spring 1898 recommended, "I think the Holland submarine boat should be purchased. Evidently she has in her great possibilities for harbor defense."[24] Roosevelt's comment revealed an understanding of the value of such vessels. The technology did not yet offer blue-water capability, but submarines could operate in protected waters and, perhaps, harass marauders or blockaders. Second, Roosevelt expressed an early interest in the military potential of aviation. Professor Samuel Langley's flight experiments near Washington, D.C., drew his attention. On 25 March 1898, Roosevelt informed Secretary of the Navy John D. Long that he had seen "some interesting photographs of Professor Langley's flying machine. The machine has worked. It seems to me worth while for this government to try whether it will not work on a large enough scale to be of use in the event of war." Roosevelt proposed that the secretary "appoint two officers of scientific attainment and practical ability" to join two Army officers in an examination of Langley's invention. The resulting panel recommended support of Langley's work.[25]

Flight, however, would have to wait, for momentous events now summoned Roosevelt. He joined the war against Spain in May 1898 and by 1901 had ascended to the presidency. There, however, he would have the chance to involve himself again in the technological issues of his favorite service. In naval affairs, Roosevelt the president mirrored Roosevelt the Assistant Secretary of the Navy. Policy, strategy, and major technologies continued to captivate him, but now he possessed greater capacity to act. He advanced a foreign policy with naval power at the core, and he wanted the mightiest military technology of the day, battleships, to carry it out. Roosevelt also engaged in matters more esoteric, from ship design to gunnery, to propulsion systems. In this work, his instincts as a dabbler were indulged, and his view of himself as an innovator was given freer rein.

Within two months of becoming president, Roosevelt demonstrated the importance that he attached to the building of battleships. On 2 November 1901, he asked for a report on the battleships then under construction. He was anxious to learn if contractors were making adequate progress on the ships being built and if the work needed to be hurried. Roosevelt also wanted to know about the building of smaller vessels.[26] His request stemmed from worries that naval funding might decline; he wanted to complete as many ships as possible before Congress applied the brakes. That same day, he expressed alarm to Senator William Chandler about naval expenditures: "But if by conservatism in naval expenditures you mean that we should stop building up the navy, I radically and totally differ with you." Roosevelt declared that he had proposed three battle-ships for authorization but had thought about asking for four; he wanted cruisers, gunboats, and torpedo boats as well, to round out the fleet.[27] When the report arrived from the Navy Department, it likely alleviated some of the president's anxiety. Manufacturers were providing more armor than expected and were striving for even more output.[28]

Negotiations with Congress over the number and size of ships would be nearly constant during Roosevelt's presidency. During his first years in office, however, Roosevelt benefited from a consensus about expanding the battleship force. Congress set limits, however, on tonnage, which resulted in ships of questionable military qualities. In March 1903, Congress authorized five battleships but struck a compromise between members who wanted larger ships and those who demanded smaller ones. Three of the new vessels would be 16,000 tons, and two would be 13,000 tons.[29] Roosevelt was apparently willing to take whatever increase he could get, but the two lesser vessels, the *Idaho* and *Mississippi*, would lack speed, power, and endurance. Rear Adm. George Melville, the engineer in chief of the Navy, assessed that "it is difficult, if not impossible, to construct a thoroughly satisfactory up-to-date battle-ship whose capacity is limited to 13,000 tons."[30] Some felt Congress had acted to restrain costs and also in response to philosophical objections to big ships. One claim had a prominent member wanting the smaller ships because larger vessels no longer fit the shipyards in his state.[31] No matter the reason, the design of these vessels played a role in a controversy over the quality of battleships that erupted later in Roosevelt's presidency.

In October 1904, Roosevelt presented his views to Rear Adm. George Converse, the chief of the Bureau of Navigation. He did so after studying how the Russian battleship *Tsesarevich* had performed during the first year of the Russo-Japanese War. The *Tsesarevich* mounted six-inch guns as its secondary battery. Roosevelt relayed, "I remain very doubtful about the six- and seven-inch guns, and certainly there should be no quick fire [i.e., quick-firing guns] below three inches."[32] The president never convinced naval engineers to make a change. Every battleship incorporated six-inch or seven-inch guns until the United States departed from a mix between big guns and intermediate batteries and adopted an all-big-gun configuration of ten- or twelve-inch main batteries.

As part of his concerns about ship design, Roosevelt studied the armor protection on vessels. He felt that the armor of the *Tsesarevich* was better located than what was proposed for new American ships. "I am not sure," Roosevelt observed, "that our battleships would have stood the hammering as well as the *Cesarevitch* [*Tsesarevich*], but I am absolutely certain that our officers would have fought her far better than she was fought."[33] *Tsesarevich* had sustained thirteen twelve-inch-caliber and two eight-inch hits during the battle of the Yellow Sea but had survived to reach port.

Roosevelt first learned about possible problems with armor from Lt. William S. Sims. Sims had bypassed established lines of communication and written the president directly in November 1901. Roosevelt was already familiar with the lieutenant. As assistant secretary, he had read intelligence reports from Sims, who was naval attaché in Paris at the time. Although each man knew of the other, Sims risked the wrath of superiors by going over their heads to contact the president. The brash Sims bridled against thinking that seemed rooted in bureaucratic priorities. He was drawn to the image of Roosevelt as a bold leader, one who would immediately order a new course when stark facts were presented. Sims did not know Roosevelt as well as he thought, for despite popular perceptions of impetuousness, the president was usually a cautious man, who weighed all sides before making a decision. Still, the two men formed a combination that would be consequential for the modern Navy. Sims would go on to become the Navy's inspector of target practice and a foremost voice for naval administrative reform. In matters of technology, his collaboration with the president ranged from battleship design to gunsights.

In his blunt November 1901 report, Sims decried "the protection and armament of even our most recent battleships" as "glaringly inferior in principle as well as in details, to those of our possible enemies, including the Japanese." He went on to condemn American marksmanship as "so crushingly inferior to theirs, that one or more of our ships would, in their present condition, inevitably suffer humiliating defeat at the hands of an equal number of an enemy's vessels of the same class and displacement."[34]

Sims spoke in language that made his charges accessible to a nonexpert like Roosevelt. He also wrote in alarmist terms, with an intention of stirring Roosevelt to action. Roosevelt's response conveyed his natural caution, yet he did not censure Sims for contacting him. He told the lieutenant that he thought him "unduly pessimistic," for Sims, he recalled, had not long before taken "a very gloomy view of our vessels even as compared with those of Spain."[35] Still, Roosevelt thought it prudent to err on the side of pessimism in such cases and so, most importantly, encouraged Sims to write again. Indeed, in March 1902 the lieutenant alerted Roosevelt to flaws in the protection of ships' batteries. Sims argued that the ports on the five-inch-caliber guns of the armored cruiser *Brooklyn* were too large. The excessively large opening increased the likelihood of enemy fire passing through and bursting inside the turret, causing devastating damage. Sims made similar charges about the main turrets and magazines of the battleship *Kentucky*, which, he claimed, were even more exposed than those on the *Brooklyn*.[36]

With Sims, the president was cultivating an alliance with an officer who could offer him a different, nonbureaucratic perspective. Roosevelt wanted to balance the advice he received from Navy Department bureau officers with that of seagoing officers. During his presidency, he seeded such men in the higher ranks. He would work closely with Sims in particular to expedite the acquisition of better gunsights, and the lieutenant would be an important sounding board on ship design.

In matters of gunnery, Roosevelt's appreciation had been long-standing, even if the technology had changed from the cannon of old. As a result, after Sims became inspector of target practice in 1902, Roosevelt assisted him in his effort to improve American marksmanship. Sims wanted to adopt a British system of continuous-aim firing. This technique involved keeping sights on target throughout the roll of a ship rather than the current practice of waiting for a particular point in the roll and then targeting.[37] Roosevelt eagerly read target practice results from ships testing the new system. For example, in September 1903 he wrote Taylor, now the chief of the Bureau of Navigation, "I am especially struck at the radical difference between ships like the *Chicago* and *Panther*, which have not tried the new system, and the others which have tried it, as shown by the actual results of target practices."[38]

The proposed method required new technology, and Roosevelt helped Sims to secure it. In March 1904, Sims reported that the Navy's gunsights were inadequate for continuous-aim firing. He had been arguing about the sights since 1903 and even suggested a new telescopic design. The president read Sims's report and penciled in suggestions about the gunsights.[39] The Navy Department informed Roosevelt that furnishing new gunsights would require seven years. Suspicious of bureaucratic foot-dragging, Roosevelt acted. He summoned junior officers and learned that industrial firms could manufacture the sights and that they could be installed in a year. He meant to spur the naval bureaus into action. According to Sims, the president declared, "I shall give the Bureaus an alternative: either they must find the money to re-sight the Navy with the best possible design of instruments or I shall take the matter up with Congress and tell them that the Navy's sighting devices are obsolete and inefficient." Roosevelt was doing what he did well, using the force of public revelation to force results. He summoned the Navy bureau chiefs, told them to find the money, and "then admonished them to 'get busy.'" The Navy received the new sights the following year.[40]

A technological matter greater than gunsights weighed on Roosevelt at the same time. The design of battleships, the keystone technology of his naval and diplomatic policies, was at issue. In 1903, Lt. Homer Poundstone proposed the construction of larger battleships designed around the main batteries—all-big-gun ships. Intermediate-sized guns would be removed completely. Poundstone proposed a vessel of about 20,000 tons' displacement of which eleven-inch-caliber guns would be the principal armament. The design promised an advantage in hitting power and would make fire control simpler because there would be fewer differences in the calibers of guns.[41] Roosevelt took up the idea in 1904. He was ever intrigued by technological innovation, and the fact that the proposal came from Poundstone was also compelling. The lieutenant represented the men of push and intelligence that Roosevelt admired, as they mirror-imaged his conception of himself. The president's knowledge of naval history also drew him to the proposition. He had only to think of naval duels during the War of 1812, when the vessels with bigger guns, and more of them, tended to prevail. In October 1904, Roosevelt wondered if the recently authorized *New Hampshire* could be built to the new specifications.

The president looked to Sims for advice. Roosevelt asked if "we ought to have on our battleships merely big twelve-inch guns and fourteen-pounders, with nothing between."[42] Sims's response was immediate, that "this is the only logical battery for a fighting vessel."[43] The president then suggested to the Navy Department that the armament of the *New Hampshire* "be composed simply of 12- or 11-inch guns and a secondary battery of 3-inch guns."[44] There the matter died. The Board on Construction responded that changing designs would require about a year and that present American battleships were as powerful as "any vessel built or building."[45] Roosevelt felt in no position to overrule the board, and, as a result, it was Great Britain that introduced the all-big-gun type in 1906 with the *Dreadnought*.

Roosevelt may have been rebuffed, but he did not lose interest in the all-big-gun concept. In the period before Britain launched the *Dreadnought*, the president consumed an enormous amount of technical information on the proposed design. The Russo-Japanese War triggered this presidential appetite. Roosevelt eagerly read reports regarding the performance of the Russian and Japanese fleets at the battle of Tsushima Straits in 1905. He was especially interested in what the battle might indicate about the all-big-gun proposal, and he was even more intrigued after Mahan published an article arguing for a standard design of smaller, mixed-battery vessels. The president turned repeatedly to Sims for data. In response, he received a steady diet of material in favor of all-big-gun ships.[46] Sims ultimately dispelled any lingering doubts in Roosevelt's mind. On 27 September 1906, Roosevelt wrote to Sims, "I regard your article as convincing and have modeled the recommendation in my message accordingly."[47] About two weeks later, the president described a conversation with a British Admiralty official who confirmed "that ordinary ships will be absolutely powerless before these ships."[48] Thereafter, Roosevelt would push for dreadnoughts only. The big stick needed bigger guns.

Roosevelt's decision on the dreadnought design followed his usual pattern in matters of technological uncertainty. He demonstrated great caution, to the point that a casual observer might sense indecisiveness. He simply could not afford to make a mistake on something so expensive and so central to American security, especially when the august Mahan had argued against the bigger ship in a public forum. Still, given Roosevelt's proclivities and knowledge of the American tradition of equipping ships with powerful guns, his eventual backing of the dreadnought design came as no surprise. Even without the prod from Britain's *Dreadnought*, a sense of inevitability hung about the decision.

Ironically, the same man who inspired Roosevelt's confidence in the new ship type would end up causing presidential headaches over the quality of American battleships, both older models and dreadnoughts. Sims, along with other like-minded officers, wanted to reform the Navy bureau system and saw battleship design as a means to drive change. In late 1907, these "insurgents" seized upon the departure of the U.S. battle fleet on its world cruise to claim a series of defects in battleship design. These charges first involved only the older mixed-caliber ships then in service—the new dreadnoughts were just then being constructed—and involved the placement of armor, design of gun turrets, and height of freeboard. Congressional hearings tamped down public concerns, and no change to naval administration resulted.[49]

The vessels under scrutiny were actually on the world cruise to be tested. Roosevelt and the Navy wanted to know whether they could stand the wear of such a long voyage. The strained condition of the Russian Baltic Fleet after its transit to the Pacific in 1905 warranted the trial. Japanese-American tensions after the Russo-Japanese War raised the possibility that the American fleet might have to endure a similarly long voyage in case of a clash. In spite of the reformers' criticism, the ships' performance exceeded expectations. At the end of the cruise in February 1909, a delighted Roosevelt proclaimed, "As a war machine, the fleet comes back in better shape than it went away."[50]

Controversy over battleship design, however, had not ceased. In 1908, the frustrated reformers made a second attempt, and this time they asserted incompetence on the part of bureaus in the design of the first American dreadnoughts. These new charges alarmed Roosevelt, for they involved the future of the Navy. "Last year," he wrote to Assistant Secretary of the Navy Truman Newberry, "while I became convinced that Sims, [Cdr. Albert L.] Key, [Capt. Cameron McR.] Winslow, and other junior officers had greatly exaggerated the defects of which they complained, I was left with the very uncomfortable feeling that there might be some real defects, and I want if possible to avoid any slip-up."[51] Again, the president waded into technical details. He would valiantly immerse himself in the issues to help ensure that the next generation of American battleships consisted of the best possible vessels. The *North Dakota*, which was near launch, received criticism of the placement of the number-three turret, the armor belt, the twelve-inch guns, and the armor protection on the funnels and smaller batteries.[52]

Roosevelt acted swiftly. He wanted errors corrected in ships presently being built and designs improved for vessels still in the planning stages. Above all, he wanted the bickering to stop between reformers like Sims and bureau officers. Roosevelt convened a conference at Newport, Rhode Island, to demand that seagoing officers and bureau officers confer on the best qualities for American dreadnoughts. He called the meeting to order, and then over the weeks it deliberated, followed the proceedings closely. As he told Assistant Secretary Newberry, "Bring with you the full report of the conference. This is a matter in which I am personally interested."[53] Unhappily for Roosevelt, the *North Dakota* and *Delaware* were too far along for significant modification. He focused instead on making the next two vessels, *Florida* and *Utah*, "immeasurably more powerful ships. . . . We have been following and not leading, as we ought to be, in battleship construction, and I want now to step ahead of all other nations."[54] Roosevelt preferred fourteen-inch guns rather than twelve-inchers in the main battery, along with heavier armor, and he desired "the whole matter before me for judgment."[55] He remained disappointed. The modifications to the *Florida* and *Utah* would involve a construction delay of fifteen months, so Roosevelt reluctantly agreed to maintain the original design. He lamented that the ships could have been "much more formidable vessels than will actually be the case."[56] Roosevelt hoped that the next ships would be stronger and looked forward to reviewing plans for them.[57]

The outcome at Newport frustrated Roosevelt's ambition for a historic accomplishment in naval and national affairs. Battleships were not only central to his foreign policy, but symbols of American technological know-how and cultural vigor. In short, as prestige weapons, these steel castles validated America's right to great power status. They also embodied for Roosevelt one of the major accomplishments of his presidency. Roosevelt's sense of history told him that a mighty battleship force signaled that America had cemented a place in the front ranks of the naval powers. He took great pride in that achievement and wanted to be remembered for having done so. The fact that the newest ships would not exceed the leading vessels of other navies diminished that legacy.

Beyond appeals to history, Roosevelt also gravitated toward battleships simply because they were a fascinating technology. They were the product of complex engineering that brought together the latest in propulsion, armor, and weaponry. Thus when the president got the chance to explore one in detail, his enthusiasm was boundless. When in November 1906 he sailed to Panama on the *Louisiana*, he explored nearly every inch of the ship. Assistant electrician Walter Whitehead reported that the president "is now going down in one of the firerooms to shovel coal for a while. He likes to do a little of everything."[58] Roosevelt wanted to know what improvements could be made to the ship, and he particularly fastened on a problem brought to his attention by the chief engineer. The brasses, critical engine parts, wore prematurely, and Roosevelt learned that the problem was not limited to the *Louisiana*. He ordered an investigation and also wanted to know if the lubricating oils were of sufficient quality.[59] The level of his interest was striking, as was his expectation of reading the resulting reports, but such involvement was understandable given the importance of the vessels involved.

Roosevelt's attention to technological detail extended to other systems. Roosevelt focused attention on devices that threatened battleships—torpedoes and explosive shells. In 1908 he expressed concern about a torpedo designed by Lt. Cdr. Cleland Davis that might "prove to be a very dangerous implement of warfare." Davis claimed to have a torpedo that could penetrate the armored bottoms of warships. The device promised an advantage to the United States but also posed a threat if an antagonist developed the same weapon. Roosevelt wanted to know if the Navy had studied incorporating into ship designs protection against attack from a Davis-type torpedo.[60] As for shells, another inventor, Willard Isham, presented a design that purportedly could pierce armor effectively. Having no success with the War Department, Isham turned to the Navy in hopes of a test against armor plate. The Navy was not responsive, so the matter was brought to the White House, and as a result trials against twelve-inch-thick armor plate were approved. The Navy, however, resisted a proposal to test the shell against the armor belt of an actual ship, the *Texas*. Isham did not get all that he wanted, but an appeal to the executive had pushed the matter along.[61]

It was the president's reputation for catalyzing action that led others as well to approach him in hopes of attracting attention to their devices. For example, one man proposed a dirigible torpedo, which appears to have been an early form of radio-guided weapon. Another conceived of a ship that would transport submarines with the battleship fleet—thus overcoming range limitations—and dispense them in the midst of battle. Presidential assistance was not rendered in either of these instances.[62] Rather, Roosevelt's reputation as innovator stemmed less from supporting untested ideas than from his promoting new devices already in use.

In 1905, Roosevelt revisited the potential of submarines, an interest that he had first demonstrated as assistant secretary. That August, the president witnessed the submarine *Plunger* go through various exercises in Long Island Sound. He could not resist taking a dive himself, so the following day he boarded the vessel and in it descended forty feet. Roosevelt expressed delight at the maneuverability of the *Plunger*, especially its efficiency at stopping, quickly regaining full speed, and traveling in reverse before resuming course. He was also amazed at the crew's ability to operate in complete darkness when the interior lights were extinguished as a demonstration. Afterward, the press remarked how the president "behaved like a delighted schoolboy" during the venture and condemned his risk-taking on such a new technology.[63]

Roosevelt may have had a thrill, but his trip also helped with the development of submarines. He called attention to the utility and relative safety of the vessel. More importantly, he became the champion of a technology that was struggling for acceptance in the Navy. Roosevelt informed Secretary of the Navy Charles Bonaparte that he had "become greatly interested in submarine boats" and that "they should be developed." He worried, though, about "old-style naval officers . . . who hamper the development of the submarine boat in every way." Finally, Roosevelt wanted submariners to receive the same recognition for service that officers and crews on surface ships got.[64]

The submarine voyage pulled together many of the elements that drew Roosevelt to military technology. First, relatively new technologies such as the submarine were fascinating for their own sake, and by going on board the *Plunger*, Roosevelt underscored his belonging to a generation defined by the industrial revolution and a post–Civil War sensibility. Such ventures additionally allowed him to stress the reformer's instinct that he brought to government. With the submarine he could take on a familiar foil, the rooted bureaucrat who had become too invested in the status quo—the turf protector. Finally, again with his well-developed sense of history, Roosevelt understood that if he was seen to have ignored a promising technology, he risked condemnation in the future.

The presidency put Roosevelt center stage, and he loved the attention. His submarine voyage fit what the public had come to expect of him, and, as the *New York Times* observed, "He is liked all the more whatever he does."[65] Roosevelt used that platform for more than personal image building, however. He needed public support for a grand strategic design in which America's continued greatness hinged on an expansive foreign policy, a modernized military, and leaders with drive and vision. Roosevelt would never obtain the technological expertise of the naval constructor, but for a busy executive, his knowledge of naval engineering and quest for information were impressive. Innate energy and intense curiosity drove him, as did his basic understanding that up-to-date technology was essential in an age of rapid industrial development. As a result, Roosevelt was receptive to technologically innovative ideas, and he used his influence to expedite change.

In technological terms, Roosevelt's impact on the Navy was as significant as that of any American president. He presided over the adoption of the all-big-gun battleship and pushed for ever-larger vessels. He also assisted in efforts to make American ships more effective as weapons of war. This work ranged from urging better designs during the defects controversy to his specific interest in lubricants and brasses. Roosevelt's involvement was crucial to the improvement of American naval gunnery, and he encouraged the Navy to devote more attention to submarines, torpedoes, and armor protection. Technology was just one part of the larger strategic vision, but without it the enlarged foreign policy that Roosevelt promoted would be difficult to sustain. The sum of these efforts was that the United States was one of the leading sea powers when Roosevelt left office. A most fitting tribute to Roosevelt's devotion to building such a force was the awarding of his name to a troop transport during World War I, then a ballistic-missile submarine in the 1950s, and, finally, a *Nimitz*-class aircraft carrier in the 1980s. Fittingly, USS *Theodore Roosevelt* (CVN 71) was completed ahead of schedule, boasted the most advanced combat information capabilities at the time, and kept alive the Roosevelt spirit with the call sign "Rough Rider" and the nickname "The Big Stick."[66]

Notes

1. "Ready for Canal Trip," *Washington Post*, 8 November 1906, 3.
2. Theodore Roosevelt, *An Autobiography* (New York: Macmillan, 1913; repr. New York: Da Capo, 1985), 12–13; TR to Henry Cabot Lodge, 16 December 1888, in *The Letters of Theodore Roosevelt*, ed. Elting E. Morison (Cambridge, Mass.: Harvard University Press, 1951–1954), 1:151; Theodore Roosevelt, *The Naval War of 1812*, in *The Works of Theodore Roosevelt, National Edition* (New York: Charles Scribner's Sons, 1926), 6:xxv; Walter Wilson and Gary McKay, *James D. Bulloch: Secret Agent and Mastermind of the Confederate Navy* (Jefferson, N.C.: McFarland, 2012).
3. Roosevelt, *Naval War of 1812*, 59–63, 65–71.
4. Roosevelt, *Naval War*, 50.

5. Roosevelt, *Naval War*, xxxvi.

6. Roosevelt, *Naval War*, xxiv.

7. Roosevelt, *Autobiography*, 221; "Throngs See the *Terror*," *New York Times*, 14 March 1898, 2; "Old Monitors to be Refitted," *New York Times*, 31 March 1898, 2; "Where Our Warships Are," *New York Times*, 1 April 1898, 2.

8. TR to Richard Henry Dana, 8 May 1897, Morison, *Letters of Theodore Roosevelt*, 1:609–10; TR to Richard Henry Dana, 21 May 1897, Morison, 1:616–17.

9. TR to Richard Henry Dana, 8 May 1897, Morison, 1:610.

10. "Battleships," *America's Navy: Forged by the Sea*, https://www.navy.mil/navydata/ships/battleships/bb-list.asp (accessed 28 December 2018).

11. TR to Alfred T. Mahan, 3 May 1897, Morison, *Letters of Theodore Roosevelt*, 1:607.

12. Roosevelt, *Naval War of 1812*, 51.

13. Holden Evans, *One Man's Fight for a Better Navy* (New York: Dodd, Mead, 1940), 113–15.

14. TR to Henry C. Taylor, 24 May 1897, Morison, *Letters of Theodore Roosevelt*, 1:617.

15. TR to John D. Long, 18 June 1897, Morison, 1:628; TR to John D. Long, 23 June 1898, Morison, 1:631.

16. Richard V. Simpson, *Building the Mosquito Fleet: The U.S. Navy's First Torpedo Boats* (Charleston, S.C.: Arcadia, 2001), 53.

17. TR to John D. Long, 22 June 1897, Morison, *Letters of Theodore Roosevelt*, 1:630; TR to Charles H. Davis, 28 June 1897, Morison, 1:632–33.

18. TR to John D. Long, 4 September 1897, Morison, 1:668.

19. TR to Charles H. Davis, 28 June 1897, Morison, 1:633.

20. Roosevelt, *Naval War of 1812*, 50–51.

21. TR to William Laird Clowes, 3 August 1897, Morison, *Letters of Theodore Roosevelt*, 1:637.

22. Roosevelt, *Naval War of 1812*, 58.

23. Thomas Parrish, *The Submarine: A History* (New York: Viking, 2004), 23.

24. TR to William W. Kimball, 19 November 1897, Morison, *Letters of Theodore Roosevelt*, 1:716; as quoted in Parrish, 31.

25. TR to John D. Long, 25 March 1898, Morison, 1:799; TR to John D. Long, 30 March 1898, Morison, 2:806; Mark L. Evans and Roy A. Grossnick, *United States Naval Aviation, 1910–2010* (Washington, D.C.: U.S. Naval History and Heritage Command, 2015), 1:1.

26. George B. Cortelyou to John D. Long, 2 November 1901, File 5936–18, Record Group 80, General Correspondence, Secretary of the Navy, National Archives and Records Administration, Washington, D.C. [hereafter RG 80, General Correspondence, SECNAV].

27. TR to William E. Chandler, 2 November 1901, Morison, *Letters of Theodore Roosevelt*, 3:186.

28. John D. Long to TR, 4 November 1901, File 5936–18, RG 80, General Correspondence, SECNAV.
29. "Agreement on Naval Bill," *Washington Post*, 4 March 1903, 4.
30. "Plans for New Battle-Ships," *Washington Post*, 12 June 1903, 9.
31. Elting E. Morison, *Admiral Sims and the Modern American Navy* (Boston: Houghton Mifflin, 1942; repr. New York: Russell & Russell, 1968), 156.
32. TR to George A. Converse, 31 October 1904, Morison, *Letters of Theodore Roosevelt*, 4:1006.
33. TR to Converse.
34. As quoted in Morison, *Admiral Sims*, 103; Brief Summary of Lieut. Sims' Criticism Contained in His Reports from the Asiatic Station, 7 December 1901, Theodore Roosevelt Papers, Manuscript Division, Library of Congress, Washington, D.C.
35. TR to William S. Sims, 27 December 1901, Morison, *Letters of Theodore Roosevelt*, 3:212.
36. William S. Sims to TR, 11 March 1902, Papers of William S. Sims, Subject Files, Container 96, Folder 1, Manuscript Division, Library of Congress, Washington, D.C. [hereafter Sims Papers].
37. Morison, *Admiral Sims*, 82–83.
38. TR to Henry C. Taylor, 15 September 1903, Morison, *Letters of Theodore Roosevelt*, 3:601–2.
39. TR to William H. Moody, 1 April 1904, Morison, 4:766.
40. William S. Sims, "Roosevelt and the Navy: Recollections, Reminiscences, and Reflections," *McClure's Magazine* 54, no. 9 (November 1922): 37.
41. Homer C. Poundstone, "Size of Battleships for U.S. Navy," U.S. Naval Institute *Proceedings* 29, no. 105 (March 1903): 161–74; Homer C. Poundstone, "Proposed Armament for Type Battleship of U.S. Navy, with Some Suggestions Relative to Armor Protection," U.S. Naval Institute *Proceedings* 29, no. 106 (June 1903): 377–411; Morison, *Admiral Sims*, 160.
42. TR to William S. Sims, 5 October 1904, Morison, *Letters of Theodore Roosevelt*, 4:973.
43. William S. Sims to TR, 6 October 1904, File 18711, RG 80, General Correspondence, SECNAV.
44. Charles Darling, Memorandum for the Board on Naval Construction, 8 October 1904, File 18711, RG 80, General Correspondence, SECNAV.
45. Memorandum as to Armament of "New Hampshire," 8 October 1904, File 18711, RG 80, General Correspondence, SECNAV.
46. To President, Information on the Battle of Sea of Japan, Subject File, Relations with T.R., 1905, Container 96, Folder 4, Sims Papers; To President Roosevelt, Comment on "Mahan's Small Ship" article, 4 September 1906, Relations with T.R., 1905, Container 96, Folder 5, Sims Papers.

47. TR to William S. Sims, 27 September 1906, Morison, *Letters of Theodore Roosevelt*, 5:427.

48. TR to William S. Sims, 13 October 1906, Morison, 5:455.

49. Henry Reuterdahl, "The Needs of Our Navy," *McClure's Magazine* 30, no. 1 (January 1908): 251–63; James R. Reckner, *Teddy Roosevelt's Great White Fleet* (Annapolis, Md.: Naval Institute Press, 1988), 65–73.

50. "Brilliant End of World Cruise," *New York Times*, 23 February 1909, 1.

51. TR to Truman Newberry, 1 July 1908, Morison, *Letters of Theodore Roosevelt*, 6:1102.

52. Reckner, *Teddy Roosevelt's Great White Fleet*, 127–28.

53. TR to Truman Newberry, 10 August 1908, Morison, *Letters of Theodore Roosevelt*, 6:1166.

54. TR to Newberry.

55. TR to Truman Newberry, 15 August 1908, Morison, *Letters of Theodore Roosevelt*, 6:1174.

56. TR to Newberry, 15 August 1908, and note; the quote is from TR to Truman Newberry, 28 August 1908, Morison, 6:1199.

57. *Arkansas* and *Wyoming* would be authorized in 1909 and when constructed did not carry the fourteen-inch guns that Roosevelt had hoped for; rather, the main batteries of both vessels were of twelve-inch caliber.

58. "Roosevelt as Stoker in Hold of Warship," *New York Times*, 14 November 1906, 1.

59. TR to Charles Bonaparte, 28 November 1906, Morison, *Letters of Theodore Roosevelt*, 5:511–13.

60. TR to Victor H. Metcalf, 8 October 1908, Morison, 6:1278.

61. File 16319–2, File 16319–5, 16319–6, 16319–8, 16319–12, RG 80, General Correspondence, SECNAV.

62. File 24970, File 26045, RG 80, General Correspondence, SECNAV.

63. "President Takes Plunge in Submarine," *New York Times*, 26 August 1905, 1–2.

64. TR to Charles Bonaparte, 28 August 1905, Morison, *Letters of Theodore Roosevelt*, 4:1324.

65. "Our Submerged President," *New York Times*, 27 August 1905, 6.

66. "*Theodore Roosevelt* III (CVN 71)," *Dictionary of American Naval Fighting Ships*, https://www.history.navy.mil/research/histories/ship-histories/danfs/t/theodore-roosevelt-iii-cvn-71.html (accessed 20 December 2018); "Traditions, USS *Theodore Roosevelt* (CVN 71)," *Commander, Naval Air Forces*, https://www.public.navy.mil/AIRFOR/cvn71/Pages/TRADITIONS.aspx (accessed 20 December 2018).

7

CHECKING THE WAKE WHILE LOOKING BEYOND THE HORIZON

President Theodore Roosevelt and "Our Navy, Peacemaker"

David Kohnen

The mythology of great naval heroes and big guns remained a key ingredient in the systematic effort to indoctrinate future U.S. naval officers in the era of President Theodore Roosevelt. Amplifying the stature of the sea services, Roosevelt exploited opportunities to engage American voters through organizations like the Daughters of the American Revolution, the Naval Order of the United States, and the Navy League.[1] Historical truths rarely thwarted Roosevelt as president, particularly when he sponsored the expedition to locate and recover the remains of the Revolutionary War hero, John Paul Jones.[2] Riding on the razor's edge of the future, Roosevelt repackaged American myths and past glories at sea in framing his strategic vision of the U.S. Navy as a global "peacemaker."[3]

The naval outlook of Roosevelt reflected the confidence associated with industrialization and economic prosperity. Americans viewed the U.S. Navy as a symbol of national unity, as the Reconstruction era culminated in the stunning success of the 1898 Spanish-American War. The oceanic borders having been connected with the transcontinental railroad, the armored warships driven by coal-fired steam propelled the U.S. Navy forward in the global maritime arena. The economic rise of the

United States remained closely connected to the watery lines of maritime communications—as the empires of Europe and Asia also competed for economic dominance through naval power.

Roosevelt took a personal interest in shaping the U.S. Navy of the future as a global force designed to protect American economic interests through command of the seas. His entrepreneurial strategy centered upon creating opportunities for American investors in foreign markets. Reflecting the times, Roosevelt also created the mandate for Americans to embrace the mission of "civilizing" other cultures—such as those recently conquered through military force in the Caribbean and Philippines. Looking beyond the horizon into the twentieth century, Roosevelt envisioned China as the untapped gold mine with the capacity to propel the United States forward in the global maritime arena.[4]

The progressive rise of Roosevelt as a global leader coincided with efforts to expand the U.S. Navy. At the turn of the twentieth century, Roosevelt required American naval officers to understand their role in securing global interests in both peace and war. He instituted fitness programs and expected officers to seek opportunities to attain a more informed perspective as naval professionals. To these ends, Roosevelt frequently corresponded with officers affiliated with the Naval War College in Newport, Rhode Island. Given new technological developments and warship designs, Roosevelt solicited their perspectives in considering the decision to abandon the future construction of coal-fired warships of multiple-caliber guns in favor of oil-burning warships of single-caliber guns.

The debate over the transition from coal to oil held vast ramifications for Roosevelt as a politician and as a naval strategist. In general, older naval officers tended to remain conservative—favoring established technologies and doctrinal procedures. Fired by the debates ongoing within the pages of the U.S. Naval Institute *Proceedings*, younger officers frequently spoke out in loyal defiance of the older generation. Roosevelt ultimately stood at the center of the debate, as older and retired officers like Capt. Alfred Thayer Mahan sparred with the younger Turks affiliated with Lt. Cdr. William S. Sims.

Imperial Federations

The future of the U.S. Navy remained undefined as Roosevelt considered potential foreign naval threats against the opportunities and grander strategic objectives. He relied heavily upon the seasoned advice of Mahan, although he remained impressed by the confident assertions of the younger Sims. Within the cloistered ranks of the U.S. Navy, Mahan treated Sims as overconfident in his assertions about naval strategy and warship design. Likewise, Sims considered Mahan overly set in his ways and out of touch with the contemporary realities of naval technology. Their differences of opinion concerning the battle of Tsushima eventually appeared in the media. Mahan lost the public battle with Sims, which forced Roosevelt to intervene and safeguard the image of the U.S. Navy in the arena of public opinion.[5]

Roosevelt understood Mahan's global celebrity status as a maritime historian and theorist of naval strategy. Mahan's works inspired the American surge in the global arms race at sea. He advocated the British model, pressing American readers to embrace the notion of "imperial federation."[6] In his memoirs, he explained, "I am frankly an imperialist, in the sense that I believe no nation, certainly no great nation, should henceforth maintain the policy of isolation."[7] Mahan's worldview reflected the influence of the British Empire upon concepts of American sea power, as illustrated by the heroic exploits of the great heroes of the Royal Navy—particularly Lord Horatio Nelson.

As the Royal Navy constructed warships of more advanced capability, the ornately fitted warships of the U.S. Navy seemed equally impressive. Just as the mythology of Nelson fueled the image the Royal Navy, Roosevelt found propaganda value in Mahan's 1897 biography, *The Life of Nelson: The Embodiment of the Sea Power of Great Britain*. Roosevelt, for his part, supported a team of archaeologists in France, under the leadership of U.S. ambassador Horace Porter, in their quest to find the remains of the mythologized hero of the American Revolutionary War John Paul Jones.[8] In doing this, Roosevelt sought a historical analogy to Nelson for use in framing future American naval strategy. By 1904, Roosevelt had chosen the Scottish naval mercenary to serve as the Nelsonian figure of the U.S. Navy in the twentieth century.[9]

The nostalgic mix of historical examples and future strategy proved an effective means for Roosevelt to place the Navy on course to assume a global mission in the maritime arena. Yet, the European empires held a crucial advantage that set limits to the aspirational American naval strategy of Roosevelt. Coal-fired warships required access to land bases in order to sustain operations beyond the continental reach of the American hemisphere. U.S. naval forces deployed to foreign waters had to rely upon the hospitality of European empires.

Maritime crossroads in the Asiatic connected the British Empire and United States in both peace and war. Given the European presence in China, American enclaves throughout the Asiatic kept an open door for the United States to participate in the greater game.[10] Anglo-American involvement in Japan also reflected broader efforts to create a military proxy in the Asiatic.[11] Acknowledging this underlying fact, Mahan encouraged readers to recognize the historical influence of "sea power" in framing the military policy of the United States within a global context.[12] In an 1890 essay, "The United States Looking Outward," Mahan identified key maritime commercial lines of communication as the transcontinental railroad and American plans to complete the Panama Canal. Ten years later, in *The Problem of Asia*, Mahan portrayed the British Empire and United States as inextricably connected by maritime lines of communication between Europe and Asia. Given common historical connections and contemporary economic interests, Mahan suggested, an alliance between the British Empire and United States remained "out of the question, but a cordial recognition of the similarity of character and ideas will give birth to sympathy, which in turn will facilitate cooperation beneficial to both."[13]

To secure future economic opportunities, Mahan required changes in the military policy of the United States. Mahan argued that the "Monroe doctrine has been and continues to be a good and serviceable working theory." Continuing, he suggested that "we may have to readjust our views of its corollary—that being apartness of European complications."[14]

Anticipating the erosion of the British Empire, Mahan warned that the "declension of a European state might immediately and directly endanger our own interests; might involve us in action, either to avert the catastrophe itself or to remedy its consequences."[15]

Asia provided an area of common Anglo-American strategic interest, which Mahan considered strategically essential to the future of the United States. Mahan also worried about the limits of European imperial order, as he coined the phrase "Middle East" in describing the vast and largely unconquered region surrounding the Persian Gulf.[16] He emphasized the importance for the British to strengthen the imperial order in the region, encouraging Americans to recognize the opportunities inherent with Anglo-American collaboration in the maritime arena.

Younger American naval professionals generally embraced the ideas of Mahan, as the Royal Navy and U.S. Navy sailed on parallel courses to meet common objectives in global maritime affairs. Foreign involvement in Asia always centered upon strategic exploitation and imperial subjugation. Humanitarians and religious evangelicals always followed an imperial path to Asia. Ultimately, the indigenous populations of Asia would revolt. After the 1898 Spanish-American War, the Boxer Rebellion in China drove the Royal Navy and U.S. Navy together to defend common interests in Asia. Under the hastily organized Eight Power Alliance, Royal Navy and U.S. Navy warships operated together in Chinese waters.

Common interests in the Asiatic provided purpose in exploring Anglo-American collaboration in the global maritime arena. Considering the strategic questions of culture and geography, Sir Halford Mackinder portrayed the British Empire as the defender of high humanistic ideals, whereas political control in the great geographical "island" of Asia represented the decisive global economic "pivot" in determining the future course of humanity.[17] Mackinder envisioned collaboration among the maritime powers as a crucial element in the survival of what he characterized as the "British Imperial system."[18]

The United States, itself a derivative of the British Empire, appeared to Mackinder a promising potential ally in the global arena. For nearly a century, Royal Navy warships had sailed to the China Station to protect East India Company interests in the greater Asiatic. British entrepreneurs also relied upon American brokers, like Warren Delano, to facilitate trade. From Hong Kong to Shanghai, Delano had coordinated the exchange of opium, whale oil, furs, and other Asiatic commodities since the 1830s.[19] The Royal Navy and U.S. Navy often worked together during the Opium Wars.

Fraternal Spirits

Personal associations and individual personalities provided the foundations for strategic collaboration in Asia. In 1900, Royal Navy captain John R. Jellicoe served as the skipper of HMS *Centurion* during operations in Chinese waters. He assumed additional duty as chief of staff under Vice Adm. Sir Edward Seymour, commander in chief of the China Station. Seymour in turn relied heavily upon Jellicoe, as the Boxer Rebellion exploded in the streets of Peking, along rivers, and in coastal ports.[20] In combat, Jellicoe himself forged lasting connections with many American naval personnel. He suffered a severe chest wound at the battle of Beicang along the Hai River leading to Peking.[21] Barely surviving, Jellicoe developed a close friendship with the U.S. Navy's Lt. Joseph Taussig while convalescing in the combined Anglo-American naval hospital near Hong Kong.[22] Serving on the fringes of empire, Jellicoe became acquainted with other American veterans of the Boxer Rebellion as well, including Capt. Bowman H. McCalla and Lt. Dudley W. Knox.[23]

Combat experiences during the Seymour Expedition against the Boxer insurgency inspired uniquely close friendships among the British and American personnel involved. In official reports Jellicoe emphasized the impressive combat performance of U.S. Navy sailors.[24] Although "all the foreign nationalities co-operated very loyally with the British," the official history noted, "none perhaps showed quite the same fraternal spirit as the Americans."[25] Through friends, Jellicoe first discovered Sims in China, thereafter keeping close watch as he ascended the ranks of the U.S. Navy.[26]

The traditional rivalry between the British Empire and United States blossomed into a collaborative relationship in China. Jellicoe departed the Asiatic as Sims arrived in 1901, although the Boxer Rebellion provided a common point of reference as Jellicoe and Sims worked separately in fusing ties between their respective navies. Where centuries of tradition underpinned the image of supremacy for the Royal Navy, the U.S. Navy was an upstart by comparison with all the other navies of the world. Nevertheless, Jellicoe understood the potential of an Anglo-American alliance. The two also followed radically different paths to higher command. By 1902, Jellicoe stood in the rarified role of a naval hero befitting the highest traditions of the Royal Navy, while Sims had earned a reputation as an outspoken critic of the U.S. Navy. Given their respective reputations, Jellicoe considered Sims an ideal American counterpart with whom to do the global business of Britannia.

Newspapers throughout the British Empire highlighted the exploits of Jellicoe in the Boxer Rebellion. He earned popular renown as a figure reminiscent of Lord Nelson as the Royal Navy prepared to mark the centennial of Trafalgar in 1905. His image appeared on cigarette boxes, lager bottles, teapots, and on the signs of public houses throughout the empire. The First Sea Lord, Sir John "Jackie" Fisher, capitalized on the opportunity by referring to Jellicoe as the "future Nelson."[27] Typical of the burdens inherent in unanticipated popularity, Jellicoe carried the millstone of Nelson for the remainder of his career.[28] Still, with his international celebrity status, Jellicoe greatly influenced—through trusted intermediaries, particularly Sims—the development of the U.S. Navy.

To Win or Lose All

The U.S. Navy churned at full speed to create an image of greatness, a goal that Roosevelt fostered with political support and financial appropriations. In his efforts to frame American maritime strategy within the broader global context, he often found the image of strength more important than the actual facts. Reacting to the propaganda surrounding the U.S. Navy, Sims stood among the young Turks who zealously attacked ranking rivals within the ranks. Undeterred by naval protocols whenever politics appeared to hinder progress, Sims rallied peers to follow his lead. He encouraged junior naval professionals to question outdated doctrinal assumptions. Frequently breaking ranks, Sims openly ridiculed the stale ideas and assertions of senior civilian officials, politicians, and fellow officers.[29]

The bureaucratic and hierarchical culture of the Navy obliged Sims to rally younger associates to challenge the prevailing winds of the Navy Department. He referred to his friends within the service as the Society for Repression of Ignorant Assumptions.[30] Sims threw caution to the wind, openly challenging his friend and former Naval Academy roommate Albert P. Niblack about the failure of the Navy Department to make improvements.

> I am playing this game to win or lose all. . . . I am perfectly willing that those honestly holding views differing from mine should continue to live; but with every fibre of my corpse I loathe indiscretion and shiftiness, and where it occurs in high places, and is used to save a face at the expense of the vital interests of our great service (in which silly people place such a childlike trust), I want that man's blood and I will have it, no matter what it costs me personally.[31]

Navy Department bureaucracy fueled in Sims a slow and steady rage, until he decided to risk his future prospects for promotion—jumping multiple chains of command—by writing a direct complaint about the routines of the Navy Department to the president of the United States. Although he wrote with the confidence of his convictions, Sims also understood the potential consequences for the slippery ladder to higher command.

Sims often appeared arrogant, unhesitatingly dismissing regulations in circumventing bureaucratic chains of command. He even risked dismissal from the service on one occasion, writing in the newspapers about embarrassing problems with American warship designs. Sims's complaint concerned the configuration of guns and other instances of poor design in the newest battleships in the U.S. Navy. In so doing, Sims earned many enemies within the Navy Department. Sharing the opinions of other bureau chiefs, Admirals George A. Converse and Washington L. Capps attempted to thwart Sims, a mere lieutenant commander. Fighting survivors of the age of sail in an era of steam and steel, Sims disregarded the bureaucratic authorities and defended his insubordination. He had acted under a higher call to duty as an American citizen, risking his commission as a naval officer to take a strong stand against the Navy Department for the greater good of the service.[32]

While British naval traditions inspired U.S. naval culture, Sims identified with the industrial progressiveness of American culture. Having spent thirteen years in his youth in Port Hope, near Ontario on the Canadian side of the Great Lakes, Sims had returned with his family to the United States shortly after the Civil War. In those years he constantly sought adventure, avoided working for grades in school, and assumed the nickname "Bloody Bill."[33] Sims considered pursuing a career as an artist until he earned an appointment to the U.S. Naval Academy. He performed well as a student but earned a reputation for collecting demerits. Sims later proudly remembered running afoul of one instructor, Cdr. Alfred Thayer Mahan, who punished Sims for being "disorderly on the quarterdeck and disrespectful to the officer of the deck." Sims graduated from the U.S. Naval Academy in 1880.

Sims directly participated in a period of revolutionary changes in technology and in American strategy. He developed a firm appreciation for the emergent threats of France and imperial Germany during service as the naval attaché in Paris between 1897 and 1900. Previously he had lived a bohemian lifestyle there in 1889, living among the artisans and social fringes. During his service as the U.S. naval attaché, he met the ambassador to imperial Russia, Ethan Allen Hitchcock, and his family as they traveled through Paris. This meeting later proved important for Sims and his career in the naval service.[34]

As the U.S. Navy continued pressing the limits of the Monroe Doctrine in the global maritime arena, Sims reinforced his reputation as being out of step within the hierarchical ranks of the service. His sojourn in Paris ended with orders to join the *Kearsarge*-class battleship *Kentucky*, sailing on a maiden voyage to the Asiatic during the final months of the Boxer Rebellion in 1901. Observing foreign warships in Asiatic waters, Sims studied the continuous-aim method of firing as developed by Capt. Percy Scott of the Royal Navy. Sharing notes with Niblack and Cdr. Albert L. Key, Sims found U.S. Navy warships wholly unprepared to measure against potential enemies—such as those of Europe.

Sims grew equally annoyed, as his newspaper exposés showed, by American warship design, which remained untested beyond the theoretical and faulty in function. For Sims, American warships were deathtraps for their crews, fated to sink after the first few shots. *Kentucky* featured various design elements of an experimental nature that Sims found dangerous by comparison with European warships. The double-turreted configuration of *Kentucky* looked very impressive, but Sims found the design fundamentally flawed. He carefully noted the problems and offered solutions in correspondence to the Navy Department.

The bureaucrats within the Navy Department suppressed such reports, but seagoing officers generally sided with Sims. His friend and Naval Academy classmate Niblack, in the Bureau of Ordnance, kept Sims informed about the politics. Key also encouraged Sims to fight the good fight. Among junior officers, Niblack and Key shared notes with Sims in identifying supporters of more senior rank. One of them, Capt. Charles H. Stockton, encouraged Sims to stand in the "light and not be afraid of the truth. . . . [T]he pathway of the reformer is hard and my experience at the War College leads me to sympathize with you in your efforts and rebuffs."[35]

The political costs of acting upon recommendations from Sims proved too high for his superiors inside the Navy Department. In June of 1901, Niblack advised Sims that "everyone is 'mum'" about serious problems in American warship design and gunnery.[36] Fighting the political battles of Washington, Niblack and Key recognized how Sims threatened the cozy relationship between the Navy Department and American industrialists. Yet technical problems experienced by Sims on board U.S. warships during operations against the Boxers proved too profound to dismiss. While assigned to *Kentucky*, Sims embarked on the monitor *Monterey* for a voyage up the Yangtze River from Shanghai to Nanking. He lambasted the warship as the "USS *Terror-of-the-East* . . . high-huffen-buffen, double-turreted, back-actin', submarine war junk."[37] On basic levels, Sims found that American warships floated too deeply in the water, their armor belts falling below the surface, that they were inadequately configured for action and technically unsound. Worse still, his gun crews lacked sufficient training and practice to hit targets during exercises.[38]

It was in this situation that Sims circumvented the Navy Department and directly corresponded with the White House. In complete defiance of restrictions imposed by the Navy Department, Sims warned President Theodore Roosevelt that "foreigners are keenly alive to these defects in our ships."[39] Roosevelt used the reports of Sims to force changes inside the Navy Department and shape policy in Congress. Roosevelt ordered the observations and recommendations of Sims published for widest circulation within the seagoing ranks of the Navy.[40] Roosevelt also recognized that Sims needed to be careful and yet affirmed him, declaring, "I think you unduly pessimistic [but that] I would a hundred fold over that you erred upon the side of thinking us not good enough than of thinking us too good."[41]

Roosevelt recognized Sims as an officer capable of overcoming bureaucratic obstacles in order to solve strategic problems. In 1902, he arranged orders for Sims to serve in the Bureau of Ordnance as an inspector of naval gunnery at the Navy Department in Washington. In this role, Sims enjoyed unique authority to address fundamental problems in American warship designs. He also used the assignment to compare American concepts with those found in foreign warships. During a visit to New York in 1903, Sims examined the armored cruiser HMS *Drake*, under the command of Jellicoe. Sharing Sims's interest in addressing fundamental problems in warship design and naval gunnery, Jellicoe embraced him as a kindred spirit. Jellicoe hosted Sims and other American naval officers in *Drake*, during which they compared notes about Royal Navy and U.S. Navy warship design. Jellicoe and Sims also agreed about strategic opportunities for the Royal Navy to collaborate with the U.S. Navy in global maritime affairs.

Recalling their mutual experiences in the Asiatic, Jellicoe and Sims agreed about the emergent challenge of the Imperial Japanese Navy. They also considered the influence of new technologies, such as wireless, in examining questions of command and naval tactics. Marconi equipment provided greater range and reliability for Royal Navy communications; the U.S. Navy lagged far behind. By 1903, the First Sea Lord, Fisher, had recognized the potential of standardized warship designs such as HMS

Dreadnought but also pressed for the speedier battle cruisers, destroyers, and submarines. To coordinate the global operations of the Royal Navy, Fisher foresaw and capitalized on the central role of wireless communications by organizing a centralized headquarters within the Admiralty in London.[42] As a result of such reforms, the Royal Navy maintained critical strategic advantages over the U.S. Navy.

Propaganda influenced strategic debates about the course of maritime strategy, as the Royal Navy sought means to establish a system of alliances with other naval powers. Facing challenges on a global scale, Fisher used the British media to fuel the idea of "six panics," as an overt argument to expend vast sums in expanding the Royal Navy.[43] With the Admiralty in London serving as the strategic hub, the British employed the warships of the Royal Navy in conjunction with naval forces of the dominions, colonies, and protectorates.[44] By 1900, Fisher had created a mandate to engage in a race to preserve his service's technological and numerical advantage against the other navies of Europe, namely those of Germany, France, and Russia. In the Asiatic, the Imperial Japanese Navy, along with its liaisons in the United States, represented another major threat to the British Empire.[45]

Battleships defined concepts of naval strategy, although technological innovations inspired close friendships among naval practitioners. Sharing professional interests, Royal Navy captains John R. Jellicoe and Percy Scott influenced Sims in the fight to build all-big-gun dreadnoughts for the U.S. Navy.[46] As Fisher worked the higher political ropes from within the Admiralty, Jellicoe and Scott sought means for the Royal Navy to establish partnerships with other navies in order to sustain the empire. Rivalries with France and Germany, in particular, drove the British to seek closer ties with their American cousins.[47]

Taking for granted the traditional role of the Royal Navy, Fisher and Jellicoe saw the U.S. Navy as a useful counterbalance in the grander competition for control at sea. Following this logic, Fisher and Jellicoe recognized Sims as an officer of sufficient rank and potential influence within the U.S. Navy to work with. After 1903, Fisher and Jellicoe wrote a series of encouraging letters to Sims. Many of these included details about the range and accuracy of British twelve-inch guns, Jellicoe expressing concern to Sims that their performance was better than those of American warships. Jellicoe mused that it would "be most unfortunate should a British commander face the dilemma of having to sink an American in an unfair fight."[48] In 1904, Sims argued in an essay in the Naval Institute *Proceedings* that improvements in gunnery required more time in the classroom followed by practical exercise at sea.[49]

Dread Not

If Sims used his pen as a strategic weapon, circumventing the Navy Department with his personal correspondence to Roosevelt, the president for his part used Sims to rattle the Navy Department. Together, Roosevelt and Sims placed the U.S. Navy on course to perform a global mission. In the State of the Union address of 1904, Roosevelt updated the Monroe Doctrine with the Roosevelt Corollary, which essentially defined the strategic mission of the U.S. Army as defensive in focus, its operations restricted to the Americas. Roosevelt portrayed the mission of the U.S. Navy, however, as worldwide, using the expeditionary branch of the U.S. Marine Corps as the primary means to defend the economic stakes of the United States that existed beyond its direct sphere of interest.

In framing a global maritime mission for the United States, Roosevelt relied heavily upon advice from naval professionals. In particular, Roosevelt greatly valued the forthright nature and bureaucratic courage of Sims. Given the reluctance of more senior advisors to discuss strategic problems concerning the future, Sims offered a refreshing approach in examining the bureaucratic challenges that hindered the U.S. Navy on the global stage. Association with Roosevelt also placed Sims in an unfamiliar role on the grander stage of the American media. Newspapers described Sims as forty-seven years old and, more distressingly for the period, "hopelessly a bachelor."[50]

Roosevelt took a personal interest in Sims, recognizing his potential for a future on the American political stage. He encouraged Sims to rekindle connections with the former ambassador to imperial Russia, Hitchcock. Hitchcock also had experience in China, as did Sims. Having returned to America with his family to serve as secretary of the interior, Hitchcock guided Sims in understanding the global diplomatic aspects of American naval strategy. Tutoring by Roosevelt and Hitchcock enabled Sims to refine his understanding of imperial Russia and China as the strategic pivots of European and Asiatic affairs.

Under the wings of Roosevelt and Hitchcock, Sims enjoyed unique influence, far beyond his station as a commander in the U.S. Navy.[51] Shortly after arriving in Washington, Sims again met with the daughter of the ambassador, Anne Hitchcock. At age forty-nine, Sims was sixteen years older than Anne when they married, on 21 November 1905, with encouragement from Roosevelt. The president attended the Sims wedding, making the match a national media spectacle. As a descendent of Ethan Allen, among other great Yankee heroes of the American Revolution, Anne also placed Sims in another social category, that of the social elite of the East Coast.

Sims cut a dapper image, augmented by the glamorous aura provided by Anne's storied and historic family. Roosevelt celebrated Sims and his family, which by extension helped further the propaganda of the U.S. Navy as a rising force in the global maritime arena. In popular media, the Sims family appeared in idealized terms as its ranks expanded to five children. Sims often read the newspaper on the front porch of their home, surrounded by his children—cheerfully dressed in naval costume. As an officer on the rise, Sims also enjoyed a reputation among the naval circles of Europe, as a naval innovator.

Rivalries between the Royal Navy and the European continental powers reinforced the idea of seeking closer transatlantic connections with the rising maritime power of America. Sailing in the battleship *Alabama* to coordinate gunnery exercises in British waters in 1905, Sims nurtured his personal connections with Royal Navy officers like Jellicoe and Scott. Through their good offices, Sims received special access to the Admiralty. Dinner meetings with Fisher and Jellicoe in London inspired Sims to write about London in letters to Anne, the gist of which she passed on to her father who indirectly shared the information with Roosevelt. In such a letter Sims proudly claimed that his procedures made sure that the "gunnery of the United States was superior to that of England."[52]

The tactical focus of discussions among naval professionals often over-shadowed the broader questions, that shaped European and American concepts of global strategy. Recent battles and technical developments in naval affairs dominated discussions between personalities like Fisher, Jellicoe, and Sims. For example, they recognized the battle of Tsushima Straits in the previous year to be palpable evidence of the potential threat to European and American influence in the greater Asiatic sphere.[53] Wire-less communications, warship maneuverability, and superior coordination in naval gunnery loomed large in the Imperial Japanese Navy's victory at Tsushima, leaving the landlocked armies of imperial Russia with few options other than to seek a negotiated settlement.

Seizing the global stage, Roosevelt sponsored peace negotiations between the empires of Russia and Japan. He received the Nobel Peace Prize for facilitating the Portsmouth Agreement, which formally ended the Russo-Japanese War. Behind closed doors, Roosevelt agreed to a secret memorandum between Secretary of War William H. Taft and Japanese general Katsura Tarō. By implication, the Roosevelt administration ceded the Korean Peninsula to imperial Japan. In turn, the Japanese recognized the Philippines as a protectorate of the United States. Such haggling over territorial control in the Asiatic set the stage for future conflict, which many American naval professionals understood.[54] Within the ranks, many compared the British- and French-designed warships of the Imperial Japanese Navy far superior to the various American classes.

Inside the Navy Department, industrialists' representatives and ship constructors dominated the process of ship design. Sims challenged this cozy relationship between civilian appointees in higher echelons of the Navy Department and civilian entrepreneurs seeking to build warships that the U.S. Navy did not need. As professional naval officers, Sims and his associates also questioned the appropriateness of giving civilians full strategic authority over the administration and future operations of the U.S. Navy.[55] For example, industrialists favored the continued construction of coal-burning warships; Sims pressed for experimentation in oil-burning warships, fast destroyers, and submarines. He also perceived the future potential of aircraft in naval operations.[56]

Sims worried about the bureaucratic culture that characterized the bureaus of the Navy Department. In official reports, Sims pushed all bureaucratic limits by highlighting uncomfortable facts. As we have seen, for example, he faulted the armor protection of recently constructed battleships.[57] His observations undermined those of Mahan, which remained focused on guns of various calibers and high freeboards. By 1905 Sims had grown more concerned with Mahan's criticism of the Royal Navy's concept of the all-big-gun warship. The talk surrounding the construction of HMS *Dreadnought* suggested standardized parts, interchangeable guns, heavy armor, and speed.[58]

Although *Dreadnought* remained under a veil of official secrecy, Mahan dismissed its design. Basing his opinions upon rumors and unconfirmed media accounts, Mahan characterized *Dreadnought* as fundamentally flawed. He preferred warships with multiple-caliber guns and heavy armor. By contrast, Sims recognized that the true innovation of *Dreadnought* lay in its interchangeability and standardization. In 1906, Roosevelt sent Sims to visit London in order to gather more information about *Dreadnought*.

Recognizing the need to create opportunities for a younger generation, Roosevelt hoped to clear the decks of the U.S. Navy by encouraging older, retired officers—many of whom had returned to work, on "special duty"—to accept fully their retired status. Mahan, for instance, who had requested transfer to the retired list in the rank of captain after forty years of service ten years earlier, had continued working for the Navy on numerous fronts inside and outside the lifelines of the service by 1906. He dominated the international stage on questions of naval strategy and command. Hoping to nudge Mahan and others of his generation into full retirement, Roosevelt influenced Congress to promote retroactively officers in the rank of captain with Civil War service to the retired rank of rear admiral, though without the extra pay. Mahan would not take the bait, refusing to accept the title unless he received the equivalent pay. He also refused to fade quietly into retirement, and thereby upstaged younger American naval thinkers like Sims.

Fisher and Jellicoe respected the strategic contributions of Mahan to an overarching vision of sea power. On tactical and technical questions, however, Fisher and Jellicoe found the ideas of Mahan stale, outdated, and predictable. Fisher and Jellicoe embraced Sims instead as the American with potential to shape the future of sea power. Upon Sims's arrival in London in December of 1906, Fisher invited him for dinner at Admiralty House. Fisher and Sims discussed the *Dreadnought*, in the final phases of construction in Portsmouth. Fisher shared details but denied permission for Sims to visit *Dreadnought*. He did, however, offer Sims the option of asking Jellicoe to arrange the visit. At that time, Jellicoe served as director of naval ordnance and as the aide-de-camp to King Edward VII.

Whatever their motives, Fisher and Jellicoe allowed Sims to gather information of great strategic value to the United States. On Christmas Eve in 1906, Sims toured *Dreadnought* and became one of the few foreigners to know anything useful about it. Sims submitted a detailed report, which Roosevelt used to force the Navy Department to build dreadnoughts for the U.S. Navy. Sims also highlighted British design achievements in an article, "The Inherent Tactical Qualities of All Big Gun, One Caliber Battleships of High Speed, Large Displacement and Gun-Power."[59]

Roosevelt used Sims as a hammer to force strategic changes from within the Navy Department. Sims offered unique ties with the British but also the perspective of seagoing experience in framing the strategic future of American sea power. In 1907, Roosevelt appointed Sims to serve as a White House naval aide. Given his connections and proximity to power, Sims followed the example of Mahan in pressing opinions inconsistent with the official line of the Navy Department. He shared personal views with influential personalities outside the Navy. With encouragement from the naval artist Henry Reuterdahl and the muckraking journalist George Kibbe Turner, Sims contributed to an article revealing politics and fraud affecting the Navy Department.

In clear violation of Navy Department General Order 252, which restricted U.S. Navy personnel from writing about or criticizing official government policy, Sims provided Reuterdahl all the information he required to publish "The Needs of Our Navy" in *McClure's Magazine* in January 1908. (Roosevelt knew about Sims's concerns before reading about them in *McClure's*.) Also, having advocated improvements in gunnery and American naval ship design, Sims, by the vehicle of Reuterdahl's article, challenged the coal-fired norms of the U.S. Navy. By running again outside the lifelines of the U.S. Navy, Sims had stirred a heated political debate, which prompted an official congressional inquiry.[60] In a telephone conversation, Roosevelt stated to Sims in a stern tone, "Well, you have been insubordinate, haven't you?"[61]

Standards and Oil

In the age of sail, captains and crew artfully managed wind and oceanic currents to maneuver warships. In battle, warships danced to achieve the "weather gauge" advantage as the crews prepared for close-quarters combat with boarding pikes, cutlasses, and carronades. The introduction of coal-fired steam in the nineteenth century revolutionized warship design, enabling greater capacity for incorporating larger-caliber guns and steel armor protection. In combat, warships squared off at greater distances.[62] Although wind was a virtually unlimited source of propulsion, coal was abundant and provided efficient means to run against the wind. In this respect, Sims reflected the technological character of the armored steel warships with heavy rifled guns and steam-driven speed. "He was a born propagandist with a keen appreciation for the value of publicity," Capt. Joseph Strauss remarked about Sims. His "plea for better gunnery was in a good cause and his efforts placed us in an advanced position with respect to scientific shooting long before we would have arrived there without him."[63]

Having rebelled as a midshipman against the regimented culture of the Navy, Sims aggressively pursued opportunities along the fringes of the active ranks of the service to earn a reputation and to satisfy personal interests in the arts, politics, and history, where his technical education had failed him. In so doing Sims drew either the respect or intense hatred of fellow officers of the U.S. Navy. Strauss described Sims as "a tall, handsome man of striking appearance and manner" who was "energetic in movement and positive in his statements—a fluent talker on not too sure a foundation of knowledge."[64] Strauss observed Sims's debating tactics: "If he arrived at an impasse and was checked up on it his reply was, 'well, that is what they tell me.'"[65]

Innovations in technology drove Sims to grapple with the unknowns of engineering as the U.S. Navy approached the decisive transformation from coal to oil. Looking to the past to gain perspective, Sims took a humanistic approach, fostering personal ties with innovators of foreign navies to recall the debates that had surrounded the inevitable transitions from sail to steam and from wood to steel, in preparation for those to come in connection with advances to oil propulsion and rifled big guns of standard caliber. Innovation also cost money, which influenced politics within the Navy Department.

Sims and his associates aggressively sparked explosive debates about the future design of American warships among civilian policy makers and U.S. Navy practitioners. Coal, cumbersome and dirty, had proven unstable in certain conditions. The 1898 explosion in the battleship *Maine* inspired the Navy to investigate other options, though coal-firing remained standard in warships of major navies into the twentieth century. The destruction of the imperial Russian fleet at the battle of Tsushima further drove efforts for change within the U.S. Navy.[66] In that episode, British and American collaboration helped the Japanese to monitor the locations of Russian colliers during the long voyage of the Baltic Fleet to ultimate defeat at Tsushima.[67]

Within the U.S. Navy, reliance on land bases appeared to represent a strategic vulnerability. Given the cheapness and abundance of oil, John D. Rockefeller and William Vanderbilt saw seemingly boundless financial opportunities in pushing the Navy Department to develop warships with boilers that burned it. Within the ranks, Sims championed experiments with alternative fuels. Lt. Henry C. Dinger articulated the perspective of other younger officers in articles he published in *Proceedings*. He recognized strategic problems in the coal-fired U.S. Navy, arguing that the global "system of supply must be simple and move with dispatch."[68]

Coal required facilities ashore, which in turn required warships to protect their maritime lines of supply. In addition, constant rotation of colliers was required to deliver the bulky fuel to distant stations. Naval bases ashore were also vulnerable on land, requiring significant investments in ground forces to defend and diplomacy to maintain good local relations. Coaling at sea was difficult, requiring ships to be stationary in calm, protected waters for extended periods. Mobile refueling appeared nearly impossible.[69] The Royal Navy relied upon just such a global network, but the U.S. Navy increasingly sought alternatives that would bring it an advantage in the maritime arena. "The use of oil for fuel is being constantly extended by the German navy," U.S. Naval Academy professor Philip R. Alger noted in *Proceedings*; a "special transport for supplying oil to ships at sea or in port has been finished and another is about to be built."[70] Oil offered means to counter the coal-fired navies of Europe, which enhanced the U.S. efforts to consolidate control in the American sphere of influence.

The Royal Navy's coaling stations were along routes first established in the age of sail. The five strategic keys of the British Empire, said the First Sea Lord, Fisher, in 1904, lay on those traditional trading routes: Gibraltar, Alexandria and Suez, Singapore, the Cape of Good Hope, and the Straits of Dover. Sir Julian Corbett repeated the idea in *Some Principles of Maritime Strategy*.[71] He applauded Fisher for recognizing the landward underpinnings of maritime command at sea. Fisher nevertheless pressed the Admiralty to begin the transition from coal to oil. At the same time, Fisher turned westward. Sitting at the center of the modern world in London, Fisher recognized the strategic imperative of reconstituting the transatlantic connection between the British Empire and the United States—fully returning the Americas to the good graces of Britannia.

Oil remained a scarce commodity on the European continent; the Americans held a decisive strategic advantage in both coal and oil reserves. Mahan too recognized the future potential of oil in naval affairs, in connection with the vulnerable position of the Royal Navy in the Middle East and Asia.[72] He also saw the Anglo-Dutch and French competition for control over oil resources in the Asiatic as a potential flashpoint for war among the Europeans. As for the United States, Mahan considered its garrison in the Philippines strategically vulnerable in the Asiatic.[73]

Unlike the Royal Navy, the U.S. Navy found the maintenance of land bases strategically unnecessary and potentially dangerous as it progressively abandoned coal in favor of oil. Seeking the strategic advantage in naval affairs, President Roosevelt led the U.S. Navy in its charge away from coal to oil. Among his other protégés, Sims helped orchestrate the transition. He advised Roosevelt to make the difficult initial decision during a series of meetings held at the Navy Department and at the Naval War College between 1904 and 1909. The summer conference of the General Board of the Navy in 1908 marked the decisive point; by that time Roosevelt saw the future in oil-fired battleships.[74] Roosevelt listened to Sims and made the revolutionary decision to abandon coal-fired warships and to build the first "Standard-type."[75]

Liquid fuels simplified the strategic challenges involved with global naval operations, reducing the dirty task of coaling and the burden of defending worldwide coaling stations ashore. Oil provided the advantages of portability and reliability.[76] Sims stood among the key innovators in tactics for use by the oil-fired warships envisioned for the future. His perspective reflected the direct influence of close British associates like Fisher and Jellicoe, who faced resistance from the Admiralty in their support of a transition to oil. Knowing about these unique connections within the Admiralty, Roosevelt empowered Sims to drive major changes inside the Navy Department and in the seagoing forces of the U.S. Navy. By his departure from office, Roosevelt had placed the U.S. Navy on course to become "second to none."

Theoretically, the Royal Navy continued to dominate the global maritime arena. However, the rapid development of the Imperial German Navy forced the British to consolidate their naval forces in European waters. The British presence in the Asiatic and greater Middle East waned after 1910, providing opportunities in those regions for the Germans, Dutch, French, and Americans. Notwithstanding the rivalries on the grander international stage, informal special relationships among individuals, like Jellicoe and Sims, provided means for the Royal Navy and U.S. Navy to foster collaboration.[77] Information supplied by Jellicoe to Sims about British designs inspired Roosevelt to press the dreadnought concept. In testimony, Sims convinced Congress of correctness of the all-big-gun concept.

Sims further emphasized the potential of battle cruisers, which featured big guns but sacrificed armor protection for higher speed. Roosevelt empowered Sims to argue the case to Congress, thereby undermining other Navy Department officials in the debate over future strategic priorities.[78] Before leaving office in 1909, Roosevelt rewarded Sims with a choice command: he influenced the chief of the Bureau of Navigation, Rear Adm. John E. Pillsbury, to adjust the hierarchical list of potential candidates for command assignments as necessary to place Commander Sims in command of the pre-*Dreadnought* battleship *Minnesota*—an assignment usually reserved for officers of a higher "lineal" seniority, or with the rank of captain. Notably, Sims stood seventieth on a list of 120 officers in the rank of commander at that time.[79]

Sims held significant political influence as a protégé of Roosevelt, which annoyed many competitors within the service. Roosevelt's successor, William H. Taft, was also a firm supporter of Sims. However, Sims's appointment to command *Minnesota* caused considerable controversy within the service. Capt. William S. Benson warned Sims that the Navy had "established a dangerous precedent of giving battleships to Commanders."[80] Captain Strauss described the problem in these terms: "Sims' dominance had reached the captains (all his superiors in rank and age) and there was a scarcely concealed hostility to him and all his works. It is human nature," Strauss wrote, "not to want to be set right by one inferior in place and authority."[81] Notwithstanding, Jellicoe—now Rear Adm. Sir John Jellicoe, Third Sea Lord of the Royal Navy—warmly encouraged Sims. "I congratulate you and the United States Navy," Jellicoe wrote Sims in February. "I hope if you do come over [to Britain] I shall see you."[82]

Workups in the Caribbean provided foundations for Sims's preparation for a widely anticipated cruise to European waters. In 1910, the U.S. Navy remained vastly inferior to the imperial German, French, and British navies. Yet, the Americans showed the flag with confidence—carrying out the big-stick strategy of Theodore Roosevelt. Responding to developments in Europe, Mahan published a pamphlet, "Britain and the German Navy: Admiral Mahan's Warning," in which he articulated the threat of Germany for Britannia and the principles of the Monroe Doctrine.

Like many American naval officers, Mahan and Sims shared the confidence that arose from being isolated from the imperial competitions of Europe and Asia. Nevertheless, Mahan noted that Germany "will be decidedly stronger at sea than we in the United States expect to be and we have over her no military check such as the interests of Canada impose upon Great Britain."[83] Mahan warned that the people of Great Britain "should not depend upon the apprehension of Germany's intentions to attack in order to appraise their naval necessities." Arguing the point by implication, Mahan cautioned British readers that otherwise, "resolutions based upon such artificial stimulus are like the excitement of drink, liable to excess in demonstration, and misdirection and ultimate collapse in energy."[84]

Given their mutual global strategic interests and limitations in relation to the threat of Germany, Mahan envisioned the prospect of maritime collaboration between the British Empire and United States. The idea held significant appeal among American naval practitioners. Sims shared that view, having benefitted from his special connections with Roosevelt. As for Mahan, in late 1914 he died, as did the era of coal and multicaliber battleship guns. Sims held command of the oil-burning Destroyer and Torpedo Boat Flotilla of the Atlantic Fleet.

The death of Mahan enabled the generation of Sims to pick up the torch in defining the future of American sea power. The tactics he developed for destroyers included replenishment at sea, tactical maneuver in support of the battleship line, and command through wireless communications. Roosevelt, the staunch advocate of the U.S. Navy, ultimately mitigated the generational differences separating those associated with Mahan and Sims.[85] Mahan influenced Roosevelt with the quasi-historical relationships between economic prosperity and sea power. Sims led him to understand the variables of technology, while accepting the fundamental vision of Mahan. Following the deployments of American military and naval forces to European waters in World War I, Roosevelt in his writings provided common ground on which American naval professionals could embrace their postwar mission of creating "Our Peacemaker, the Navy."[86]

Notes

1. Robert O'Connell, *Sacred Vessels: The Cult of the Battleship and the Rise of the U.S. Navy* (New York: Oxford University Press, 1994), 9–101, 302–22.
2. James C. Bradford, *John Paul Jones and the American Navy* (New York: Rosen, 2002), 92–100; Evan Thomas, *John Paul Jones: Sailor, Hero, Father of the American Navy* (New York: Simon & Schuster, 2003), 1–13, 299–312; Samuel Eliot Morison, *John Paul Jones: A Sailor's Biography* (Boston: Little, Brown, 1959), 406–10.
3. Theodore Roosevelt, *America and the World War, and Fear God and Take Your Own Part*, vol. 18 of *Works of Theodore Roosevelt* (New York: Charles Scribner's Sons, 1925), 122–35.
4. Frank Ninkovich, "Theodore Roosevelt: Civilization as Ideology," *Diplomatic History* 10, no. 3 (July 1986): 221–45.
5. Elting E. Morison, *Admiral Sims and the Modern American Navy* (Boston: Houghton Mifflin, 1942), 163–71.
6. Alfred Thayer Mahan, *The Problem of Asia and Its Effect on International Policies* (Boston: Little, Brown, 1900), 38, 62, 125, 175.
7. Alfred Thayer Mahan, *From Sail to Steam: Recollections of a Naval Life* (Boston: Little, Brown, 1907), 324.
8. O'Connell, *Sacred Vessels*, 9–101, 302–22.
9. Bradford, *John Paul Jones and the American Navy*, 92–100; Thomas, *John Paul Jones*, 1–13, 299–312; Morison, *John Paul Jones*, 406–10; and Charles W. Stewart, comp., *John Paul Jones: Commemoration at Annapolis, April 24, 1906* (Washington, D.C.: Government Printing Office, 1907), 9–21.
10. Yoneyuki Sugita, "The Rise of an American Principle in China: A Reinterpretation of the First Open Door Notes toward China," in *Trans-Pacific Relations: America, Europe, and Asia in the Twentieth Century*, ed. Richard J. Jensen, Jon Thares Davidan, and Yoneyuki Sugita (Westport, Conn.: Greenwood, 2003), 15–20.
11. Jacques M. Downs and Frederick D. Grant Jr., *The Golden Ghetto: The American Commercial Community at Canton and the Shaping of American China Policy, 1784–1844* (Hong Kong: Hong Kong University Press, 2014), 179–92, 365–74.
12. The phrase "sea power" may be found in the nineteenth-century works of Professor Sir John Knox Laughton of King's College London and of Spenser Wilkinson, Chichele Professor of Military History at Oxford University. In conceptualizing the strategic role of navies, American naval professionals generally deferred to the theoretical musings and quasi-historical works of Rear Admirals Stephen B. Luce and Alfred Thayer Mahan. The death of Mahan in 1914 and then of Luce three years later marked a radical transition in U.S. naval history as a new generation of American naval officers staged a bureaucratic revolution within the service. See Donald M. Shurman, *The Education of a Navy: The Development of British Naval Strategic Thought, 1867–1914* (Chicago: University of

Chicago Press, 1965), 1–14, 85–90; John B. Hattendorf, B. Mitchell Simpson III, and John R. Wadleigh, *Sailors and Scholars: The Centennial History of the U.S. Naval War College* (Newport, R.I.: Naval War College Press, 1984), 115–16, 122; Andrew Lambert, *The Foundations of Naval History: John Knox Laughton, the Royal Navy, and the Historical Profession* (London: Chatham, 1998), 30, 121–22, 231–32.

13. Alfred Thayer Mahan, "United States Looking Outward," *Atlantic Monthly* 66, no. 398 (December 1890): 824.

14. Mahan, *Problem of Asia*, 16-17.

15. Mahan, *Problem of Asia*, 93.

16. Alfred Thayer Mahan, *Retrospect and Prospect: Studies in International Relations—Naval and Political* (Boston: Little, Brown, 1902), 237.

17. Halford J. MacKinder, "The Geographical Pivot of History," *Geographical Journal* 23, no. 4 (April 1904): 421–37.

18. MacKinder.

19. Downs and Grant, *Golden Ghetto*, 179–92, 365–74.

20. Jonathan D. Spence, *God's Chinese Son: The Taiping Heavenly Kingdom of Hong Xiuquan* (New York: W. W. Norton, 1997), 2–16, 192–200, 204–9.

21. Established in 1900, the Eight Power Alliance included the empires of Britain, France, Italy, Russia, Germany, Austria-Hungary, Japan, and the United States. The British assumed the leading role in organizing operations, although the other participants often spearheaded tactical efforts against the Boxer insurgency. In his memoirs, concerning operations against the Boxers, Sims referred to Peking (contemporary Beijing) as "Tientsin." Sims, *Victory at Sea* (New York: Doubleday, Page, 1920), 54.

22. Sims, *Victory.*

23. Paulo E. Coletta, *Bowman H. McCalla: Fighting Sailor* (Washington, D.C.: University Press of America, 1979), 1–62. Also see David Kohnen, ed., *21st Century Knox: Influence, Sea Power, and History for the Modern Era* (Annapolis, Md.: Naval Institute Press, 2016), 1–19. After service together in the Boxer Rebellion, Knox became the son-in-law of McCalla and the brother-in-law of Arthur MacArthur II and his brother Douglas.

24. John R. Jellicoe to William S. Sims, 22 June 1910, Folder 110, Correspondence File, Papers of Admiral of the Fleet John Rushworth Jellicoe, Lord Jellicoe, vol. XLVII (1900–1916), Add. Ms 49035, British Library, London.

25. William Laird Clowes, with Clements Markham, Alfred Thayer Mahan, Herbert Wrigley Wilson, and Theodore Roosevelt, *The Royal Navy: A History from the Earliest Times to the Death of Queen Victoria* (London: Sampson Low, Marston, 1903), 7:530.

26. Jellicoe to Sims, 22 June 1910.

27. Arthur J. Marder, *Fear God and Dread Nought: Years of Power, 1904–1914* (London: Jonathan Cape, 1956), 479.

28. James Goldrick, *Before Jutland: The Naval War in Northern European Waters, August 1914–February 1915* (Annapolis, Md.: Naval Institute Press, 2015), 64–66.

29. James Goldrick, "The Irresistible Force and the Immovable Object: The *Naval Review*, the Young Turks, and the Royal Navy, 1911–1931," in *Mahan Is Not Enough: The Proceedings of a Conference on the Works of Sir Julian Corbett and Admiral Sir Herbert Richmond*, ed. James Goldrick and John B. Hattendorf (Newport, R.I.: Naval War College Press, 1993), 87.

30. Benjamin J. Armstrong, ed., *21st Century Sims: Innovation, Education, and Leadership in the Modern Era* (Annapolis, Md.: Naval Institute Press, 2015), vii.

31. William S. Sims to Albert P. Niblack, 14 March 1902, William S. Sims Papers, Correspondence File, Naval War College, Newport, R.I.

32. Morison, *Admiral Sims and the Modern American Navy*, 176–215.

33. Nathaniel Sims, Correspondence of William S. Sims, William S. Sims Jr., notes of "Recollections" circa 1934, 3–4, sent by William S. Sims Jr. to Anne Sims on 18 December 1984, digital copy provided by Nathan Sims to author on 27 April 2016.

34. Morison, *Admiral Sims and the Modern American Navy*, 18, 29–30, 48–57.

35. Charles H. Stockton to William S. Sims, 21 May 1901, Correspondence Files, box 145, William S. Sims Papers, Library of Congress, Washington, D.C.

36. Albert P. Niblack to William S. Sims, 20 June 1901, Sims Papers, Library of Congress.

37. Morison, *Admiral Sims and the Modern American Navy*, 94.

38. Morison, *Admiral Sims*, 86–90.

39. "Brief Summary of Lieut. Sims' Criticisms Contained in his Reports from the Asiatic Station," 8, Theodore Roosevelt Papers, Library of Congress, Washington, D.C.

40. Morison, *Admiral Sims and the Modern American Navy*, 103–5.

41. TR to William S. Sims, 12 December 1901, box 92, Sims Papers, Library of Congress.

42. Nicholas A. Lambert, "Strategic Command and Control for Maneuver Warfare: Creation of the Royal Navy's 'War Room' System, 1905–1915," *Journal of Military History* 69 (April 2005): 361–410.

43. Francis Wrigley Hirst, *The Six Panics and Other Essays* (London: Methuen, 1913), 1–165, 247–59.

44. Spencer Wilkinson, *The Brain of the Navy* (London: Archibald Constable, 1895), 97–99.

45. Lambert, "Strategic Command and Control for Maneuver Warfare," 361–410.

46. Morison, *Admiral Sims and the Modern American Navy*, 3–14, 280, 389–92.

47. Paul A. Kramer, "Empires, Exceptions, and Anglo-Saxons: Race and Rule between the British and United States Empires," *Journal of American History* 88 (March 2002): 1315–53.

48. John R. Jellicoe to William S. Sims, 8 December 1908, Correspondence Files, box 68, Folder 1906–1918, Sims Papers, Library of Congress.
49. William S. Sims, "Training Ranges and Long-Range Firing," U.S. Naval Institute *Proceedings* 30 (September 1904): 511–31.
50. Sims, "Training Ranges," 150.
51. Sims, "Training Ranges," 50–54, 147–52.
52. William S. Sims to Anne Hitchcock Sims, July 1905, Folder 16, Sims Papers, Naval War College.
53. Morison, *Admiral Sims and the Modern American Navy*, 164–75.
54. Armstrong, *21st Century Sims*, 1–12, 51, 75, 154–57; Henry J. Hendrix, *Theodore Roosevelt's Naval Diplomacy: The U.S. Navy and the Birth of the American Century* (Annapolis, Md.: Naval Institute Press, 2009), 104–10, 114–17, 123–24; Donald Chisholm, *Waiting for Dead Men's Shoes: Origins and Development of the U.S. Navy's Officer Personnel System* (Stanford, Calif.: Stanford University Press, 2001), 514–16.
55. Peter Karsten, *The Naval Aristocracy: The Golden Age of Annapolis and the Rise of American Navalism* (Annapolis, Md.: Naval Institute Press, 2008), 1–15; O'Connell, *Sacred Vessels*, 9–101, 302–22; Hattendorf, Simpson, and Wadleigh, *Sailors and Scholars*, 1–35.
56. Morison, *Admiral Sims and the Modern American Navy*, 184–86.
57. Morison, *Admiral Sims*.
58. Morison, *Admiral Sims*, 155–75.
59. William S. Sims, "The Inherent Tactical Qualities of All Big Gun, One Caliber Battleships of High Speed, Large Displacement and Gun-Power," U.S. Naval Institute *Proceedings* 32 (December 1906): 1337–66.
60. Kenneth J. Hagan, "Radical but Right: William Sowden Sims (1878–1936)," in *Nineteen-Gun Salute: Case Studies of Operational, Strategic, and Diplomatic Leadership during the Twentieth and Early Twenty-First Centuries*, ed. John B. Hattendorf and Bruce A. Elleman (Newport, R.I.: Naval War College Press, 2010), 1–12; Dean C. Allard, "Anglo-American Differences during World War I," *Military Affairs* 45 (April 1980): 75–81; and David F. Trask, "The American Navy in a World at War, 1914–1918," in *In Peace and War: Interpretations of American Naval History, 1775–1978*, ed. Kenneth J. Hagan (New York: Greenwood, 1978), 169–81.
61. William S. Sims, "Roosevelt and the Navy: Recollections, Reminiscences, and Reflections—Part II," *McClure's Magazine* 54, no. 9 (November 1922): 62.
62. John H. Maurer, "Fuel and the Battle Fleet: Coal, Oil, and American Naval Strategy, 1898–1925," *Naval War College Review* 34 (November–December, 1981): 60–77.
63. Joseph Strauss, "As I Recall It: Being the Recollections of Forty-Four Years Spent in the U.S. Navy" (unpublished typescript), 171, Strauss Papers, Naval Historical Collection, Naval War College, Newport, R.I.
64. Strauss.

65. Strauss.

66. David C. Evans and Mark R. Peattie, *Kaigun: Strategy, Tactics, and Technology in the Imperial Japanese Navy, 1887–1941* (Annapolis, Md.: Naval Institute Press, 1997), 83–87.

67. Constantine Pleshakov, *The Tsar's Last Armada: The Epic Journey to the Battle of Tsushima* (New York: Basic Books, 2001), 75–88.

68. Henry C. Dinger, "Some Notes on Naval Needs and Requirements," U.S. Naval Institute *Proceedings* 30 (January 1904): 91.

69. Spencer Miller, "Refueling Ships at Sea," Society of Naval Architects and Marine Engineers *Transactions* (December 1914): 1.

70. Philip R. Alger, ed., "Professional Notes," U.S. Naval Institute *Proceedings* 30 (October 1904): 848.

71. Julian Corbett, *Some Principles of Maritime Strategy* (London: Longmans, Green, 1911), 105–107.

72. Alfred Thayer Mahan, "The Persian Gulf and International Relations," *National Review* 40 (September 1902): 39.

73. Mahan, *Problem of Asia*, 42, 46–47, 98–105, 164, 196, 214.

74. "Battleship Conference, 1908," RG 8, Series 1, box 168, Folder 1, Naval War College.

75. Hattendorf, Simpson, and Wadleigh, *Sailors and Scholars*, 60–65; Morison, *Admiral Sims and the Modern American Navy*, 313–36.

76. Peter V. Nash, *The Development of Mobile Logistic Support in Anglo-American Naval Policy, 1900–1953* (Gainesville: University Press of Florida, 2009), 1–77.

77. John R. Jellicoe to William S. Sims, 3 February 1909 and 25 December 1910, box 68, Folder 1906–1918, Sims Papers, Library of Congress; Invitation from the Commander and Officers of the Third Division–U.S. Atlantic Fleet to "Mrs. E. A. Hitchcock and the Whole St. Louis Family Push [*sic*]," box 101, Sims Papers, Library of Congress; Jellicoe to Sims, 22 June 1910.

78. Morison, *Admiral Sims and the Modern American Navy*, 176–200.

79. *Register of the Commissioned and Warrant Officers of the United States Navy and Marine Corps* (Washington, D.C.: Navy Department, January 1909), 14.

80. William S. Benson to William S. Sims, March 1909, box 48, Folder 1909–1916, Sims Papers, Library of Congress.

81. Strauss, "As I Recall It," 172.

82. Jellicoe to Sims, 3 February 1909.

83. Alfred Thayer Mahan, "Britain and the German Navy: Admiral Mahan's Warning," as reprinted by the *Daily Mail* (1910), 2.

84. Mahan, "Britain and the German Navy: Admiral Mahan's Warning."

85. Mathew Oyos, *In Command: Theodore Roosevelt and the American Military* (Lincoln: Potomac Books of the University of Nebraska Press, 2018), 285–300.

86. Roosevelt, *America and the World War*, 122–35.

8

USEFUL ALLIES

Theodore Roosevelt's Secretaries of the Navy and America's Naval Ascendancy

Branden Little

T.R. turned secretaries over like pancakes. —*Robert Seager II*

In an era in which Congress wielded tremendous power in U.S. foreign policy, President Theodore Roosevelt appointed Secretaries of the Navy to strengthen his campaign for fleet expansion and departmental reform. He needed able executives and apostles for sea power to obtain congressional approval and thereby accomplish his grand designs. Roosevelt's larger-than-life personality and deep interest in naval affairs have obscured his six secretaries' tenures. Historians have frequently claimed that the rapid turnover in secretaries signaled that Roosevelt cared little for who held the post.[1] But Roosevelt did not wish the department to experience such frequent change in its leadership. The revolving door of Roosevelt's secretaries was made necessary by many factors outside the president's control. In his secretaries Roosevelt sought useful allies to secure America's naval ascendancy.[2]

John D. Long (6 March 1897 to 30 April 1902)

John D. Long and Roosevelt had sparred since 1897, when President William McKinley appointed Long secretary and Roosevelt the assistant secretary of the Navy. Long had little prior knowledge of naval affairs but was a longtime friend of McKinley's. Long believed that a small navy had adequately protected American interests in the long nineteenth century. Comfortable with a gradual pace of naval construction, Long felt no urgency to initiate a breakneck program of fleet expansion. He was the custodian of American naval traditions that Roosevelt sought to upset. In Roosevelt's estimation, Long represented the entrenched political establishment that had historically made bad decisions concerning national security. Roosevelt detested Long's opposition to the creation of a naval general staff. Long's failure to resolve positively the Sampson-Schley dispute, a scandal in which two ranking American officers disagreed over who should receive credit for destroying the Spanish fleet in Cuban waters in 1898, strengthened Roosevelt's convictions that McKinley's old friend was ill-suited to lead the Navy.[3]

McKinley's assassination in September 1901 brought Long's reign to an end. Long remained secretary for seven months, however, until President Roosevelt was ready to form his own cabinet.[4] When Long resigned, Roosevelt publicly praised his lengthy service to the nation. Privately, Roosevelt considered Long's rule disastrous: "Wholly unfit to be Secretary of the Navy because of his ignorance on naval matters," Roosevelt declared.[5] Despite Long's passivity, the U.S. Navy was a more powerful force when Long left the department than it had been when he entered office. Congress had lavished appropriations on Long's Navy. Dozens of new warships had been built or were under construction when he retired. By most standards of measurement, the U.S. Navy ranked as one of the world's strongest by 1901. That Roosevelt inherited a respectable Navy was thanks, in part, to Long's leadership.

William H. Moody (1 May 1902 to 30 June 1904)

When Roosevelt sought a replacement for Long, he did not ignore candidates with naval expertise, but it was not a paramount concern. Roosevelt favored two U.S. representatives out of a small pool of prospects: George E. Foss of Illinois, the chair of the House Naval Affairs Committee, and William H. Moody of Massachusetts, whose portfolio included

Appropriations and Insular Affairs. Roosevelt found no good reason to displace Foss from a position of leadership. Roosevelt also discovered that he disliked Foss and considered him "a weakling."[6]

Moody emerged as Roosevelt's front-runner. The two Harvard alums had first become acquainted in early 1898. They shared a common desire to promote America's power internationally. Roosevelt also admired Moody's law-practice mentor, the famous mariner and author of *Two Years Before the Mast* (1840) Richard Henry Dana Jr. For many years Roosevelt and Dana had strategized about civil service reform and even matters of warship design.[7] In Moody, Roosevelt found an ideological counterpart.

Moody was a rising star in the Republican Party (the "GOP") and well regarded by Democrats. Champ Clark, a popular Democratic representative, characterized Moody as "one of the ablest men in the House."[8] Clark admired how Moody triumphed in "spirited debates which have arisen over items in the appropriation bills that have come from his committee." Appropriations Committee chair Joseph G. Cannon heavily relied on Moody to advance GOP projects. In just two congressional terms, Moody was catapulted into consideration for Speaker of the House.[9]

His selection as naval secretary signaled the president's desire for a loyal deputy who could strengthen the administration's ties to Congress. Moody was the only member of Roosevelt's early cabinet who had any legislative experience.[10] Roosevelt anticipated (correctly) that Moody's dynamic leadership, bipartisan rapport, and knowledge of appropriations could spearhead his battleship program. Roosevelt also wished to make a clean break with the partisan fighting over Sampson and Schley that had long divided American opinion on the Navy. The final congressional report on the inquiry would soon be released, Roosevelt knew. It could reenergize the dispute, smear the Navy Department, and threaten his plans for modernization. Unlike Foss, however, Moody had not been entangled in the contretemps. Moody could take the department's helm without bias for one faction or another. Reinforcing the political value of Moody's selection was that the powerful and cantankerous Rear Adm. Arent S. Crowninshield, who was a fierce partisan of Sampson's, had just relinquished the Bureau of Navigation. Into Crowninshield's place had stepped Rear Adm. Henry C. Taylor, a reformer with whom Roosevelt had worked cooperatively while assistant secretary. It seemed that a clean slate for a new secretary and chief of this important bureau heralded a glowing future for Roosevelt's Navy.

To many observers, Roosevelt's nomination of Moody came as a pleasant surprise.[11] If Moody was highly regarded, however, he had hardly any more expertise in naval affairs than Long had at first possessed. Secretary Moody nevertheless soon promoted a vigorous construction policy and departmental reform campaign. Rear Admiral Taylor and the president of the General Board, Adm. George Dewey, supported Moody's leadership. An articulate administrator, Moody quickly became a powerful figure in Roosevelt's cabinet.

Moody's baptism by fire came almost instantly upon his oath of office. On 8 May, a volcanic eruption devastated the French Caribbean islands of Martinique and St. Vincent. Moody ordered the cruiser *Cincinnati* and collier *Sterling*, then active in nearby waters, to aid survivors. The Brooklyn Navy Yard dispatched the training ship *Dixie* with humanitarian aid.[12] Roosevelt approved of these actions. He directed Moody to "go to the furthest limits of Executive discretion in the world of relief and rescue in the afflicted Islands of the Caribbean."[13] Congress appropriated $500,000 for supplies. The French president, Émile Loubet, praised American generosity; "France will never forget this proof of fraternal amity," he exclaimed.[14] The U.S. Navy's swift response demonstrated its readiness for action and the government's willingness to save beleaguered peoples.

At precisely the same time, in May 1902, Roosevelt dedicated a statue of Marshal de Rochambeau in Washington.[15] The project had been planned for months, but the timing was symbolic given American aid to French volcano survivors. Events ranged from the White House to Annapolis, Maryland, where the French warship *Gaulois* hosted a luncheon to honor Roosevelt, with Moody in tow. The battleships *Kearsarge* and *Alabama*, the cruiser *Olympia*, and the dispatch vessel *Dolphin* participated in the celebrations by firing salutes that echoed across Chesapeake Bay. Ambassador Jules Cambon professed "that the splendid friendship between the French and American people which had continued unbroken for more than a century would continue for generations."[16] Roosevelt recalled France's seminal contributions to American independence. Moody declared that the United States owed "an obligation" to France.[17]

Within a few days of this Franco-American fête, Moody addressed Republicans in Detroit. Hundreds gathered to hear the president's emissary. Moody recounted the glories of American victory in the war with Spain: "We changed the geography of the globe. It brought to this nation as great responsibilities as ever rested upon a nation. We have discharged some of them. Some of them are still bearing heavily upon us." He continued, "The war with Spain . . . disclosed the character of our people." Moody blasted the anti-imperialist critics who advocated "the policy of scuttle." He argued that disaster would have resulted "if we had sailed away and left those islands [the Philippines] floating uncared for upon the sea of chance." Moody rejected Democratic criticism of McKinley's Republican administration for "plundering, exploiting and oppressing the people who had come under American rule." American tutelage, Moody insisted, "means order, it means the rule of law, it means respect for the rights of others, it means education, it means self government, it means civilization, it means—thank God—it means everything which makes life worth living to an American, and we are going to keep it there." An otherwise brief war with Spain had created enduring responsibilities for the United States.[18]

Germany's ambitions factored into Moody's advocacy of Roosevelt's "large policy" of hemispheric and international ascendancy. The two Americans wished to build a fleet equivalent to Germany's, then ranked the world's second largest after Britain's.[19] In 1902, Moody facilitated fleet exercises in the Caribbean that were envisioned as a counterweight to Germany's ambitions there. He launched an assessment of Venezuelan beaches suitable for German landing operations and ordered the development of plans to prevent Germany's seizure of Caribbean islands. He encouraged joint operations between the fleet and the Marine Corps detachments that would guard Culebra Island and Panama. The following year, Moody's warships supported Roosevelt's seizure of the Panamanian Isthmus from Colombia.[20]

Encouraged by Roosevelt and Moody, Congress accelerated the construction of battleships. Steel shortages and strikes delayed completion of many vessels, but in just eleven months three *Illinois*-class battleships had been commissioned. A *Maine*-class battleship was commissioned in each of the next three years. The keels of five *Virginia*-class battleships were laid in the eleven months between August 1901 and July 1902. Even larger and more powerfully armed designs were being developed—the *Connecticut* and *Mississippi* classes. Five *Connecticut*-class keels were laid in 1903–4. The furious pace of battleship construction pleased the president and his secretary. As their lobbying achieved success, Roosevelt and Moody collaborated on the politically important naming of ships. George B. Cortelyou, secretary to the president, informed Moody, "The President requests me to say that he will be likely to adopt any suggestions which you may submit on the subject."[21]

Moody acted to improve the fighting efficiency of the fleet. He campaigned for funds to recruit more officers and men to ensure ships were fully crewed. He intensified training regimens for sailors. "Preparedness for war," Moody insisted, "is the best guaranty of the continuance of peace."[22] Moody and Secretary of War Elihu Root established the Joint Board of the Army and Navy to facilitate interservice coordination.

Recognizing that modern warships required extensive basing infrastructure, Moody lobbied to expand or build bases and dry docks along America's coastlines and on insular possessions. Moody became a vanguard of hemispheric interventionism, shepherding a congressional visit to the Caribbean and Gulf Coast. Eugene Hale, the fiscally conservative chair of the Senate Naval Affairs Committee, and James A. Hemenway, who chaired the House Appropriations Committee, accompanied Moody on a three-week excursion. They toured naval stations throughout the region. Guantánamo Naval Base was soon established with their support.[23] Moody's campaign to build bases in the Philippines and Cuba and establish civil governance on Guam and Tutuila, however, achieved little; Congress never wished to appropriate funds for distant territories where its members had no constituents.[24]

In 1904, Moody deftly orchestrated the passage of the naval appropriations bill. He understood that Republican legislators were "eager to avoid controversy over expenditures . . . which might give the public the impression that money was flowing too freely in Washington." Recognizing Hale's authority, Moody ascertained the budget ceiling that the senator would consider palatable. Armed with Hale's figure of $30 million, Moody ordered his department to design a budget less than this amount. Moody requested $1.5 million less than Hale would have accepted. Democrats offered only token resistance. The bill sailed through Congress.[25]

Resistance to proposals to reform the bureau system and to create a naval general staff plagued Moody's tenure. Shortly before Congress adjourned in spring 1904, Moody submitted a general staff bill drafted by Admiral Dewey and Admiral Taylor. Instantly sparks flew that illuminated the internal division within the Navy.[26] In testimony before the House Naval Affairs Committee, Assistant Secretary of the Navy Charles H. Darling vehemently objected to Moody's proposal. Darling claimed that the bill "was but an opening wedge for militarism." Several bureau chiefs who feared their considerable powers would wane with the staff's formation so strongly objected that not even Foss, who supported Moody, could obtain his committee's assent. The bill died in committee.[27]

Following the abrupt death of Moody's bill, Hale promised to block similar legislation.[28] Rather than waste political capital on this controversial subject, Roosevelt focused elsewhere. He wanted to enlarge basing infrastructure, enhance readiness for war with greater training, and improve warship designs. Roosevelt disappointed reformist officers by silently abandoning the general staff crusade.[29] Unable to circumvent Hale's opposition, the president had no viable alternative.

By summer 1904, Roosevelt felt satisfied that the biggest obstacles to his campaign of fleet modernization and expansion had been overcome. The massive construction program Long and Moody had catalyzed would soon provide the battleship force he desired. The United States was on pace to beat Germany's fleet strength. No guarantee existed that the favorable tide of popular support for the Navy would continue to rise. Growing voices objected to the U.S. Navy's seemingly insatiable appetite for taxpayer's dollars. Champions of nonmilitary projects believed that bridge and road construction suffered because the Navy was siphoning away available funds. Other critics like Rear Adm. Alfred Thayer Mahan and Senator

Hale decried as myopic the administration's emphasis on battleships, which were vulnerable to obsolescence and asymmetric weapons, including sea mines. They objected to the diversion of resources from smaller warships that had traditionally protected trade and interests in distant waters.[30]

An unexpected Senate vacancy brought Moody's term as secretary to a close. The death of a powerful Republican senator from Pennsylvania, Matthew S. Quay, in late May 1904 resulted in a deck chair–like rearrangement of cabinet members. Roosevelt orchestrated it. By temperament and political instinct, Roosevelt made swift decisions regarding political appointments. He feared that uncertainty would prove corrosive to his leadership. One editorialist from Kansas observed this trait: "Indeed, it is one of the president's particular characteristics that he does not allow important appointments to hang fire."[31] Philander C. Knox, the attorney general, filled the newly vacated Senate seat, and Roosevelt nominated Moody as Knox's replacement.[32] "The President is now trying to find a man to take Mr. Moody's place," the *Boston Globe* reported. "The navy department is his hobby and he will not place it in the hands of a man who does not exactly suit him."[33]

Paul Morton (1 July 1904 to 30 June 1905)

With the sudden displacement of Moody, Roosevelt searched for a replacement who could achieve his reformist objectives. Throughout June 1904, Roosevelt considered several possible successors. Foss remained a perennial candidate. Roosevelt interviewed Victor H. Metcalf, who sat on the House Ways and Means and Naval Affairs Committees. A transplant to the Bay Area of California, Metcalf had vigorously promoted Republican goals and shipbuilding at Mare Island Naval Shipyard.[34]

Assured of Foss's loyalty, Roosevelt negotiated the Navy Department's future with Metcalf and another prospective cabinet official, the railroad magnate Paul Morton. At first Roosevelt wanted the industrialist Morton to organize the newly formed Department of Commerce and Labor.[35] Morton declined. He had never entertained public service before because cabinet officials earned less than a third of his executive salary.[36] Undaunted, Roosevelt shifted direction. Turning to Metcalf, Roosevelt promised that he would eventually appoint him Secretary of the Navy if the representative would first "accept the more onerous and distasteful task of completing the organization of the commerce and labor department."[37] Metcalf agreed.

Roosevelt then invited Morton to take the reins of the Navy Department. Morton declined. He knew little about the U.S. Navy or Washington politics. Roosevelt sweetened the offer by indicating he would consider Morton a suitable secretary of the treasury if he first served in the Navy Department. Roosevelt predicted that Morton's intuition as a prominent industrialist might revitalize the Navy's antiquated corridors of power and fix its myriad inefficiencies. Roosevelt assured Morton that naval expertise was unnecessary. "Any honest, fairly able man can do such work. . . . It is this military efficiency of the fleet which needs to receive most attention."[38]

At a private dinner at the White House, Roosevelt overcame Morton's reluctance.[39] Roosevelt invoked their long-standing relationship. The two had first met in 1884, at the Republican national convention. At the time, Roosevelt was an assemblyman from New York and Morton a rising star in the railroad industry who had cut his teeth as a clerk, like Andrew Carnegie. Morton's meteoric ascent had since culminated in the presidency of one railroad and the senior vice presidency of another.[40] Roosevelt was also a friend of Morton's father. Invoking these personal ties, Roosevelt sought a four-year commitment by Morton to serve as his Secretary of the Navy. Morton refused to serve more than a year.[41] The two titans compromised, Morton accepting Roosevelt's offer and Roosevelt accepting Morton's demand.

In July 1904, Roosevelt announced his nominees for a dramatically reconfigured cabinet. Roosevelt surprised the nation again with his choice of Morton to lead the Navy Department. Metcalf became the secretary of commerce and labor, and Roosevelt's "much beloved" Moody became attorney general.[42]

The Russo-Japanese War, which had begun in February 1904, intensified Roosevelt's appreciation of America's geostrategic vulnerabilities. He tutored Morton about sea power.[43] In July, Roosevelt forwarded to his secretary an article printed in a popular British magazine. "Japan's Object-Lessons in Naval Warfare" praised Japan's leadership and warned about Russia's lackadaisical preparations. Japan "has illustrated the fruits of intelligent, careful organization and the meaning of being ready for war. She has humbled a Power against whom even Napoleon could not prevail." The article also blasted Senator Hale's allegedly "hasty and ill-founded conclusions" about the purported disadvantages of battleships.[44] After Roosevelt read more reports of Japanese naval supremacy, he warned Morton that American warships were undergunned.[45]

Morton, Roosevelt's new disciple of sea power, wholeheartedly accepted these claims. They both believed that American preparations for war with powers such as Japan were inadequate. In his first annual report to Congress, submitted in December 1904, Morton parroted the magazine article. "The lessons of the war in the East," Morton insisted, "thus far are the same as those of the Spanish war with respect to the relative value and uses of battleships, torpedo boats, and destroyers. Weight of metal, heavy guns, and hard hitting, whether at long or short range[,] still do the most effective work." Certain of American vulnerability to surprise attack, Morton insisted that only a powerful fleet could prevent war. Diplomacy offered no panacea. He exclaimed: "We want such a Navy in size, style, and 'sand' that no other navy will ever desire an engagement with us."[46]

However, alternative interpretations of the implications of the Russo-Japanese War abounded. The *Nation* argued "that Secretary Morton's jingo call for a very great navy meets with Mr. Roosevelt's approval"; "No foreign navy has attacked us or tried to attack us for nearly a century"; "No periods in our national history were more full of peace with honor than those years during which our navy was smallest."[47] The *Nation* warned against an aggressive shift in American foreign policy that would likely result in war. Moreover, the war between Russia and Japan had hardly demonstrated the primacy of the battleship. Sea mines and torpedoes had inflicted most naval casualties. A seemingly decisive battle at Port Arthur had mirrored Dewey's in Manila by demonstrating the limits of battleship accomplishment. To achieve victory, Japan and the United States had both been compelled to transport ground troops overseas to engage enemy forces.[48] This heresy did not immediately register in the Roosevelt administration.

Undaunted by the limitations of capital ships displayed in recent wars, Morton lobbied for battleship construction. In February 1905, he requested three more behemoths; Congress agreed to build two. In just four years Congress had approved ten battleships. Morton's emphasis on construction instead of on reforming the Navy Department helped to retain Hale's favor, even though Hale was fast becoming an opponent of building more "battlewagons." Hale praised Morton: "He is one of the best . . . administrator[s] . . . I have ever known in the Navy Department, and we have had good Secretaries of the Navy heretofore."[49]

Morton labored, however, to lead a bitterly divided Navy. The surprise death of Rear Admiral Taylor, the chief of the Bureau of Navigation, left a conspicuous absence as a senior advisor. Morton understood that Roosevelt's effective moratorium on administrative reforms in the Navy Department meant he could do little to resolve intensifying discord within the Navy's leadership. Foes of change were content to bide their time. Crusading reformers felt betrayed by Morton. Their scathing remarks indicated sharp disappointment with Morton's unwillingness to reintroduce general staff legislation. In correspondence with the retired rear admiral Stephen B. Luce, Capt. William J. Barnette equated the secretary's demeanor to "a bag of cold mush."[50] The reformers' unwillingness to support Morton's leadership produced paralysis in the Navy Department.

Scandal soon enveloped Morton. His predecessor and now attorney general, Moody, unintentionally sparked a crisis in May 1905. An allegation of illegal freight rebates triggered an investigation by Moody of the Santa Fe Railroad—a company over which Morton had recently been vice president. Morton proclaimed his innocence, but cries of corruption quickly mounted. Embattled and perhaps desiring an end to an unpleasant tenure in Washington, a city he disliked, Morton made a statement interpreted as challenging the president. In a speech given at the International Railway Congress, Morton rejected Roosevelt's claim that railroad rates were unfairly set by monopolies. Morton's new counterpart in the War Department, William H. Taft, a Roosevelt protégé, was present at the convention.

Predictably, Taft rallied to Roosevelt's defense. He mocked Morton: "Then here is the Secretary of the Navy, who has nothing to do but think of what he has done in the past with respect to railroads!" Laughter followed. Taft's and Morton's spat stretched into the evening at a banquet.[51]

In response to this nationally publicized airing of disagreement between cabinet officials, William Jennings Bryan, the eminent Democrat and thorn in Roosevelt's side, called for Morton's resignation. Bryan character- ized Morton's rule as "a standing embarrassment to the president's efforts to bring the railroads under efficient regulation."[52] Roosevelt remained silent on the matter, but the *Washington Post* correctly insisted that Morton had outlived his usefulness.[53] Roosevelt and Morton determined that his departure should coincide with the end of the fiscal year, in June.[54] Job offers for executive positions in major corporations flooded Morton's office. Roosevelt and Moody agreed not to prosecute Morton, on the grounds that he was not legally responsible for his railway deputies' malfeasance.[55]

The announcement of Morton's resignation prompted widespread speculation about his successor. The *Los Angeles Herald* was so confident of Metcalf's appointment that its front page featured a large portrait of the California representative and proclaimed him the incoming secretary. In apparent confirmation of this rumor, Alice Roosevelt, the president's daughter, announced she would stay with the Metcalf family during a tour of California.[56] But Metcalf's health had suffered in Washington, and he contemplated retirement.[57] While Roosevelt considered a suitable replacement for this important post, he chose a Republican from Michigan, Truman H. Newberry, to become assistant secretary. Rumors circulated that Newberry would eventually become secretary.[58]

Charles J. Bonaparte (1 July 1905 to 16 December 1906)

Roosevelt silenced speculation by appointing Charles J. Bonaparte. The great nephew of Napoleon Bonaparte, Charles Bonaparte was a Harvard- trained lawyer and ideological ally of Roosevelt.[59] Roosevelt and the "Baltimore Reformer," as Bonaparte was known, had long campaigned to reform municipal government. The two crusaders' acquaintance had begun in 1889. President Roosevelt had recently relied on Bonaparte as a special counsel on investigations of corruption on Indian reservations and the postal service.[60]

Bonaparte confessed he "was completely surprised by" Roosevelt's request to join his cabinet.[61] He knew practically nothing about naval affairs and had spent no time at sea.[62] The shock of Roosevelt's proposal was compounded by the unlikely circumstances in which it was made. At precisely the time when Roosevelt was pondering Morton's successor, Bonaparte arrived at the White House to discuss GOP strategy for Maryland. Roosevelt may not have had any prior inclination to select Bonaparte until they met for lunch and the president sensed the possibility.[63] Bonaparte's serendipitous appearance at this critical juncture likely rekindled Roosevelt's desire to reform the Navy Department. Roosevelt probably thought that this progressive giant of good governance might erase the taint of Gilded Age corruption Morton had unwittingly reintroduced.

Roosevelt promised Bonaparte that after he had taken the helm of the Navy for a year, he could have Moody's job as attorney general. (In fact, the civil service reformer would eventually become Roosevelt's chief trust buster.) The allure proved irresistible. "My dear fellow," Roosevelt wrote to his prospective secretary on 22 May 1905, "you can hardly imagine how glad I am to have you a member of my official family."[64]

Roosevelt's choice for secretary surprised Congress and the press alike. "Now, I have scooped you all!" the president boasted at a press conference.[65] Nevertheless, the *New York Tribune* predicted that this "brilliant lawyer and a man of great executive force" would surely threaten "greedy contractors" and "antiquated officials" running the Navy's bureaus.[66] The Senate confirmed Bonaparte in July. Newspapers across the United States viewed the appointment positively.[67] In an allusion to Trafalgar, one wry cartoonist depicted Napoleon reacting to his grand-nephew's selection: "I hope he does better with ships than I did."[68]

Bonaparte echoed Roosevelt's views of sea power.[69] "If we are to do our part in protecting, pacifying, and regenerating the New World," the secretary asserted, "all men must know and therefore believe that, while we prize peace, we do not fear and have no reason to fear war."[70] Bonaparte told Congress that the Russo-Japanese War had revealed "the paramount importance to a belligerent of thorough preparation, drill, discipline, target practice, and proximity to a well-supplied base at the moment of decisive conflict."[71]

Strengthening the Navy's professionalism and preparedness for war dominated Bonaparte's agenda. Construction took a distant second place. Foremost a fiscal conservative, he detested unnecessary public expenditures. His perception of necessity related to what he perceived as bona fide threats to the nation: "If [geopolitical] circumstances remain as they are now I see no reason to suppose that the number of ships in our Navy need increase."[72] Roosevelt privately agreed that the building program for battleships was adequate. He informed Maj. Gen. Leonard Wood of this conviction: "For some years now we can afford to rest and merely replace the ships that are worn out or become obsolete, while we bring up personnel."[73]

In any case, a growing chorus was loudly objecting to what it called the Roosevelt administration's myopic emphasis on naval ascendancy. Members of Congress and other politically astute commentators denounced battleship construction. They rejected the geopolitical premises upon which Roosevelt and his secretaries had advanced his building campaign. To them Roosevelt's plans seemed fiscally irresponsible, strategically unnecessary, and recklessly provocative. Roosevelt also confronted opposition from an unlikely source: Rear Admiral Mahan. The internationally influential officer and author resisted the capital-intensive construction, inspired by the naval outcome of the Russo-Japanese War and the imminent debut of Britain's *Dreadnought*, of whole classes of capital ships.[74] Specifically, Mahan objected to the all-big-gun battleship, chiefly for the reason that its wholesale adoption undermined the size and tactical flexibility of fleets. He worried that the U.S. Navy could afford only a few of the very expensive dreadnoughts. Mahan feared that if Roosevelt's plans were implemented, "we [would] be left with a few monsters, instead of a number adequate to our varied requirements."[75] Mahan's apostasy threatened Roosevelt's plans by awakening congressional resistance.[76]

Roosevelt refused to countenance anti-navalist heresy. Relying on partisans including Lt. Cdr. William S. Sims, Roosevelt undermined Mahan. Sims attacked Roosevelt's once-trusted ally with arguments that exposed the retired strategist's loosening grasp on warship design. But Roosevelt and Bonaparte needed more than Sims's sophisticated technical arguments to fulfil the president's modernization plans. They needed to convince Congress that the prophet of sea power was mistaken.[77]

HMS *Dreadnought* sparked debates about American battleship design. In May 1905, announcements of the construction of the all-big-gun marvel had circulated globally.[78] It would boast ten twelve-inch guns and displace 18,000 tons. America's newest battleships rated two thousand tons less and carried four fewer guns. The U.S. Navy was secretly aware of Britain's leviathan in advance, thanks to Sims's fraternal ties to the British Admiralty. But the U.S. Navy was internally divided over its response to *Dreadnought*'s implications. The shocking disparity of firepower it represented demanded alteration to American designs, the General Board argued. In opposition to any change stood the Board of Construction. Its engineers were smugly contented with their own handiwork.

Roosevelt wished new American battleships would match *Dreadnought*'s capabilities. In March 1906, Bonaparte requested the House Naval Affairs Committee to authorize new battleship construction. If the committee would not build two 16,000-ton vessels, he suggested, it should build one beast that would outclass *Dreadnought*. A vigorous four-hour committee-room fight followed. The leader of the opposition (and chair of the Appropriations Committee), James A. Tawney, proclaimed, "We are spending to-day on account of wars we have had and in anticipation of wars we may have, twice as much as the [Panama] canal will cost."[79] In Rooseveltian terms, Edward B. Vreeland blasted Tawney's naiveté: "Have you made up a statement of what lack of preparedness has cost us?" Congress funded the 20,000-ton *Delaware*; its keel was laid the following November. Foss was stunned by the committee's "own moderation. Not in a dozen years . . . has there been a program the tonnage of which is so small."[80]

Bonaparte also battled the Bureau of Navigation over ship names. He substituted the names *Prometheus* and *Vestal* for ships the bureau proposed calling *Orestes* and *Nestor*. Classically educated, Bonaparte associated the original names with insanity and feebleness.[81] Bonaparte himself was pressured on the naming of ships. Residents of Erie, Pennsylvania—who took great pride in the fact that Oliver Hazard Perry had built there the fleet with which he would win the 1813 battle of Lake Erie—resented the bureau's plan to name a mere collier *Erie*. Representative Arthur L. Bates persuaded Bonaparte to reconsider, "as this city was the birth-place of the American Navy." Bonaparte relented, and *Erie* became *Vestal*. But the town of Erie would have to wait until the 1930s before the *Erie* class of gunboats would jointly represent it afloat.[82]

Bonaparte also waded into controversies that derailed his proposals for reform, modest and mostly fruitless as they were. Less than three weeks after he entered office, a boiler explosion on the gunboat *Bennington* killed or injured most of its crew of 112. Bonaparte convened a court of inquiry. He rejected its conclusions that the ship had been well maintained; he believed poor training had caused an otherwise preventable accident. He rejected the court-martial verdict, which had exonerated the captain. Bonaparte's willingness to challenge senior officers so forcefully earned him few allies within the Navy.[83]

A hazing scandal at the Naval Academy during Bonaparte's tenure exposed the public to brutality among sailors. A midshipman murdered a classmate. To Bonaparte's frustration, the Navy's punishment was administrative (not criminal) and light. For want of interest within the Navy, he found, it was impossible to strengthen disciplinary measures. When rumors circulated that the accused was family friends with Speaker of the House Joseph Cannon, cries of corruption surfaced.[84]

If American society, however, accepted that its sailors were licentious and uncouth, it waxed nostalgic about old warships whose glories were seemingly undimmed by age. Bonaparte caused a national furor by recommending that Congress either scrap or use for target practice the ailing *Constitution*, the celebrated frigate of the War of 1812. A nationwide letter-writing campaign inspired children from St. Louis to Brooklyn to denounce Bonaparte's proposal. They inundated his office with such pleadings as "Please do not blow it up" and "spear [*sic*] the old battleship."[85]

In Congress, the chaplain of the House of Representatives prayerfully denounced "the ruthless destruction of the good old ship."[86] "Oh what a delicious rumpus you have stirred up!" Roosevelt chided Bonaparte. Roosevelt loved anything that inspired passion for naval history.[87]

Bonaparte found few supporters for his *Constitution* plan. Unfavorable comparisons between American indifference to and British reverence for naval heritage were easily made in the immediate aftermath of the Trafalgar centennial in October 1905. The British had preserved HMS *Victory*, Adm. Horatio Lord Nelson's flagship. But, Bonaparte insisted, so many repairs had been made to "Old Ironsides," as *Constitution* was affectionately dubbed, that little of the original ship remained. To call it the same ship as the one that fought long ago was a fiction. The cost savings to the Navy that its destruction would achieve could be better used in building an armored cruiser named *Constitution*. "So long as one of her planks remains," Representative William Sulzer countered, "she will represent an heroic and patriotic sentiment that is all that we are, all that we have been, and all that we hope to be." Congress disgorged adequate funds to stabilize the patchwork vessel but not enough to make it seaworthy. The "clamor" over *Constitution* quickly subsided.[88] On another occasion, the entombment of John Paul Jones at the Naval Academy, Bonaparte proved he was not indifferent to naval heritage. Jones was an icon of the Revolutionary War the exhumation of whose remains in France Roosevelt had supported.

In the autumn of 1905, Roosevelt embraced an opportunity to strengthen America's relations with Britain by hosting a British rear admiral, Prince Louis of Battenberg, who was visiting the United States in command of a flotilla of six warships. Bonaparte began planning for the event that summer. Battenberg and a large entourage would visit the White House, the U.S. Naval Academy, the U.S. Military Academy, and New York City. A flurry of opposition by the United Irish-American Societies of New York deluged Bonaparte's office. Battenberg's visit would "blast the hope of Irish freedom." "Anglomaniacs," the critics asserted, were distorting American traditions of isolationism. Death threats would keep Battenberg on guard and under the protection of the Secret Service, but his visit was undisturbed.[89]

When asked about naval affairs generally, Battenberg stressed the importance of leadership over technology. "I don't know that the construction of [the *Dreadnought*] is of such importance," he suggested, "except that the more strong and better prepared a nation is, the more chance that nation has for peace. . . . Your navy has been making wonderful strides these last few years."[90] Battenberg praised Roosevelt as a peacemaker. He explained that King Edward "very much desires that the good feeling between the two countries should be increased, and it was mainly by his wish that our squadron came here."[91]

The president appreciated that Bonaparte's unusual pedigree strengthened his own bid for closer ties to European monarchs. Roosevelt also enjoyed Bonaparte's friendship.[92] The two allies sparred on occasion, but that did not diminish their affection.[93] An apparently insincere suggestion to the president that he, Bonaparte, resign elicited this response: "You are a trump!" A jocular Roosevelt protested, "I put you in the Navy Department as a stop-gap. You must not leave the Cabinet even temporarily."[94]

Bonaparte never defined his cabinet role narrowly. Wielding influence in communities having shipyards and bases, Bonaparte had encouraged temperance among naval personnel by pressuring municipal authorities to restrict the licensing of saloons. From various sources, including the wives of American sailors, he was aware that drunken sailors were being victimized. Alcohol-related desertion and courts-martial flowed like libations. City officials near Mare Island, California, however, opposed Bonaparte's intervention in their city's liquor trade. In December 1906, recognizing that his departure from the Navy Department—he was slated to become attorney general—was imminent, they chose to drag their feet. "It is openly stated now that the plan . . . is to delay the matter . . . until you [Bonaparte] are relieved by Secretary Metcalf, believing that he will allow matters to drop, as he is from California."[95]

Victor H. Metcalf (17 December 1906 to 30 November 1908)

In Metcalf, Roosevelt appointed yet another lawyer as Secretary of the Navy. A graduate of Yale, Metcalf broke the monopoly on the secretaryship that Harvard had long maintained. An East Coaster by birth, Metcalf immersed himself in West Coast politics. Oakland, California, served as his base of operations.[96] A three-time Republican member of Congress, Metcalf sat on the House Ways and Means Committee and the Naval Affairs Committee. He championed GOP policies and ingratiated himself with Roosevelt.[97]

As noted, Roosevelt had considered Metcalf a suitable candidate for Navy secretary since Moody's promotion to attorney general in 1904, but he had appointed Metcalf secretary of commerce and labor instead. While still in that post, Metcalf was deputized by Roosevelt, to intercede to ease the antagonisms the San Francisco School Board had created with the government of Japan by its racist mistreatment of Japanese schoolchildren. When in December 1906 Roosevelt decided to reshuffle his cabinet again and elevated Bonaparte to attorney general, Metcalf transferred to the Navy Department. Roosevelt elevated their predecessor, Moody, to the Supreme Court.[98] The president anticipated that Metcalf would positively resolve labor disputes at steel mills and shipyards that had hampered warship construction.[99]

Nevertheless, and as fervently as he sought to build America's navy, Roosevelt wished to bring an end to the world's naval arms race. He welcomed Andrew Carnegie's vision of arms limitations. To the tycoon Roosevelt wrote, "I have been thinking more and more that we might at least be able to limit the size of battleships, and I should put the limit below the size of the *Dreadnought*. . . . [L]et all nations agree that hereafter no ship to exceed say fifteen thousand tons shall be built."[100] "I would be delighted," Roosevelt informed Hale, "if the Hague Conference would agree that thereafter all battleships should be limited in size; but after sounding France, Germany, England and Italy in the matter, I see no hope of accomplishing this result."[101]

Failing to secure an international agreement on naval limitations at the Hague Conference in late 1907, Roosevelt rallied to enlarge the Navy. "In my judgment we should this year provide for four battleships," Roosevelt declared in his annual message of December.[102] He appreciated that Hale would oppose his recommendation. To overcome Hale, Roosevelt encouraged Metcalf to "make the stiffest kind of a fight to put them [battleship authorizations] thru the Senate. . . . Fight to the last gasp without any compromise." Roosevelt's desperation was evident in his fervor to dislodge Metcalf from complacency. "Push it thru if you possibly can," Roosevelt implored. "I do not think we can afford to yield to Mr. Hale." Hale infuriated Roosevelt. "He is a conscienceless voluptuary," Roosevelt complained to Elihu Root, his former secretary of war turned secretary of state. Roosevelt vilified Hale as "unscrupulous" and "a physical coward."[103]

Roosevelt sought to harness public opinion to overcome Hale's intractable opposition to American naval ascendancy. At the Oyster Bay, New York, naval review in September 1906, Roosevelt and Bonaparte had delighted in the processional. Addressing the members of Congress he had invited on board the presidential yacht *Mayflower*, Roosevelt declared, "This [display of warships] is the direct result of your work, gentlemen."[104] He explained to Root why he had invited to the event particular journalists and candidates for public office: "I wanted [them] to grow to have a personal feeling for the navy—to get under the naval spell—because I want them both to be our allies in keeping the people awake to what it means to have such a navy."[105]

For many of the same reasons as he offered Root, Roosevelt dispatched the Great White Fleet around the world. Its "epoch-making cruise," Metcalf recalled, began in December 1907. At Hampton Roads, Virginia, Roosevelt and Commander Sims, then his flag aide, bid sixteen battleships smooth sailing. Hale's opposition to funding this extravagance collapsed under the weight of Roosevelt's unprecedentedly bold assertion of executive power and the extraordinary popularity of the cruise.

The armada's fourteen-month global circumnavigation "enlisted the interested attention of the naval world."[106] In May 1908, Metcalf journeyed westward from Washington to celebrate the fleet's arrival in San Francisco. As Roosevelt had hoped, the twelve days' visit of the fleet to the Bay Area awakened enthusiasm for the Navy along the West Coast. After completing its long voyage, the fleet returned to joyous celebrations in Virginia. The thousands of enthusiastic spectators that thronged to the waterfront to greet their returning "heroes" confirmed Roosevelt's expectations of the cruise building support for American naval power.[107]

While the battle fleet was under way, the design characteristics of new battleships had produced sharp disagreements. Frustrated by the failures to achieve reforms in the Navy and keenly aware that Roosevelt was in his waning days as president, Commander Sims launched a broadside attack against complacency. Sims arranged the publication in *McClure's Magazine* of an article titled "The Needs of the Navy." With Sims's help, Henry Reuterdahl, a popular painter of naval subjects and a respected editor of *Jane's Fighting Ships*, had penned a damning indictment of the Navy's blindness to major defects in its warships. Reuterdahl documented flaws that made American battleships highly vulnerable to destruction. The article appeared in January 1908.

A shaken Senate investigated the allegations. Metcalf resented Reuterdahl's attack, which he correctly attributed to Sims and the radical reform faction of the Navy. Before Hale's committee the secretary reflexively defended the location of the armor belts on the in-production *Delaware*-class battleships; Reuterdahl had identified improperly placed belts as one of the critical vulnerabilities.[108] When Metcalf demanded that Sims admit his insubordination, Sims appealed directly to Roosevelt, who shielded his protégé. Sims hoped to use his testimony to disclose the Navy's organizational woes as well; Hale silenced him. At sea with the Great White Fleet, the artist-journalist Reuterdahl returned to Washington to defend his article's claims. His detractors suggested that Rear Adm. Robley D. Evans, who was severely ill but in command of the armada, had demanded his departure. In any case, Reuterdahl did not ingratiate himself when he causticly commented, "The navy is bedridden by a lot of old fogies who hold their jobs just because they blindly follow ancient traditions."[109] Roosevelt remained loyal to Reuterdahl—"No man has done better work for the American Navy, my dear fellow, than you."[110] The uncertainty about the fighting capabilities of the Navy that Sims and Reuterdahl created in the public mind, however, proved unsettling to Roosevelt. His labor seemed to have produced a large but ill-designed navy. A summer conference convened at the Naval War College failed to resolve definitively the problems Sims had identified. The U.S. Navy remained deeply divided.[111]

Plagued by illness for more than a year, Metcalf struggled to retain control of his department. The Navy's fighting forces had swelled in size. "We have twenty-five battleships in service and four building," he exclaimed. "We should have a number more."[112] Steadfast, he publicly repeated Roosevelt's conception of sea power: "A great navy is a preserver of peace. Diplomacy, of course, is a fine thing, and so is arbitration, but a strong navy backs up a nation's contentions better than a statesman or a diplomat can."[113] Yet no meaningful reforms were undertaken within the Navy while Metcalf presided. He understood that Roosevelt no longer relied on him, and he resented his assistant Truman Newberry's ambition.[114] After a two-month-long absence from the department, an ailing Metcalf resigned in November 1908.[115] "I accept your resignation with real reluctance," Roosevelt replied. "I had earnestly hoped that you would be able to continue with me throughout my term." He praised Metcalf's "faithful and efficient service."[116]

Retiring to California, Metcalf signaled ambivalence about the Navy's future. In his last annual report published in December 1908 and in an interview with the *Los Angeles Herald*, he asserted that the efficiency of the fleet hinged on shipyards and dry docks. This infrastructure remained sorely underfunded.[117] Despite loud voices of support for basing the fleet in California, Metcalf cared little where the battle fleet was stationed.[118] "As a matter of fact the battleships are not really needed [on the West Coast]. They can be moved swiftly. The world cruise demonstrated that. It is not a question of keeping them on the Pacific or the Atlantic. It is a question of keeping them at sea." Metcalf considered war unlikely and felt no urgency to reform the inner Navy. "We are at peace with the world now. . . . Patience is needed for the growth of the navy in all its phases."[119]

Truman H. Newberry (1 December 1908 to 5 March 1909)

With little time left as president, Roosevelt acquiesced to Newberry's de facto status. Like Metcalf, Newberry was a Yale graduate. Like Morton, he had been a railroad executive and industrialist before entering the cabinet. Alone among the naval secretaries in Roosevelt's administration, however, Newberry had prior military service. He had participated in the Spanish-American War as a lieutenant in the Michigan Naval Brigade, on board a U.S. cruiser engaged in blockade duty.[120] In 1905, Roosevelt had selected him as Assistant Secretary of the Navy. During Metcalf's long vacancies for travel and ill health, Newberry had acted ably in his stead. Newberry was dissatisfied with the innumerable inefficiencies that marred bureau coordination but firmly opposed the creation of a general staff. He feared a general staff would undermine civilian rule. Newberry apparently misunderstood Roosevelt's appointment of him in December 1908 as confirmation that his modest ideas for restructuring the Navy would meet with the president's satisfaction. They did not.

In office merely three hours, Secretary Newberry announced an order to reorganize the General Board by enlarging its membership. Newspapers pondered the implications. Some journalists speculated that Roosevelt had abandoned his quest to create a general staff. The *Baltimore Sun* thought that Newberry had in effect created a general staff. Confusion reigned.[121] Roosevelt bristled. In his eighth annual message, given several days later, Roosevelt blurted, "There is literally no excuse whatever for continuing the present bureau organization of the Navy." Roosevelt did not wish to rearrange deck chairs among the bureaus and the board.

Roosevelt and Newberry thus reignited a public debate about the Navy's future. In January 1909, Roosevelt convened two study groups: a day-long conference in Washington and a Commission on Naval Reorganization. Moody, Morton, and Mahan participated in both groups.[122] Mahan penned the commission's report and defended the general staff concept: "There should be no shock or change of method in expanding from a state of peace to a state of war. This is not militarism."[123] Its delivery in late February left no time for Roosevelt to use his presidential powers of persuasion to convince Senator Hale's Naval Affairs Committee to embrace the proposal. Roosevelt passed the torch to President William H. Taft on 4 March. Predictably, the old foe of the general staff, Hale, praised Newberry as the most "able administrator" to direct the Navy Department in many years.[124] Newberry served as Secretary of the Navy for barely three months. Hale remained in the Senate for two more years. In retirement, Roosevelt pondered how much he had accomplished with the Navy and what critical tasks remained.

Conclusion

By 1909, Roosevelt's prized battle fleet was complete, American sailors were more prepared for combat than ever before, and the rudiments of a general staff had been proposed. Only Britain possessed a stronger navy than the United States. Roosevelt's secretaries of the Navy never received the credit they deserved for their central role in this complex achievement. The revolving door that ushered five new secretaries into the cabinet position during Roosevelt's tenure proved less disastrous than might have been the case had either the president been uninterested in the department or the appointees less capable executives. The president did not desire the frequent changes to the secretaryship, but he was enthusiastic about Long's departure, and he was ever willing to rearrange Republican leadership to strengthen the party and reward loyal service. In three instances—Moody, Morton, and Bonaparte—Roosevelt made deals with prospective secretaries that loyal service would result in promotion to a more prestigious cabinet post. After serving as the Navy's head, Moody, in fact, was twice promoted. He served as Roosevelt's attorney general and then on the Supreme Court. Bonaparte became attorney general when Moody ascended to the pinnacle of the nation's judiciary. Morton's scandal and Metcalf's illness demanded their respective replacements. Two veteran assistant secretaries, Darling and Newberry, provided continuity in departmental leadership during the length of the Roosevelt administration. Empathetically appreciative of their yeoman's duty, Roosevelt appointed the outgoing Darling as a customs collector and elevated Newberry to the secretaryship.

Roosevelt's appointees advanced his navalist agenda. They proved useful allies in leading the president's favorite department. Moody's dynamic leadership, bipartisan rapport, and knowledge of appropriations spearheaded Roosevelt's battleship program. Morton maintained the momentum Moody had begun. The short-serving industrial executive

Morton, in contrast, proved incapable of satisfying Roosevelt's ambition to restructure the Navy's antiquated bureaus and resolve its myriad inefficiencies. Bonaparte too proved unequal to the task of eliminating graft and repairing the rift between zealous reformers and their circumspect foes. But the popular descendant of Napoleon and respected civil service dynamo attracted interest to the department, attention that paid benefits domestically and abroad. Chronically ill, Metcalf was incapable of strenuously improving the Navy's often-troubled partnerships with shipyards and labor. Newberry's perennial presence as assistant and acting secretary ensured that many of the daily chores of running the Navy were nevertheless well handled. Secretary Newberry's particular vision for reform foundered in part because he failed to secure Roosevelt's approval. The president and his secretaries, then, did not accomplish every goal they championed. On occasion they worked at cross-purposes. Also, in many instances they discovered that an obstructionist Congress possessed preponderant political power. Nevertheless, together they helped to forge the U.S. Navy into an instrument of international power.

Notes

The epigraph is in Robert Seager II, *Alfred Thayer Mahan: The Man and His Letters* (Annapolis, Md.: Naval Institute Press, 1977), 542.

1. Kenneth J. Hagan, *This People's Navy: The Making of American Sea Power* (New York: Free Press, 1991), 232; George T. Davis, *A Navy Second to None: The Development of Modern American Naval Policy* (New York: Harcourt, Brace, 1940), 135; Matthew Oyos, *In Command: Theodore Roosevelt and the American Military* (Lincoln: Potomac Books of the University of Nebraska Press, 2018), 118–19. Dudley W. Knox, *A History of the United States Navy* (New York: G. P. Putnam's Sons, 1948), makes no reference to Roosevelt's secretaries.

2. On congressional power in foreign policy, see Colin D. Moore, *American Imperialism and the State, 1893–1921* (Cambridge, U.K.: Cambridge University Press, 2017). See also TR to Henry Cabot Lodge, 27 September 1906, in *The Letters of Theodore Roosevelt*, ed. Elting E. Morison (Cambridge, Mass.: Harvard University Press, 1951–1954), 5:428.

3. Paolo E. Coletta, "John Davis Long," in *American Secretaries of the Navy*, ed. Paolo E. Coletta (Annapolis, Md.: Naval Institute Press, 1980), 1:446.

4. TR to Long, 9 January 1902, in *Papers of John Davis Long, 1897–1904*, ed. Gardner W. Allen (Boston: Massachusetts Historical Society, 1939), 415; "Mr. Long Resigns," *Evening Star* (Washington, D.C.), 10 March 1902.

5. Quoted in Coletta, "John Davis Long," 436; Morison, *Letters of Theodore Roosevelt*, 8:912–13.
6. TR to Lodge, 13 February 1906, and Charles Bonaparte to TR, 19 August 1906, in Eric F. Goldman, *Charles J. Bonaparte, Patrician Reformer: His Earlier Career* (Baltimore: Johns Hopkins University Press, 1943), 114–15.
7. See TR to Lodge, 27 December 1888, Morison, *Letters of Theodore Roosevelt*, 1:151; TR to Dana, 28 December 1891, Morison, 1:269; TR to Dana, 8 and 11 May 1897, Morison, 1:609–10, 616–17; John Hay to William H. Moody, 26 April 1889, and Hay to Moody, 22 October 1900, May 9, 1879–May 17, 1902, box 1, William H. Moody Papers, MSS33274, Library of Congress, Washington, D.C. [hereafter LC].
8. "Champ Clark's Letter," *Ukiah Dispatch Democrat* (Ukiah, Calif.), 4 April 1902.
9. "Moody for Attorney General," *Hutchinson Daily News* (Kans.), 16 June 1904; "The New Secretary of the Navy," *Chetopa Advance* (Kans.), 18 April 1902.
10. "Mr. Long Resigns."
11. "John D. Long Resigns," *Baltimore Sun*, 11 March 1902.
12. Louis Klopsch to Moody, 12 May 1902, May 9, 1879–May 17, 1902, box 1, Moody Papers, LC; "Ordered to Stricken Island," *Nebraska State Journal*, 13 May 1902; "America Leads Nation in Succoring Stricken," *Evening Times* (Washington, D.C.), 13 May 1902.
13. John Hay (transmitting Roosevelt's directive) to Moody, 12 May 1902, May 9, 1879–May 17, 1902, box 1, Moody Papers, LC; "U.S. Government Prompt to Relieve the Sufferers," *Detroit Free Press*, 13 May 1902.
14. Loubet to TR, 22 May 1902, *Papers Relating to the Foreign Relations of the United States* [hereafter FRUS], *1902* (Washington, D.C.: U.S. Government Printing Office, 1903), 413.
15. TR to Loubet, 27 March 1902, FRUS, 409.
16. "Honor to Roosevelt," *Omaha Daily Bee*, 24 May 1902.
17. Quoted in "Honor to Roosevelt."
18. Moody speech, 31 May 1902, May 9, 1879–May 17, 1902, box 1, Moody Papers, LC; TR to Charles W. Eliot, 4 April 1904, TR to Arthur T. Hadley, 6 April 1904, Letterpress Copybooks, 1897–1916, vol. 46, April 5–21, 1904, reel 334, series 2, Theodore Roosevelt Papers, MSS38299, LC, http://hdl.loc.gov/loc .mss/ms009253.mss38299.0379 (accessed 22 October 2018).
19. Paul T. Heffron, "William H. Moody," in Coletta, *American Secretaries of the Navy*, 462; Davis, *Navy Second to None*, 166; *Annual Report of the Secretary of the Navy, 1903* (Washington, D.C.: U.S. Government Printing Office, 1903), 33.
20. Henry J. Hendrix, *Theodore Roosevelt's Naval Diplomacy: The U.S. Navy and the Birth of the American Century* (Annapolis, Md.: Naval Institute Press, 2009), 40–42.

21. George B. Cortelyou to Moody, 12 July 1902, May 20–Aug. 20, 1902, box 2, Moody Papers, LC.

22. *Annual Report of the Secretary of the Navy, 1902* (Washington, D.C.: U.S. Government Printing Office, 1902), 5, 13.

23. Heffron, "William H. Moody," 463.

24. *Annual Report of the Secretary of the Navy, 1902*, 37; *Annual Report of the Secretary of the Navy, 1903*, 13–15.

25. "The Naval Bill: Senate Will Lose Little Time in Passing Measure," *Times-Democrat* (La.), 3 March 1904.

26. *Annual Report of the Secretary of the Navy, 1903*, 3–6.

27. "That Naval Staff Idea," *Baltimore Sun*, 2 May 1904.

28. Paul T. Heffron, "Paul Morton," in Coletta, *American Secretaries of the Navy*, 470.

29. Oyos, *In Command*, 319.

30. "May Stop Maneuvers," *Lawrence Weekly World*, 29 December 1904; Goldman, *Charles J. Bonaparte*, 107, 116.

31. "Moody for Attorney General."

32. "Knox May Resign," *Daily Independent* (Kans.), 15 June 1904.

33. "Moody Chosen to Replace Knox," *Boston Globe*, 15 June 1904.

34. "Distinguished Alamedan Is Selected to Succeed Secretary Cortelyou," *San Francisco Call*, 25 June 1904; Metcalf to Moody, 9 June 1902, May 9, 1879–May 17, 1902, box 1, Moody Papers, LC; "Small Politics in Congress," *San Francisco Chronicle*, 7 April 1904.

35. "Has a Cabinet Slate," *Chicago Tribune*, 23 June 1904.

36. "Morton Soon to Quit," *Washington Post*, 20 May 1905.

37. "Metcalf Is to Succeed Morton," *Los Angeles Herald*, 20 May 1905.

38. Morison, *Letters of Theodore Roosevelt*, 4:847–48.

39. "Changes in the Cabinet," *San Francisco Call*, 25 June 1904.

40. Heffron, "Paul Morton," 469–70; "New Head for Equitable," *Marengo Republican News* (Ill.), 30 June 1905.

41. "Morton to Retire in Fall," *Washington Post*, 14 May 1905.

42. "Moody for Attorney General."

43. TR to Bonaparte, 21 February 1906, Morison, *Letters of Theodore Roosevelt*, 5:159–61.

44. Heffron, "Paul Morton," 470; Excubitor, "Japan's Object-Lessons in Naval Warfare," *Living Age* 24, no. 3130, 2 July 1904, "has illustrated" on 12, "hasty" on 4.

45. TR to Morton, 6 October 1904, Morison, *Letters of Theodore Roosevelt*, 4:974.

46. *Annual Report of the Secretary of the Navy, 1904* (Washington, D.C.: U.S. Government Printing Office, 1904), 3–4; Heffron, "Paul Morton," 471.

47. "Our Naval Policy," *Nation* 79, no. 2058 (1904): 454.

48. John H. Russell, "The Preparation of War Plans for the Establishment and Defense of a Naval Advance Base," 23 May 1910, RG8, Naval Historical Collection Archives, Naval War College, Newport, Rhode Island.

49. Quoted in Heffron, "Paul Morton," 472; *Congressional Record*, 58th Congress, 3rd Sess., 39, part 4:3489.

50. Quoted in Oyos, *In Command*, 118.

51. Taft quoted in "At Foot of Monument," *Washington Post*, 4 May 1905; "Fight to a Finish," *Evening Star* (Washington, D.C.), 10 May 1905.

52. "Says Morton Should Go," *Topeka State Journal*, 19 May 1905.

53. James B. Morrow, "Paul Morton's Rise," *Washington Post*, 7 May 1905; "Railway Rate Crisis," *Washington Post*, 11 May 1905; "To Leave Cabinet Soon," *Star Tribune* (Minn.), 18 May 1905.

54. "At the White House," *Evening Star* (Washington, D.C.), 20 May 1905.

55. "Right on Paul Morton, Roosevelt to Moody," *New York Times*, 18 December 1905.

56. "Metcalf Is to Succeed Morton," and "Alice Roosevelt Is Coming Here," *Los Angeles Herald*, 20 May 1905.

57. "Morton to Wall Street," *Los Angeles Times*, 19 May 1905; "Coming Changes in President's Cabinet," *Morning Post* (N.C.), 30 May 1905.

58. "Morton Soon to Quit."

59. On shared political beliefs, see Bonaparte's address "Drastic Means for Suppression of Anarchism," *Philadelphia Inquirer*, 13 August 1906.

60. Quoted in "Bonaparte to Head Navy," *New York Tribune*, 1 June 1905; Goldman, *Charles J. Bonaparte*, 23.

61. Charles J. Bonaparte, "Experiences of a Cabinet Officer under Roosevelt," *Century Magazine* 79 (March 1910): 752, https://babel.hathitrust.org/cgi/pt?id=mdp.39076002641251;view=1up;seq=766 (accessed 4 February 2019).

62. "Mr. Bonaparte for the Cabinet," *Buffalo Evening News*, 1 June 1905; "The New Navy Secretary," *Winston-Salem Journal* (N.C.), 18 June 1905.

63. Bonaparte indicated they had met on a Friday and two days later, on 21 May, had replied to Roosevelt's offer. Bonaparate, "Experiences of a Cabinet Officer under Roosevelt," 752; Paul T. Heffron, "Charles J. Bonaparte," in Coletta, *American Secretaries of the Navy*, 475–76.

64. Quoted in Joseph B. Bishop, *Charles Joseph Bonaparte: His Life and Public Services* (New York: Charles Scribner's Sons, 1922), 102.

65. Quoted in Goldman, *Charles J. Bonaparte*, 86.

66. "Bonaparte to Head Navy," *New York Tribune*, 1 June 1905.

67. "A Leader of Reform," *Baltimore Sun*, 1 June 1905; "A Cabinet Change," *Omaha Daily Bee*, 2 June 1905; "A Bonaparte at the Head of the American Navy," *American Monthly Review of Reviews* 32, no. 1 (July 1905): 35–38.

68. Quoted in Bishop, *Charles Joseph Bonaparte*, 103.

69. Quoted in Bishop, 100.

70. Quoted in Goldman, *Charles J. Bonaparte*, 104.

71. *Annual Report of the Secretary of the Navy, 1905* (Washington, D.C.: U.S. Government Printing Office, 1906), 19–20; Tyler Dennett, *Roosevelt and the Russo-Japanese War* (New York: Doubleday, 1925), 159–67.

72. *Annual Report of the Secretary of the Navy, 1905*, 23.

73. TR to Wood, 9 March 1905, Morison, *Letters of Theodore Roosevelt*, 4:1136; Davis, *Navy Second to None*, 169.

74. See for example, TR to Mahan, 3 May 1897, Letterpress Copybooks, 1897–1916, vol. 1, 1897, April 9–July 12, reel 313, Roosevelt Papers, LC, http://hdl.loc.gov/loc.mss/ms009253.mss38299.0319 (accessed 22 October 2018).

75. Quoted in Seager, *Alfred Thayer Mahan*, 522.

76. Mahan outlined his views in the U.S. Naval Institute *Proceedings* in June 1906.

77. Seager, *Alfred Thayer Mahan*, 521–33; Davis, *Navy Second to None*, 141–50.

78. "Dreadnought Battleship," *Sydney Morning Herald*, 29 May 1905.

79. Quoted in "$10,000,000 Battleship Voted for by the House," *New York Times*, 17 May 1906.

80. Quoted in Goldman, *Charles J. Bonaparte*, 111.

81. "Reverses Paul Morton," *Baltimore Sun*, 16 July 1905.

82. "A Duty of Congressman Bates," *Erie Evening Herald* (Pa.), 25 October 1905; Bates to Bonaparte, 27 October 1905, Folder Ba–Be, box 122, 53.9, Charles J. Bonaparte Papers, MSS13151, LC.

83. *Annual Report of the Secretary of the Navy, 1905*, 6.

84. *Annual Report of the Secretary of the Navy, 1906* (Washington, D.C.: U.S. Government Printing Office, 1907); J. J. Doan to TR, 20 December 1905, Folder Coo–Conl, box 122, 53.9, Bonaparte Papers, LC.

85. Pauline Schriever to Bonaparte, 20 December 1905; Sophie Wartmann to Bonaparte, 21 December 1905; Folder Coo–Conl, box 122; Rock Spring School, James Matthews postcard, and Robert Rälsen to TR, 3 December 1905, Folder R, box 125, 53.9, Bonaparte Papers, LC.

86. Quoted in Goldman, *Charles J. Bonaparte*, 96; Henry N. Couden quoted in *Congressional Record, House*, 18 January 1906, 1238.

87. Quoted in Goldman, *Charles J. Bonaparte*, 98.

88. Charles F. Adams to Bonaparte, 14 February 1906, box 122, 53.9, Bonaparte Papers, LC; William Sulzer quoted in *Congressional Record, House*, 18 January 1906, 1239.

89. United Irish Societies of New York City, "To the Sailors of the American Navy," 28 October 1905, Folder Bi–By, box 122, Bonaparte Papers, LC; "His Life Sought," *Los Angeles Times*, 19 November 1905.

90. Annabel Lee, "Louis of Battenberg: A Talk with the Sailor Prince," *New York Times*, 12 November 1905; see also the photo essay on pages 2–3 of the *New York Times*, 19 November 1905.

91. "Enjoyed Each Moment, Says Departing Prince," *New York Times*, 20 November 1905.

92. Goldman, *Charles J. Bonaparte*, 92–96.

93. "Cabinet Revolt at Gag; Bonaparte Hits Hard," *New York Times*, 4 November 1905.

94. Quoted in Bishop, *Charles Joseph Bonaparte*, 128.

95. Curtis to Bonaparte, 18 July 1905, Folder Coo–Conl, box 122; Forbes H. Brown to Bonaparte, 29 October and 9 November 1906, Folder Bi–By, box 122, 53.9, Bonaparte Papers, LC.

96. "Distinguished Alamedan Is Selected to Succeed Secretary Cortelyou."

97. "Small Politics in Congress"; TR to Michael H. De Young, 8 April 1904, Letterpress Copybooks, 1897–1916, vol. 46, April 5–21, 1904, reel 334, series 2, Roosevelt Papers, LC, http://hdl.loc.gov/loc.mss/ms009253.mss38299.0379 (accessed 22 October 2018).

98. "News," *Caucasian* (N.C.), 1 November 1906; "Changes in Roosevelt's Cabinet," *Boston Globe*, 3 December 1906.

99. "Shipyard Men Lay Down Their Tools," *Philadelphia Inquirer*, 18 January 1901; "Shipyard Strike of 7,000," *Sun* (N.Y.), 5 May 1904; "Investigation at Request of the President," *Oakland Tribune*, 3 July 1907; TR to Eugene Hale, 27 October 1906, Morison, *Letters of Theodore Roosevelt*, 5:473–74; TR to Metcalf, 27 November 1906, Morison, 5:510–11.

100. TR to Andrew Carnegie, 6 September 1906, Morison, 5:398.

101. TR to Hale, 27 October 1906.

102. Quoted in James D. Richardson, ed., *A Compilation of the Messages and Papers of the Presidents* (New York: Bureau of National Literature, 1917), 14:7114.

103. TR to Root, 13 July 1907, Morison, *Letters of Theodore Roosevelt*, 5:717.

104. Quoted in "Big Guns Salute President," *New York Tribune*, 4 September 1906.

105. TR to Root, 4 September 1906, Morison, *Letters of Theodore Roosevelt*, 5:394.

106. *Annual Report of the Secretary of the Navy, 1908* (Washington, D.C.: U.S. Government Printing Office, 1908), 6.

107. "Magnificent Home Coming Welcome to the Fleet That Toured the World; Received Plaudits of the Nation," *Scranton Truth* (Pa.), 22 February 1909.

108. "Victor H. Metcalf," *Star Press* (Ind.), 12 March 1908.

109. "Critic of Fleet Must Show Proof," *Star Tribune* (Minn.), 1 March 1908.

110. TR to Reuterdahl, 23 July 1917, *Signature House Auctioneers* (Bridgeport, W. Va.); https://www.invaluable.com/auction-lot/theodore-roosevelt -tls-1p-81-2-x11-new-york-546-.c-ow8y7dmln3# (accessed 2 March 2019).

111. Elting E. Morison, *Admiral Sims and the Modern American Navy* (Boston: Houghton Mifflin, 1942), 182–210.

112. "Big Navy Is Peace Maker," *Leavenworth Post* (Kans.), 18 May 1908.

113. "Big Navy Is Peace Maker."

114. Paul T. Heffron, "Victor H. Metcalf," in Coletta, *American Secretaries of the Navy*, 486; C. C. Carlton, "Metcalf Gained Victory in Dispute with Newberry," *San Francisco Call*, 6 December 1908.

115. "Victor Metcalf Out," *Sedalia Democrat* (Mo.), 1 December 1908; "Secretary of Navy Metcalf Resigns," *Trenton Evening Times*, 14 November 1908.

116. "Metcalf Steps Out of Cabinet," *Missoulian* (Mont.), 14 November 1908.

117. "Navy Yard Calls Big Cruise Success," *Dispatch* (Ill.), 11 December 1908.

118. "Strong Plea Made to Secretary Metcalf to Keep Fleet in Pacific," *Oakland Tribune*, 6 May 1908.

119. "Must Have Dry Docks to Take Care of Fleet," *Los Angeles Herald*, 7 December 1908.

120. Paul T. Heffron, "Truman H. Newberry," in Colleta, *American Secretaries of the Navy*, 489.

121. "Newberry Will Shake Up the Navy," *Concord Daily Tribune* (N.C.), 5 December 1908; "Creates Navy Staff," *Baltimore Sun*, 2 December 1908.

122. Heffron, "Truman H. Newberry," 490.

123. Despite his animus for Sims, Mahan gave the report a title nearly identical to that of the Reuterdahl-Sims article. U.S. Senate, "Certain Needs of the Navy," Doc. No. 743, 60th Cong., 2nd Sess., 1909, 3.

124. Quoted in Heffron, "Truman H. Newberry," 492.

9

WHY DETERRENCE FAILED

The Imperial Japanese Navy, Strategic Memes, and the Great White Fleet

James R. Holmes

Theodore Roosevelt dispatched the U.S. Navy's Great White Fleet to the Far East in hopes of reshaping Japanese geopolitical calculations to favor U.S. national interests in the region, in particular commercial access to an undivided China and a regional balance among the imperial powers that preserved access.[1] In other words, President Roosevelt intended the voyage as a deterrent. He believed mounting an impressive peacetime display of naval force buoyed by political resolve would make imperial Japanese rulers believers in American seamanship and combat prowess. If successful, the fleet's grand tour would prompt Tokyo to think twice before risking war against the United States. Peace would prevail on American terms.

At the same time Roosevelt meant the world cruise to conciliate Japan under his doctrine of the Big Stick. "I have always been fond of the West African proverb: 'Speak softly and carry a big stick; you will go far,'" he liked to say.[2] He interpreted the proverb as a mandate to combine absolute inflexibility on matters of principle with flexibility in less critical areas and to leaven diplomatic outreach with tact and good humor. He brandished the Big Stick in labor disputes, relations with Congress, and political campaigns. Roosevelt exhorted diplomats to comport themselves frankly yet magnanimously toward potential foes while also exhibiting strength and resolve should relations turn sour. America would outmuscle those it could not placate.

Big Stick diplomacy, then, sought to transmit two messages. It sent a political message about U.S. government attitudes toward relations with Japan, conveying the intent to pursue friendship in peacetime yet wage war without remorse should a trial of arms befall the two competitors. It also sent a strategic message about American sea power, meant to convince Tokyo the U.S. Navy was a force not to be trifled with. Now, there was some tension between these messages. For instance, staging too convincing a demonstration of naval might could complicate diplomatic efforts to convey goodwill. Japanese rulers could construe it as a domineering America's effort to cow them into submission, leading them to redouble their efforts to outcompete the U.S. Navy. An unconvincing display, conversely, would sap the potency from Washington's diplomatic narrative.

This dualism made choreographing U.S. naval outreach across civilizational boundaries a delicate affair. The political message appears to have resonated in Japan, giving its magnates pause. Indeed, Tokyo refrained from testing American power or resolve during the Roosevelt presidency and for long after. The strategic message elicited a mixed response at best. While the Great White Fleet's endeavors may have impressed, the fleet did not and could not overawe the Imperial Japanese Navy (IJN). Perversely, technological advancements undertaken by British shipwrights—in particular the advent of dreadnought battleships starting in 1906—undercut the U.S. Navy's reputation as a frontline fighting force. Technological change effaced some of the battle fleet's deterrent, coercive, and conciliatory power, muffling the strategic message Roosevelt hoped its Far Eastern exploits would convey.

While the global voyage could prompt the Meiji leadership to think twice before risking military adventurism, deploying American fighting ships to the western Pacific stood little chance of disabusing Japanese seafarers of the sophisticated, offensively oriented way of naval strategy engraved onto the imperial navy's culture during the Sino-Japanese War of 1894–95 and especially the Russo-Japanese War of 1904–5. I deploy the scientist Richard Dawkins's concept of "memes" in concert with strategic theory to reveal the contours of Great White Fleet diplomacy, assess its impact in Tokyo, and derive findings useful for naval diplomats in today's new, old epoch of great power competition.

American Power and Weakness

There is no gainsaying President Roosevelt's diplomatic design. Roosevelt had long admired Japan, but at the same time he feared Japan might hurl itself into imperial conquest if left unchecked by some geopolitical counterweight such as Great Britain, Russia, or America. Capt. Alfred Thayer Mahan, his close confidant on geopolitical matters, helped shape his views of American maritime strategy. Their acquaintanceship dated to 1888, when Roosevelt visited the Naval War College to lecture about the War of 1812. A decade later, while serving as Assistant Secretary of the Navy, Roosevelt praised Mahan's *The Interest of America in Sea Power, Present and Future*—a collection of essays that espoused annexing Hawaii, among other things—"in highest terms," according to historian Howard K. Beale.[3] Maintains Howard Beale, Mahan "deeply influenced" Roosevelt throughout their lifetimes.[4]

Hawaii was the immediate controversy in 1897. American navalists coveted the archipelago as a "stepping-stone" across the Pacific.[5] In other words, steam-propelled merchantmen and warships needed way stations at which to refuel and provision during their trek across the Pacific Ocean. Hawaii, which lay at the center of an empty expanse, represented the only candidate for an eastern Pacific naval station. Roosevelt was convinced Tokyo craved the islands as well and might deploy force to obtain them. "I am fully alive to the danger from Japan," he told Mahan. The Japanese leadership was "holding off in the Hawaiian matter"—meaning the debate in Washington over annexation—"to see if she won't have a chance to jump in and smash us." This was a real possibility. The U.S. Navy, insisted Roosevelt, remained inferior to Japan's "efficient fighting navy." Its Pacific fleet must "be constantly kept above that of Japan."[6]

Roosevelt's anxiety about Japan waxed and waned over the years. Tokyo's eventual forbearance in the Hawaiian controversy soothed his worries. Yet martial strife was a real prospect by 1907, when the Great White Fleet departed Hampton Roads for the South Atlantic and thence the Pacific. Japanese citizens had turned out to protest Roosevelt's handling of the Portsmouth Peace Conference in 1905, in large part because Japanese delegates failed to wring a cash payment from Russia at the bargaining table.[7] Governments along the West Coast had enacted laws discriminating against Japanese labor, injecting fresh friction into transpacific relations. Tokyo had drawn up a litany of grievances vis-à-vis Washington. Some deterrent gesture thus seemed a natural choice.

The geopolitical picture also militated for deterrence. The rising American and Japanese heavyweights' ambitions might clash in the western Pacific now, while they increasingly boasted the power to make good on their purposes. The United States had kept a squadron on station in the region since the days of Andrew Jackson.[8] But the nation was a newcomer to Asia as a resident power, having annexed the Philippine Islands after defeating Spain in 1898. Victory over Spain cemented an American presence in maritime East Asia.

Worse from the Japanese standpoint, the American presence over-shadowed sea-lanes connecting Japan with Southeast Asia. Naval forces based in Manila Bay or elsewhere in the archipelago could conceivably menace north–south maritime movement along the continental seaboard or east–west movement through the Luzon Strait. Having vanquished past contenders for naval suzerainty in Asia—namely, China and Russia— many Japanese strategists found this new competitor and this downturn in regional geopolitics bothersome. In fact, Admiral Fukudome Shigeru, the IJN chief of staff during World War II, was to recall that "the Imperial Navy made the United States its sole strategic enemy" in 1907—the same year the Great White Fleet steamed for Pacific waters.[9]

Girding against the new enemy demanded a strategy steeped in political and geographical calculations. The American posture in the Far East and the world tempted Japan to strike preemptively if it could while turning geography to operational advantage. The United States was a curious foe. It managed to combine strength with weakness in the Pacific Ocean basin. It was replete with latent military might, boasting an economy and relevant industries that dwarfed Japan's. Yet it would need time and political willpower to transmute potential strength into working combat power and bring it to bear on the far side of the world.

Thus time was Japan's ally. IJN commanders could entertain hopes of striking swiftly and fulfilling operational and strategic aims before the United States built up insuperable naval might in the theater. Japan could hand America the fait accompli of naval defeat, loss of the Philippines, and expulsion from Pacific waters west of Guam. In short, a sudden offensive stroke could undo the results of the Spanish-American War in part or in whole—leaving imperial Japan atop the regional order in East Asia.

Happily for Tokyo, Washington also did not enjoy the option of concentrating its attentions and energies exclusively on the Far East. The Pacific Ocean was neither the only nor the most pressing theater of endeavor for the U.S. government and armed services. Then as now, America was a bicoastal power accustomed to peering eastward toward Europe when contemplating international affairs. Washington could amass overpowering strength vis-à-vis Japan—but only by incurring substantial danger in the Atlantic Ocean, the traditional top priority for Eurocentric America. Political potentates balked at swinging massive forces to the Pacific absent an immediate and overbearing threat.

Grand strategic realities, then, inclined U.S. military commanders and their political masters to partition resources between the Atlantic and Pacific theaters while favoring the Atlantic. American strategists wrestled constantly with the dilemma of how much force to station in which ocean and how much risk to accept at each potential flashpoint. Only in 1940— when Congress authorized what amounted to a self-sufficient navy for each ocean under the Two-Ocean Navy Act—would new shipbuilding begin to ameliorate this strategic quandary.

During the Theodore Roosevelt presidency, however, U.S. naval power typically remained fragmented between the oceans. In all likelihood the Imperial Japanese Navy would confront whatever fraction of the U.S. Navy was stationed in Pacific waters at the time, and in all likelihood that fraction would represent a minority of the total fleet inventory. As Captain Mahan wrote, a "broad formula" for sizing fleets and fleet detachments demands that top commanders assemble a force "great enough to take the sea, and to fight, with reasonable chances of success, the largest force likely to be brought against it."[10] If a foe scatters its fleet about the seas to uphold many commitments, naval strategists should plan against that fraction that the foe's leadership is likely to commit to battle—not against the enemy navy in its entirety. By Mahanian logic the U.S. Navy's Pacific contingent—not the U.S. Navy as a whole—constituted the benchmark for Japanese naval preparations.

IJN commanders, then, had the luxury of focusing their forces and intellectual energies on accomplishing one big task. They could hope to fall on a segment of U.S. Navy forces and annihilate it before reinforcements could arrive from the Atlantic. They could then defeat the reinforcements as well. This is why strategic thinkers such as Roosevelt and Mahan warned repeatedly about the perils of strategically subdividing the U.S. Navy among theaters. In fact, Roosevelt's final official act as president was to caution successor William Howard Taft against strategically fracturing the fleet into standing Atlantic and Pacific fleets. Doing so risked leaving each parcel of American naval power weaker than the adversary it faced—and thereby invited disaster by increments. Roosevelt reminded Taft that "the entire Japanese force was always used to smash some fraction of the Russian force" during the Russo-Japanese War.[11] Woe to America if it threw a fragmented navy against Japan and replicated Russian blunders.

But the U.S. Navy would face stiff strategic headwinds even if officialdom gathered the entire battle line in the Pacific to outface Japan. Short of forward-deploying the fleet to the Philippines—a prospect unlikely in the extreme—it would call eastern Pacific seaports home. The Navy thus would need time and endurance to surmount the tyranny of distance in the Pacific and so bring the weight of its power to bear in that expanse's westernmost recesses. Succoring the Philippines would compel an expeditionary fleet to traverse thousands of miles of sea with only a few coaling stations, such as Midway Island, Wake Island, and Guam, at which to tarry after it departed Hawaii. A fatigued fleet that had gone without upkeep and repairs since leaving home port would encounter a Japanese Combined Fleet fresh from its dockyards and plying familiar waters.

The rested home team could well triumph over weary visitors. Nor could land defenses on America's post-1898 island possessions delay a Japanese offensive long enough to grant the fleet a respite there during its westward voyage. Congress constantly skimped on fortifications and gunnery for these outposts. Denied the resources to essay a meaningful passive defense, U.S. Army commanders clamored continually for the fleet to appear in western Pacific waters to act as their protector.[12]

So precarious was the situation that the analyst Walter Lippmann upbraided Washington for "monstrous imprudence" in Pacific strategy. In other words, it had taken on commitments of colossal magnitude starting in 1898 yet neglected to buttress its expansive policy with military resources. Lippmann concluded that a divide between policy and strategy gaped wide by the interwar decades—depriving American foreign policy of popular support at home while tempting foreign aggressors to attack where America remained unready. In his estimation, only the Theodore Roosevelt administration deserved even partial credit for trying to match policy with strategy and strategy with adequate resources, chiefly warships and armaments.[13]

Geostrategic realities, in short, prodded Tokyo to plot a fait accompli strategy at sea. Both time and distance were its friends. It could wrest the Philippine archipelago from its occupants, fortify Manila Bay and other strongpoints, and then dare the U.S. Navy to take its holdings back at frightful cost at the terminus of a debilitating transpacific journey. In light of these grim realities, President Roosevelt came to doubt the William McKinley administration's decision to annex the Philippines. He branded the archipelago "our heel of Achilles."[14] To make do, Roosevelt advocated tirelessly on behalf of a preponderant battle fleet. Trying to hold the islands with a fleet too feeble to carry the fight into Asian seas would amount to "a veritable national calamity."[15] An America guilty of monstrous strategic imprudence risked playing into Japanese hands.

Japan's Russo-Japanese War Meme

Japan had staged a meteoric ascent of its own as America rose to great power. Starting with the Meiji Restoration of 1868, the Japanese cast off centuries of martial rule and seclusion, embraced the industrial revolution with zeal, and vaulted into the forefront of progressive civilization. Warlike exploits constituted part and parcel of Japan's rise to regional eminence. During the Sino-Japanese War of 1894–95, for example, the Imperial Japanese Navy triumphed over Asia's leading indigenous navy, that of China's Qing Dynasty.[16] A fleet cobbled together from imported hulls and components made short work of what naval opinion had considered the superior force.

The IJN electrified domestic and foreign audiences again a decade later, when it crushed the tsar's navy bit by bit during the Russo-Japanese War of 1904–5.[17] Admiral Tōgō Heihachirō's Combined Fleet landed a surprise blow against the Russian Pacific Squadron at Port Arthur (February 1904), destroyed the Russian squadron at the battle of the Yellow Sea (August 1904), and demolished the Russian Baltic Fleet at the battle of Tsushima Strait (May 1905). Feats of Japanese arms spelled an end to Chinese sea power for a century while burying Russian sea power in the Far East until Admiral Sergei Gorshkov and the Soviet navy resurrected it to wage the Cold War.

Such deeds understandably seemed to ratify the Japanese way of sea combat. Few officers were prepared to quarrel with success. Looking eastward across the Pacific after 1905, Tokyo could entertain the idea that the imperial navy could replicate its triumph over the Russian Baltic Fleet if called upon to fight the U.S. Navy. In other words, strategists foresaw smashing another hostile Western fleet that limped into Asian seas after a wearisome voyage from far-distant naval stations. This became the IJN playbook.

Roosevelt saw the need to deter this venturesome friend while staying on good terms with him. The Great White Fleet thus circumnavigated the globe in an effort to shatter illusions that the imperial navy could overcome America's the way Tōgō's Combined Fleet had its Russian foe at Tsushima Strait. If successful the world cruise would forestall hostilities against the Philippine Islands and other American interests in the Pacific Ocean.

IJN heroics had given rise to what scientists, analysts, authors, and marketing agencies today style a "meme." *Merriam-Webster*'s defines a meme as a sort of intellectual contagion, an "idea, behavior, style, or usage that spreads from person to person within a culture."[18] Richard Dawkins coined the term in *The Selfish Gene* (1976), postulating that natural selection distinguishes among not just biological organisms, as Charles Darwin maintained, but ideas as well. Competition among ideas determines which are fittest—or, at any rate, which concepts or images seem fittest to the most observers.[19] Dawkins likens memes to "mental viruses."[20]

Memes are a mixed blessing. For example, opinion makers strive constantly to find catchphrases that will "go viral" among influential officials and mold policy. Authors want their writings to go viral, boosting book sales and advertising revenue while burnishing their reputations for excellence and clout. Memes can also captivate institutions, which are nothing more than groups of individuals. Take a group of people, put some in authority, and suppose some meme entrances those holding authority. What impact will the meme exert on institutional practices? In all likelihood, the leadership will transcribe the dominant idea into rules, procedures, and doctrine. In short, the meme will shape—or mis-shape—how the organization transacts its business.

Memes thus inhibit institutional adaptability. Bureaucracies are machinelike organizations. They exist to perform a standard repertoire of tasks using routine methods and procedures. Visceral experiences—successes, failures, big ideas thrust on them by senior leadership—have a way of encoding memes within the institutional culture. Effacing them is hard once they make up part of the bureaucratic repertoire. A fixed idea becomes an assumption from which members of the organization reason—and assumptions are taken as given rather than subjected to question or disproof.[21]

Once written into rules and procedures, memes obstruct efforts to adapt to surroundings in flux. If natural selection distinguishes among ideas, as Dawkins contends, then one meme may give way to another with relative ease among individual human beings. People are known to change their minds. Memes come and go. But bureaucracy is designed not to be as supple or adaptable as individual minds. It is a production line, designed to execute a slate of tasks again and again, the same way every time. The machinery imposes standard ways of thinking and doing on the individuals who constitute it.

The trouble with bureaucracy, then, is that it interferes with the clash among ideas that refreshes strategic debate, debunks ideas that prove false or outlive their usefulness, and assures that the ideas fittest for the surroundings and the times prevail. Writing a meme into policy exempts it from critical scrutiny. It is now axiomatic. In other words, a meme can sap an institution's dexterity of thought and action, impairing efforts to remake itself as circumstances change around it.

Martial bureaucracies are acutely susceptible to memes, perhaps more so than other enterprises.[22] Memes may manifest themselves as military doctrine, maxims, or truisms. These are good and necessary things within limits. Sayings lend unity of vision and purpose to an armed service. For instance, a Nelsonian maxim governed Royal Navy fighting doctrine during the age of sail: "No Captain can do very wrong if he places his Ship alongside that of an Enemy."[23] That's a good meme, bequeathed by Great Britain's foremost naval hero before his greatest victory. The maxim exhorts British commanders, if flag signals from the fleet commander are obscured, ambiguous, or unintelligible, to seize the initiative, go after the enemy at close quarters, and blaze away.

Individual initiative and derring-do are timeless virtues for seafarers. Lord Horatio Nelson codified these virtues in terms fitting for sea combat in the Napoleonic era. Were he alive today, however, Nelson would surely update his instructions to commanders for this age of guided-missile warfare. Closing to gunnery range would be suicidal nowadays, when naval armaments can strike from scores or hundreds of miles away. Nelson was daring but scarcely suicidal. He would comprehend that his maxim was an artifact of his day and must be updated to account for new technology and tactics.

In short, few doctrines or military maxims endure forever. They are perishable and must be regarded as such. As Dawkins contends, a meme must withstand the contest of ideas. And as he implies, it must withstand challenge in the arena again and again as the times change and people formulate contending ideas. It might need to be amended or discarded altogether. Similarly, the historian Julian S. Corbett jeered at a maxim held dear in the fin-de-siècle Royal Navy. The old guard had grown fond of proclaiming that "the enemy's coast is our frontier." "You might as well plan a campaign by singing 'Rule Britannia'" as by invoking such dogma, Corbett told one gobsmacked audience at Portsmouth.[24]

But Corbett was right. The Royal Navy would not always be the strongest force at every place and every time. Commanders might need to do things differently until they regained their customary local supremacy. Making a cult of seizing the offensive in enemy home waters would be as foolish as forever basing doctrine on Nelsonian close-quarters tactics. Doing so would disregard crucial variables such as the operational environment and the relative balance of naval might. Navies need doctrine and maxims; they submit to a tyranny of doctrine, maxims, or memes at dire peril.[25] Entrenched ideas stifle critical analysis, leave sea services maladapted to changing times, and encumber efforts to adapt.

Strategy by proverb, then, entails severe hazards. Standard methods can prove so stultifying that only some dramatic event can empower a new meme to oust and replace an ingrained but outdated one. An armed service might find itself forced to flout doctrine or established wisdom to prevail in combat. It might suffer a crushing defeat that discredits the old meme and generates demand for fresh thinking. Or hardheaded uniformed or political leadership might imprint a new meme on the institutional repertoire, displacing or overlaying the old. It takes drama—if not trauma—to jolt institutions out of obsolescent ways of doing things.

The Imperial Japanese Navy succumbed to all of these problems. The meme that came to permeate the imperial navy in the wake of its triumphs at the Yellow Sea and Tsushima proved extraordinarily durable and resilient. How could dissenters within the naval high command argue against such a record of success? Few could. The meme's tenets might be summed up thus.

First, stun the stronger foe. If the Imperial Japanese Navy could get at an enemy fleet, it should open hostilities with a surprise attack—much as it did against the Russian Pacific Squadron at Port Arthur. Such an approach was true to Japanese traditions. Russo-Japanese War historians

Denis and Peggy Warner note that surprise had long constituted a "fundamental principle" of Japanese war making.[26] For good reason—catching enemy ships unawares magnified the impact of IJN gunnery and torpedoes, boosting the likelihood of progressive flooding and sinking if watertight integrity had been relaxed when the hits came. And a sudden onslaught does more than enfeeble the material dimension of strategy. Crews lounging at ease are probably unready to return fire or undertake damage control after suffering gun or torpedo strikes. Such an attack, moreover, could stun and disorient senior commanders subjected to it. If a hostile navy's overseers already incline to defensive-mindedness, a surprise assault could induce them to act on their natural proclivities, assuming a defensive crouch. Russian commanders did so. Their passivity made them relatively easy pickings. In short, a surprise attack promises disproportionate results, degrading both the material and human dimensions of an opponent's combat power.

Second, weary the stronger foe. If a surprise assault proves impractical because the hostile fleet resides too far away, IJN commanders should let that fleet come to them and weary itself as it does. Deft diplomacy could deny the foe access to straits or narrow seas that would shorten its voyage. Diplomacy could foreclose opportunities for the enemy to refit, rest, or restock with vital supplies along its way. Japan's ally Britain closed the Suez Canal to Russia in 1904–5, forcing the Baltic Fleet to circumnavigate Africa just to reach the battleground. The French government refused to replenish Baltic Fleet vessels with full loads of coal. These troubles compounded the fleet's already arduous journey to the Far East. Tokyo envisioned reprising that diplomatic offensive should a new conflict come. Meanwhile IJN defenders could mount piecemeal asymmetric attacks, wearing away at the material and human factors as the enemy traversed intercontinental distances to reach the scene of action. Torpedo-armed surface craft and submarines would collectively play a prominent part in Japanese strategy. Combat aircraft joined the mix during the interwar decades, as military aviation started to fulfill its combat potential. After evening the naval balance, the IJN fleet could fight a decisive action somewhere in Japan's neighborhood with reasonable odds of success.

If geographic distance is a tyrant, defenders could make his rule even harsher.

In short, the Japanese high command envisioned prosecuting what the Pentagon today calls an "access denial" strategy. Access denial seeks to impose steep costs and damage on hostile fleets that venture into our off-shore waters, cutting them down to size as a precursor to a decisive military action. It is a strategy whereby the relatively weak overcome the relatively strong through patience, ingenuity, and asymmetric measures. The meme underlying IJN access denial centered almost exclusively on battle, and thus on the tactical and operational levels of war. Japanese strategists slighted the prospect of access denial to dissuade enemies from attacking altogether. Erecting imposing access-denial defenses, in other words, could bias foreign decision makers' calculations to Japanese advantage.

To be fair, history provided few grounds to think Japan's navy could altogether deter antagonists from venturing into East Asian environs. After all, the Qing navy had come out to fight. Tsar Nicholas II had accepted the hazards of ordering the Baltic Fleet on an epic 18,000-mile journey through the Atlantic Ocean and Indian Ocean into the China seas. The tsar rolled the iron dice—and risked losing the remainder of Russian sea power—in hopes of salvaging St. Petersburg's standing in maritime Asia. Japanese strategists saw little reason to assume Washington would waffle where Russian and Chinese leaders had not. After all, it had annexed the Philippines following the Spanish-American War. No nation lightly relinquishes sovereign territory to foreign conquest. It fights to preserve its rule.

It is worth noting, however, that assuming away deterrence unduly narrowed Tokyo's range of options. Access-denial defenses can deter. As martial theorist Carl von Clausewitz observed, a rational calculus juxtaposing costs against benefits should impel diplomatic and military undertakings. What a combatant wants and how much it wants it—the "political object" and the value the leadership assigns it—govern how heavy a price the leadership is willing to bear to obtain it. In Clausewitz's words, the value of the object "must determine the sacrifices to be made for [the object] in magnitude and also in duration."[27]

Magnitude is the rate at which a combatant expends lives, national treasure, and military resources to obtain its goal; duration is how long it keeps up that rate of expenditure. Multiplying the rate by the time yields the political object's final price tag. If its cost exceeds the benefits the leadership hopes to extract—if the enterprise threatens to consume resources too quickly, take too long, or both—then the leadership should abjure the effort. Combatants should refuse to pay a steep price for war aims that are not worth the time, resources, and dangers.

Impressing on a faraway foe that it would pay an unacceptable price for its war aims could induce that foe to forgo the attempt. The political and psychological dimensions of access denial seem to have eluded Tokyo. They have not eluded today's contenders. The iron logic of costs and benefits impels access-denial strategies deployed by contemporary China, Russia, and Iran, which have erected thickets of antiship and antiair missiles, missile-armed submarines and patrol craft, and land-based combat aircraft along their shorelines. These arsenals convey a threat to impose unacceptable damage on enemy forces that venture within weapons range.

It is hard to escape the conclusion that hubris—outrageous arrogance that offends the gods, or Fate, or Providence—etched the Russo-Japanese War meme on Japanese military minds while scanting these larger considerations. Experience had seemingly ratified past practice. It had brought victory over the Qing navy, while the Russo-Japanese War vindicated the full-fledged operational concept in action against the Russian navy. Japanese strategists came to believe that access denial, suitably updated to harness new technology as it matured, would garner the IJN new laurels.

Nor were the Japanese the only ones to shower plaudits on Imperial Japanese Navy prowess. The 1905 victory garnered worldwide acclaim, showing that non-Western peoples could defeat European imperial powers. In fact, foreign policy commentator Pankaj Mishra documents how the encounter at Tsushima "struck the opening chords of the recessional of the West."[28] Japanese exploits fired enthusiasm among intellectuals from China's Sun Yat-sen to Turkey's Kemal Atatürk to the American civil rights leader W. E. B. Dubois, all of whom hailed the battle as a portent of coming national liberation. That Tokyo was swept up in the acclaim is unsurprising.

In effect, then, the Russo-Japanese War went viral in Japanese minds and the naval bureaucratic apparatus. Theodore Roosevelt and the Great White Fleet had their work cut out for them if they wanted to discredit a way of Japanese naval strategy and operations that had been tested and reaffirmed in the crucible of naval warfare.

Throwing Shade at the Meme

The Russo-Japanese War thus forged the IJN's access-denial strategy. To discredit the meme and temper Japanese hubris, Washington needed to inflict a kind of virtual defeat on Tokyo, showing that its strategy offered dim prospects of success against the U.S. Navy. Deterrence had to shock Japanese military minds. This was no easy feat. Strategist Edward Luttwak urges commanders to use fleet movements in times of uneasy peace to cast a "shadow" across potential antagonists' political and strategic calculus.[29] Luttwak maintains, for instance, that the victor in a peacetime naval showdown is the contestant that most observers believe would have prevailed in wartime. If Japanese statesmen and naval officialdom regarded the Great White Fleet as an unbeatable foe—and if they believed Washington would send the entire fleet against them in wartime, accepting risk in the Atlantic—then the world cruise ought to throw a long and dark shadow across decision-making circles in Tokyo. Japanese leaders might abandon the conceit that they could repeat their triumphs over China and Russia in action against America.

Deterrence and coercion are synonyms for Luttwak's metaphorical shadow. During the 1960s, the scholar-statesman Henry Kissinger elaborated on deterrence. He was exploring how one atomic state deters another, but his ideas apply in equal measure to conventional deterrence and coercion. Deterrence is the process of convincing a prospective aggressor not to do something we wish to proscribe. We issue a threat to do something drastic if hostile leaders defy us and try to convince them we will inevitably execute our threat if they do what we forbid.

Economist Thomas Schelling goes Kissinger a step farther, declaring that we should make our threats self-executing. We must persuade opponents that the threat will automatically go into effect if they do what we forbid. The contestant issuing the deterrent threat, that is, deliberately takes away its own freedom not to fulfill the threat. In a sense we take ourselves out of the strategic picture, imposing the burden of decision wholly on our antagonist.[30] If we make believers of adversaries, and if the action we threaten would exact a penalty or inflict costs they are unwilling to bear, then, according to deterrent logic, they should desist.

On the essentials of deterrence and coercion Clausewitz, Kissinger, and Schelling seem to agree. Kissinger goes farthest, reducing the confidence-building process vis-à-vis adversary leaders to an algorithm. "Deterrence," he writes, demands "a combination of power, the will to use it, and the assessment of these by the potential aggressor." He appends a coda: "Deterrence is a product of those factors and not a sum. If any one of them is zero, deterrence fails."[31] This is basic algebra. Multiply a large number by a tiny fraction, and the product of multiplication is small. Multiply even very large numbers by zero, and the product is zero. All the physical brawn in the world, in other words, means little if its possessor lacks resolve to use it. Even overbearing might backed by dauntless willpower means little if the antagonist deems us irresolute.

It is worth noting (although Kissinger does not) that the basic logic of capability, resolve, and belief applies not just to deterrence and coercion but to reassurance. To reassure a would-be friend or ally of our commitment, we flourish the capability to keep our commitments to the common cause, impress upon the friendly government that we are deadly serious about honoring our commitments, and make believers out of our interlocutors. President Roosevelt hoped to deter the Meiji leadership while at the same time reassuring Tokyo of American friendliness. This is what Big Stick diplomacy was all about: conducting oneself with circumspection while telegraphing resolution should matters come to blows.

That dual messaging was difficult to pull off. The capability element was the same for efforts to deter and to conciliate. Namely, the U.S. fleet had to be visibly fit to fight and able to sustain itself. Otherwise it could neither execute threats nor honor commitments vis-à-vis Tokyo. And resolve? Luttwak observes that naval commanders and their political masters must attune themselves to the messages fleet movements send. He suggests assigning political advisors to naval commands to monitor and adjust "the political 'radiation' emitted by the fleet" while correcting "severe distortions in others' perceptions of the fleet—of its tactical configuration and the underlying political intent of its movements."[32] Political advisors work with diplomats to tune the messages emitted—and improve the prospects of hearers' interpreting them the way the broadcasters intend.

Calibrating dual messages was the task Roosevelt set for the diplomatic and naval apparatus. To deter—to discredit the Russo-Japanese War meme—the Great White Fleet needed to convince Japan the U.S. Navy would not be incapacitated by a surprise attack at the outbreak of war. The fleet also needed to prove it could reach Far Eastern waters in good order, withstanding (by extension) harassment from the Imperial Japanese Navy while lumbering westward. To speak softly, American diplomats and senior commanders needed to convey friendliness. They also needed to signal that Washington would shed its friendly visage and unlimber the Big Stick if forced to it.

Did the Shadow Deter and Conciliate?

Did the world cruise succeed at its messaging function? President Roosevelt feared it might not. Repeated success could intoxicate even a friendly Japan, goading it into aggression that upset the regional balance of power. Roosevelt intuitively grasped the logic espoused by strategic theorists, viewing deterrence as an effort to mold potential antagonists' perceptions of capability and resolve. It thereby bends their strategic calculus in a favorable direction.

Roosevelt seemed sincere about his professions of friendship toward Japan. He exhorted Americans to befriend the Japanese and reprimanded those who mistreated Japanese laborers on the West Coast. The Japanese "interest me and I like them," he told British ambassador Cecil Spring Rice in 1904. In fact, Roosevelt hoped Japan would maintain order in East Asia, much as the United States kept order in the Western Hemisphere under the guise of his Roosevelt Corollary to the Monroe Doctrine.[33] "I thought it for the interest of all the world," he reported telling the Japanese minister, "that each part of the world should be prosperous and well policed." Since Japan commanded a "preeminent interest" in the Yellow Sea basin, it should act as an international constable there.[34]

"My feeling...about the Japanese Nation [is] that they are a wonderful and civilized people," confided Roosevelt in 1905.[35] At the same time he feared the Meiji regime's unbroken string of successes might whet its appetite for more. While his confidant Elihu Root depicted the surprise assault on Port Arthur as a "bully" way to open hostilities—voicing a view that seemed to reflect the president's own—both leaders also saw cause for concern.[36] They feared Tokyo would contract a case of "victory fever," a malady that predisposes victors to seek more and more conquests.[37] "That Japan will have her head turned to some extent I do not in the least doubt," prophesied Roosevelt, "and I see clear symptoms of it in many ways."[38] A desire to restore sobriety among imperial statesmen constituted the prime mover behind Roosevelt's decision to dispatch battleships.

The president himself portrayed the world cruise in deterrent terms. In his autobiography he pronounced it a "striking thing" that radiated resolve and capability along with respect and friendship. "In my own judgment," he maintained, "the most important service I rendered to peace was the voyage of the battle fleet round the world."[39] President Roosevelt trusted commanders to bring the fleet from North America into Far Eastern waters in fighting trim, showing that the U.S. Navy was no Russian Pacific Squadron or Baltic Fleet. A display of physical capability backed by political willpower, he believed, would counteract hubris and induce forbearance among the island state's rulers. Clear heads would prevail. In all likelihood, deterrence theorists would approve of his handling of the cruise.

Deploying a fleet that could traverse intercontinental distances ready to do battle, then, formed the crux of Rooseveltian strategy. Casting the shadow of American maritime might across the Far East would discourage military adventurism, in particular aggression against American possessions in the western Pacific. And, hoped Roosevelt, a show of strength and resolve conveyed in a friendly spirit would channel Tokyo's ambitions toward responsible stewardship over regional order in East Asia.

Roosevelt evidently believed his show of strength did work, or else he would not—apparently sincerely—have touted the cruise as having abetted the cause of peace. The reality is murkier. Gauging the impact of deterrence can be frustrating. If an antagonist refrains from some action, it may be that deterrence worked. Or it may be that the antagonist desisted for reasons of its own, unrelated to deterrent threats. Nor do foreign leaders make a habit of disclosing their motives to rivals. Accordingly, the guesswork quotient is typically sizable when estimating the effects of deterrence.

This was true in the case of the world cruise. Taking the Great White Fleet's measure was an ambiguous undertaking. However impressively its crews acquitted themselves, the fleet itself was made up of coal-fired battleships staring at technological oblivion. In 1906 the Royal Navy had launched HMS *Dreadnought*, the world's first all-big-gun, turbine-driven battleship. Naval opinion deemed *Dreadnought* a revolutionary capital ship. Today, in fact, it is commonplace to declare that all previous battlewagons became obsolescent once *Dreadnought* took to the seas. That probably goes too far; older battleships remained useful for certain missions. But it is eminently fair to say the new ship type demoted all past battleships—including those constituting most of the Royal Navy's own battle line—to secondary status as capital ships.

In other words, the dreadnought revolution overtook the technology underwriting the U.S. Navy battle fleet and its capacity to deter. It reset the battleship race in the Pacific, much as it reset the Anglo-German naval race in the North Sea. Japanese observers seem to have been impressed with how U.S. Navy crews brought their ships around Cape Horn and into the western Pacific in good shape. But the Imperial Japanese Navy had courted close ties with the Royal Navy since its founding, developing its fleet with British counsel and material support, and thus grasped the implications of the leap-ahead warship design.

It cannot have escaped IJN strategists that the American fleet no longer stood at the forefront of capital-ship technology. The prospect of dueling a second-rate fleet cannot have been daunting enough to prompt Japan to rethink its foreign policy or a naval strategy seemingly already confirmed in combat—the final arbiter of what does and does not work in naval strategy and operations. Roosevelt's demonstration of U.S. combat capability cannot have cast a shadow deep enough to discredit the Russo-Japanese War meme in IJN minds.

Nor did it. Indeed, Japan's navy stuck to its playbook during the inter-war decades as aviation, submarine, and torpedo technology matured. Sadao Asada describes how Japanese strategists and tacticians extended the reach of their access-denial defenses as armaments took on greater range, accuracy, and hitting power. Their strategy of "interceptive operations" was a direct descendant of the strategy deployed against imperial Russia in 1904–5. "Embodying the 'principle of big battleships and big guns,'" writes Asada, "and deriving perceived lessons from Tsushima and Jutland, Japan's interceptive operations hardened into a dogma that continued to govern strategic thinking until 1941."[40]

Both elements of the meme persisted in Japanese strategy. IJN war planners added a forward component to tire the U.S. Pacific Fleet during its westward voyage from Hawaii or the West Coast. Warplanes would strike at the fleet from Pacific island airstrips, inflicting such incremental damage as they could with bombs and torpedoes. Submarines would lurk in the waters between the islands in hopes of executing torpedo attacks of their own. No one believed interceptive operations would shut the U.S. Navy out of the western Pacific altogether. But Japanese strategists increasingly believed they stood a realistic chance of evening the naval balance before a decisive battle somewhere in the western Pacific.

The second element of the meme, a preemptive assault, lay mostly dormant in Japanese planning during the interwar decades. Distance remained a tyrant. Before the advent of carrier aviation, the U.S. fleet's home ports lay too far away to make an assault reminiscent of Port Arthur feasible. But a surprise carrier air strike acquired an influential spokesman in the person of Admiral Isoroku Yamamoto, who thrust his scheme for an assault on Pearl Harbor on Japanese military commanders in 1941. In effect Yamamoto—who had taken part in the Port Arthur torpedo attack as a junior officer—rejuvenated and reinforced the IJN's habitual way of devising operations.[41]

Given the Pearl Harbor raid's galvanic impact on American fighting spirit, one suspects Tokyo would have been better off rejecting Yamamoto's scheme and staying with interceptive operations. The IJN fleet could have mounted its pinprick attacks, let the U.S. Pacific Fleet exhaust itself, and undertaken a decisive battle that however successful may not have infused American society with vengeful passion. In any event, the meme clearly persisted long past the time when Theodore Roosevelt claimed to have deterred Japan in the cause of peace. His political message arguably had its intended effect. The strategic message elicited mixed results at best.

Takeaways from the World Cruise

The voyage of the Great White Fleet abounds with insight for diplomacy and maritime strategy today. First of all, diplomats, officials, and seafarers should fathom how deterrence, coercion, and reassurance work. Revisiting the classics of strategy and political science will help them comprehend how to cast a shadow across the cost/benefit calculations of potential foes and friends—and how to respond when others attempt to cast shadows of their own.

As Luttwak notes, once again, fleet movements broadcast messages. It is an open question whether a brief appearance in the Far East—at the behest of an American president who would soon leave the White House—could have sent a resonant message to Japan. Tokyo could simply outwait the Roosevelt presidency and postpone any Pacific adventures until a later date when the Imperial Japanese Navy was ready. U.S. naval officialdom should study the world cruise and alert themselves to the messages they send today when deploying fleets and how those messages may be received. The size, configuration, and movements of a force mold the message it conveys.

Some officials are acutely conscious of navies' messaging function. During the 1980s the U.S. Navy conducted a regular series of multinational exercises aimed at convincing Soviet leaders that allied forces could operate within striking distance of Eastern Bloc shores and accomplish their goals.[42] In part the maneuvers were meant for messaging purposes. Navy leaders hoped to dishearten Soviet officials, casting doubt on the access-denial defenses the Soviet armed forces had strewed around littoral zones. It appears the allies cast a shadow long and dark enough to deter

Moscow. Undertaken throughout Ronald Reagan's eight-year presidency, such endeavors probably carried more weight than did the one-off show of strength at the close of Roosevelt's tenure.

Second, intervening factors can amplify or detract from efforts at deterrence, coercion, and reassurance. For example, the dreadnought revolution caught many unawares, including Britons. Revolutionary technologies can transform diplomatic relations and strategy almost overnight. Apply Kissinger's formula to the problem of deterrence: capability, willpower, belief. In the case of the Great White Fleet, new warship design in a foreign navy degraded American diplomats' efforts to overawe the Japanese with American capability. No matter how resolute Roosevelt and his advisors showed themselves to be, technological change imposed a ceiling on Washington's ability to make Tokyo a believer in the deterrent threat implicit in Big Stick diplomacy. The effort to deter yielded so-so results at most.

Military technology has entered now another era of tumult, raising the possibility that ships of war—long the core of U.S. deterrence and combat power—may no longer deter. For instance, questions surround the nuclear-powered aircraft carrier's durability under the threat of anti-ship cruise and ballistic missiles. If key audiences come to believe U.S. Navy carrier groups cannot withstand the threats they face, the carrier's capacity to deter, coerce, or reassure will suffer. If China, Russia, or Iran ceases to believe that carrier expeditionary forces would win during times of strife, these forces may no longer deter. It is worth pointing out, furthermore, that foreign leaders need not be right in their assessment of American forces. Even a false estimate of American naval prowess would undercut Kissinger's belief variable. Deterrence could fail despite fervent and well-founded efforts.

And third, practitioners should fathom how a contagion of ideas can constrict the bounds of strategic debate among a military service's members. Seldom are memes and the doctrines, strategies, and maxims to which they give rise amended through dispassionate debate, as strategic theory and Richard Dawkins's concept of natural selection suggest they should be. Fixed ideas must be shattered. This insight helps a competitor estimate how potential opponents may conduct themselves. It also warns us to fight lethargy and nurture dynamism within our own institutions, lest we too fall prey to memes.

Few institutions are exempt from bureaucratic dynamics—or stasis. Dynamists typically fare better in armed competition than services set in their ways. Perhaps the way to remain supple and innovative is for top leaders to inscribe one indelible precept on the institutional culture, setting it above all others: No Precept Is Forever. That is one meme worth making permanent. The Imperial Japanese Navy offers an example to avoid—or to exploit if some future foe appears likewise prone to fixed ideas.

In the end, it appears that Theodore Roosevelt and the U.S. Navy may have induced Japanese leaders to hesitate, postponing any plans for regional aggression they may have harbored during his presidency. But the Great White Fleet could not intimidate the Imperial Japanese Navy or its political masters into foregoing future conquests; neither could it dislodge the Russo-Japanese War meme from IJN strategic thought. It was encoded in Japanese war-making methods and fleet design. It shaped the Japanese way of naval warfare during the interwar years—and helped determine the character and course of the Pacific War decades later. It took the navy's downfall in 1945 to break finally the meme gripping Japanese minds.

Essaying some anxious foresight about the downrange effects and unintended consequences of deterrent threats will pay dividends for today's leaders. American leaders should study this episode—and put history to work refining maritime statecraft for an age of great power competition.

Notes

1. The classic study of Roosevelt's foreign policy is Howard K. Beale, *Theodore Roosevelt and the Rise of America to World Power* (Baltimore: Johns Hopkins University Press, 1956). See also Henry A. Kissinger, *Diplomacy* (New York: Simon & Schuster, 1994), 29–55.
2. TR to Henry L. Sprague, 16 January 1900, in *The Letters of Theodore Roosevelt*, ed. Elting E. Morison (Cambridge, Mass.: Harvard University Press, 1951–1954), 2:1141.

3. Beale, *Theodore Roosevelt and the Rise of America to World Power,* 37–38, 163, 174, 226–29, 336. See also J. Simon Rofe, "'Under the Influence of Mahan': Theodore and Franklin Roosevelt and Their Understanding of American National Interest," *Diplomacy & Statecraft* 19 (2008): 732–45.

4. Beale, *Theodore Roosevelt and the Rise of America to World Power,* 233. See also Richard W. Turk, *The Ambiguous Relationship: Theodore Roosevelt and Alfred Thayer Mahan* (New York: Greenwood, 1987). Turk portrays the relationship as a reciprocal one: TR influenced Mahan as well as the reverse.

5. Michael J. Green, *By More Than Providence: Grand Strategy and American Power in the Asia Pacific since 1783* (New York: Columbia University Press, 2017), 87.

6. Beale, *Theodore Roosevelt and the Rise of America to World Power,* 233.

7. Denis A. Warner and Peggy Warner, *The Tide at Sunrise: A History of the Russo-Japanese War, 1904–05* (1974; repr. London: Routledge, 2002).

8. Andrew C. A. Jampoler, *Embassy to the Eastern Courts: America's Secret First Pivot toward Asia, 1832–37* (Annapolis, Md.: Naval Institute Press, 2015).

9. James R. Reckner, *Teddy Roosevelt's Great White Fleet* (Annapolis, Md.: Naval Institute Press, 1988), 119.

10. Alfred Thayer Mahan, *The Interest of America in Sea Power, Present and Future* (Boston: Little, Brown, 1897), 198.

11. TR to William Howard Taft, 3 March 1909, Morison, *Letters of Theodore Roosevelt,* 6:1543.

12. Brian McAllister Linn, *Guardians of Empire: The U.S. Army and the Pacific, 1902–1940* (Chapel Hill: University of North Carolina Press, 1997).

13. Walter Lippmann, *U.S. Foreign Policy: Shield of the Republic* (Boston: Little, Brown, 1943), 42.

14. Quoted in Ishaan Tharoor, "How the U.S. Fights Its Wars," *Time,* 29 December 2010, http://content.time.com/time/nation/article/0,8599,2038003,00.html.

15. TR to William Howard Taft, 21 August 1907, Morison, *Letters of Theodore Roosevelt,* 6:761–62.

16. S. C. M. Paine, *The Sino-Japanese War of 1894–1895: Perceptions, Power, and Primacy* (Cambridge, U.K.: Cambridge University Press, 2003).

17. Warner and Warner, *Tide at Sunrise.*

18. *Merriam-Webster Online,* s.v. "Meme," https://www.merriam-webster.com/dictionary/meme.

19. Richard Dawkins, *The Selfish Gene* (1976; repr. Oxford, U.K.: Oxford University Press, 2006).

20. Mark A. Jordan, "What's in a Meme?," *Richard Dawkins Foundation for Reason & Science,* 4 February 2014, https://www.richarddawkins.net/2014/02/whats-in-a-meme.

21. On bureaucratic culture, see for instance Max Weber, *Economy and Society: An Outline of Interpretive Sociology,* ed. Guenther Roth and Claus Wittich,

trans. Ephraim Fischoff and others (New York: Bedminster, 1968), 215–23; and Robert W. Komer, *Bureaucracy at War: U.S. Performance in the Vietnam Conflict* (Boulder, Colo.: Westview, 1986), 17–18, 43–49.

22. Since the 1980s memes imported from the business world have periodically swept the U.S. Navy, going by such slogans as "Total Quality Leadership," "Lean Six Sigma," and "Just-in-Time Logistics."

23. "Nelson's Trafalgar Memorandum," *British Library: Learning English Timeline*, http://www.bl.uk/learning/timeline/item106127.html.

24. Eric J. Grove, introduction to Julian S. Corbett, *Some Principles of Maritime Strategy* (1911; repr. Annapolis, Md.: Naval Institute Press, 1988), xxix.

25. See James R. Holmes, "Strategy and the Tyranny of Maxims," *Diplomat*, 23 February 2014, https://thediplomat.com/2014/02/strategy-and-the-tyranny-of-maxims.

26. Denis Warner and Peggy Warner, "The Doctrine of Surprise," *MHQ: The Quarterly Journal of Military History* 4, no. 1 (Autumn 1991): 20–25.

27. Carl von Clausewitz, *On War*, ed. and trans. Michael Howard and Peter Paret (Princeton, N.J.: Princeton University Press, 1976), 92.

28. Pankaj Mishra, *From the Ruins of Empire: The Revolt against the West and the Remaking of Asia* (2012; repr. London: Picador, 2013), 1–11.

29. Edward Luttwak, *The Political Uses of Sea Power* (Baltimore: Johns Hopkins University Press, 1974), 11.

30. Schelling's two masterworks are *The Strategy of Conflict* (Cambridge, Mass.: Harvard University Press, 1960) and *Arms and Influence* (New Haven, Conn.: Yale University Press, 1967).

31. Henry A. Kissinger, *The Necessity for Choice* (New York: Harper, 1961), 12.

32. Luttwak, *Political Uses of Sea Power*, 14–15.

33. Theodore Roosevelt, "Message of the President to the Senate and the House of Representatives," 6 December 1904, in U.S. Department of State, *Foreign Relations of the United States, 1904* (Washington, D.C.: U.S. Government Printing Office, 1905), 41.

34. TR to Cecil Arthur Spring Rice, 13 June 1904, Morison, *Letters of Theodore Roosevelt*, 4:829–33.

35. TR to David B. Schneder, 19 June 1905, in Beale, *Theodore Roosevelt and the Rise of America to World Power*, 268.

36. Beale, 236.

37. The phrase seems to have originated in Japanese. J. J. Stephan, *Hawaii under the Rising Sun: Japan's Plans for Conquest after Pearl Harbor* (Honolulu: University of Hawaii Press, 2002), 1–64.

38. Beale, *Theodore Roosevelt and the Rise of America to World Power*, 281.

39. Roosevelt brokered an end to the Russo-Japanese War, helping manage the negotiations at the Portsmouth Peace Conference. He was awarded the Nobel Peace Prize for 1906 but did not accept the award until 1911. Theodore Roosevelt,

Theodore Roosevelt: An Autobiography, intro. Elting E. Morison (New York: Charles Scribner's Sons, 1913; repr. New York: Da Capo, 1985), 563. See also Frederick W. Marks III, *Velvet on Iron: The Diplomacy of Theodore Roosevelt* (Lincoln: University of Nebraska Press, 1979).

40. Sadao Asada, *From Mahan to Pearl Harbor: The Imperial Japanese Navy and the United States* (Annapolis, Md.: Naval Institute Press, 2006), 181.

41. Warner and Warner, "Doctrine of Surprise," 20–25.

42. John Lehman, *Oceans Ventured: Winning the Cold War at Sea* (New York: W. W. Norton, 2018).

10

"TO PROFIT BY THE LESSONS OF HISTORY"

Heritage, Modernity, and Rooseveltian Navalism, 1907–1909

Jason W. Smith

No country can ever have a powerful marine, or one likely to produce much influence in her wars, that does not pay rigid attention to the tactics of fleets. Your frigate actions and sailing of single ships, are well enough as drill; but the great practice must be in squadron. . . . It is only by using vessels together, that we find out what both ships and men can do. —*James Fenimore Cooper*

One of Cooper's best novels was *The Two Admirals*. I don't care anything for the love story in it, and neither did Cooper. He says at the end that of course his ships are his real heroes. —*Theodore Roosevelt*

The presidential yacht *Mayflower* steamed into Hampton Roads on the morning of 26 April 1907 to a chorus of ceremonial twenty-one-gun salutes from sixteen American battleships of the U.S. Atlantic Fleet swinging at their berths in the Man-of-War Anchorage. The occasion was the opening of the Jamestown Tercentennial Exposition. Beyond the battle fleet lay Sewell's Point, the piers christened "Godspeed" and "Susan Constant," and the makeshift neocolonial city in the distance. With its midway-like "War Path," Philippine Reservation, "Battle of Hampton

Roads" cyclorama, and Georgia State House—the latter a re-creation of the president's maternal homestead—the Jamestown Exposition was a paean to American industry, empire, and history. Who better to frame the enthusiasm of the fair's opening day than Theodore Roosevelt? There followed an international naval review over the same waters "where nearly a half century ago the *Monitor* and the *Merrimack* met," noted the *New York Daily Tribune.* After a seemingly endless parade of soldiers, Marines, and bluejackets, Roosevelt ascended the grandstand's pulpit—in fact, stood atop a chair to command his audience—and declared it their collective purpose to commemorate "the beginning of what has since become this mighty Republic."[1]

In all its spectacle, the fair better reflected the America of 1907 than the humble stockade of its English forebears. Like so many expositions of the era, Jamestown fused past and present with a future that Roosevelt assured the crowd was America's to seize. Drawing on his own race-based historical worldview, Roosevelt identified the "English stock" of the Jamestown settlers as the wellspring of "our national character. The Cavalier and the Puritan," he observed, "made an inheritance in which all of us share."[2] Having established the racial origins of the United States, Roosevelt extended a friendly but measured welcome to the Japanese delegation attending the fair at a moment when tensions with Japan over West Coast immigration and school segregation had worked some in the press and the American public into a war scare. Roosevelt ended by calling for righteousness and peace. "And I want to say right here," the president proclaimed, "that battleships are mighty good peacemakers." The assembled needed but look to the waters of Hampton Roads to see Roosevelt's vision partly manifest. "The cheering was prolonged," the *Daily Tribune* reported.[3] In December, less than a month after the exposition closed, the fleet's sixteen battleships departed Hampton Roads and embarked on their world cruise.

Like his remarks at Jamestown, Theodore Roosevelt's presidency and his naval policy were steeped in history and heritage. For Roosevelt, the past was prescriptive, a view rooted perhaps in his own inclinations as a historian, the author of *The Naval War of 1812* and *The Winning of the West*, but also augured by his historical kinship with the naval historian and theorist Alfred Thayer Mahan, with whom he shared a vision of American sea power derived from historical antecedents.[4] As Roosevelt put it in a 1905 speech in Mobile, he intended "to profit by the lessons of history by seeing that our navy is always kept adequate to our needs."[5] He used the past in at least three distinct ways. First, he followed and participated in debates about the lessons to be drawn from recent history, namely the Spanish-American and Russo-Japanese Wars. Second, Roosevelt often invoked heritage, or an American inheritance, which he understood as a deeper set of national stories about the past from ancient Rome through the settling and founding of English North America to the American Revolutionary era, the War of 1812, and the American Civil War. These stories defined the nation along lines of race and masculinity that Roosevelt believed were now enshrined in its past, that must be protected and cultivated, and that, for the president, were the sure signals of America's potential greatness as a nation. Lastly, Roosevelt was a shrewd craftsman of history, seeing in it as he did at the Jamestown Exposition the ways it might be framed and then linked to his own policy objectives, which by the summer of 1907 meant a significant expansion of the U.S. Navy.

This chapter places the voyage of the Great White Fleet in the context of Roosevelt's historical understanding, discerning in the past a potent and largely overlooked influence on the president's naval policy. The chapter considers neither the lessons drawn from the recent past nor Roosevelt's relationship with his fellow naval historian Mahan, which other contributors to this volume examine. Nor is it a history of the world cruise, per se, which has been ably chronicled by a number of historians.[6] Rather, this chapter examines four dimensions of the cruise in which Roosevelt's conception of history seems to have been particularly influential and that have been generally overlooked by historians. These are the ways his race-based conception of history not only informed his worldview but intersected with his naval policy and, more specifically, the world cruise of the battle fleet; the ways his historical understanding informed his view of the Navy's role in simultaneously averting and preparing to meet the challenges of international rivalry and conflict in his own time; the ways his study of naval history influenced his construction of a youthful, masculine naval officer and enlisted corps whose fighting characteristics reconciled tensions in Roosevelt, tensions at once modern and premodern; and, finally, his conjuring of the past in the production of naval pageantry for public consumption. Taken together, these views of Roosevelt underscore a historian and statesman who used history and heritage in significant ways to meet the domestic and foreign policy challenges of his presidency, culminating in the world cruise of the American battleship fleet between 1907 and 1909.

Feast, Frolic, or Fight

From the summer of 1907 to the departure of the fleet in December, Roosevelt faced a number of domestic and foreign challenges that informed his ultimate decision to send all his battleships to the Pacific. Most pressing on his mind was undoubtedly a crisis with Japan, which began in earnest after the 1906 San Francisco earthquake, erupted into nativist riots on the West Coast, and culminated in the so-called Gentleman's Agreement in which Roosevelt sought to quell unrest in California and convince the Japanese to limit emigration to the United States, goals in which he was mostly unsuccessful in the short term.[7] By the summer of 1907, these conditions had coalesced into a full-blown war scare in the United States, fed by hard-liners on both sides of the Pacific and spun by elements of the press into a war frenzy. Roosevelt himself dismissed it publicly, but privately he confessed feeling the situation sometimes "ticklish" and other times fearsome, depending on when and with whom he was corresponding.[8] He may well have sought to use the crisis—as the principal editor of his papers intimates—to further his political goals in the coming congressional appropriations battle to press the case for four dreadnoughts over the one annual battleship he had assured Congress was sufficient in 1905.[9] In any case, after the decisive victory of the Japanese in the Russo-Japanese War in 1905, a conflict whose end Roosevelt helped to negotiate, it was clear that an emergent Japan allied with Great Britain signaled a new challenge to American interests in the western Pacific.

Domestic political considerations regarding naval matters also pressed
on the president's mind. Perhaps foremost were questions of technology and battleship design ushered in by the 1906 launching of HMS
Dreadnought and the debate over the lessons of the battle of Tsushima,
questions that pitted advocates of the all-big-gun design such as Roosevelt's young inspector of target practice, Lt. Cdr. William S. Sims,
against the president's old interlocutor on naval affairs Mahan.[10] Though
Roosevelt had not yet settled the question in his own mind as summer
gave way to autumn, full commitment to a dreadnought fleet would
require a substantial expansion of the Navy. Sanction for such a program
Roosevelt deemed unlikely from a Congress split among Progressive and
probusiness Republicans and led in questions of naval affairs by Benjamin
Tillman and Eugene Hale in the Senate and Joseph Cannon and George
Foss, among others, in the House. These men were lukewarm toward
if not opposed to Roosevelt's brand of navalism, and they became only
more so after the financial Panic of 1907 gripped the nation in October.[11]
Within the Navy, too, the question of battleship design had called forth a
host of difficult—sometimes publicly embarrassing—questions about the
inefficiencies of the bureau structure relative to a more streamlined general
staff model and the problematic system of promotion by seniority rather
than merit. Roosevelt, a polymath in so many matters, to say nothing
of his engagement on a broad spectrum of naval issues, was intensely
interested in these questions. Pressed by naval planners at the Naval War
College, in Newport, Rhode Island, and the General Board of the Navy,
whose members were already considering a fleet cruise to the Pacific,
Roosevelt quickly grasped the ways such an effort could help clarify
these various issues for the Navy, Congress, the American people, and,
not least, himself.[12]

Historians have long since established that Roosevelt did not intend
the world cruise to be a provocation toward Japan.[13] Rather, given his
concern about a possible Pacific war in the near or long term, he hoped
the cruise would, in his words, "have a pacific effect," and, with a mind
toward both the disaster that had befallen Russia's Baltic Fleet in 1905
and the Americans' own logistical struggles in waters as near as the

Caribbean in 1898, "to try in time of peace to see just what we could do in the way of putting a big battle fleet in the Pacific, and not make the experiment in time of war."[14] According to James Reckner, whose history of the episode is definitive, the aims and direction of the voyage proceeded in three phases: the first, in which primarily naval concerns of fleet tactics, operations, gunnery, and a broader commitment to the Monroe Doctrine took precedence; second, calls in West Coast ports thronged by excited crowds, by which Roosevelt hoped "to impress the American people"; and third, visits to New Zealand, Australia, and, of course, Japan, among other ports, which, according to historian Henry J. Hendrix, illustrated Roosevelt's genius for using the Navy as an instrument of "coercive diplomacy."[15] The cruise—from conception to execution—was thus a multidimensional response to the domestic and foreign challenges Roosevelt faced in his second term.

By nearly all measures, the voyage was a dramatic success. Departing Hampton Roads in December 1907, the fleet's sixteen battleships steamed 46,000 miles, circumnavigated the globe, intermittently augmented by a flotilla of destroyers, colliers, cruisers of the Pacific Fleet, and by four new battleships upon its return in February 1909. The Japanese had received the fleet warmly, at Yokohama, as had the Australians, New Zealanders, and others. Roosevelt acknowledged improvements in fleet operations from the beginning and also significant advances in gunnery, a problem area that had shadowed the Navy in a glaring way at least since the battle of Manila Bay. Perhaps most importantly, the fleet's movements reported by a breathless press and piqued by visits to West Coast ports had stirred popular interest in and support for the Navy, one aspect of the cruise that has been tacitly acknowledged by historians but little studied as significant in its own right.[16]

In its triumphal return to Hampton Roads—a moment marked by naval fanfare of Rooseveltian proportions—this seven-mile-long column of ochre atop a sea of gold-crested white proved an impressive spectacle, enough to obscure for the public at least some of the more troubling questions the voyage raised about the Navy's anemic collier fleet, its lack of developed Pacific naval stations, design flaws in its battleships, and, not least, the age, health, and mindset of its senior officers.[17] Rather, as James Holmes rightly asserts, "turning America's gaze seaward was [Roosevelt's] uppermost concern," and one that would pay dividends in his quest to enlarge the Navy.[18] The fleet's homecoming, noted the *New York Times*, marked "the apotheosis of Roosevelt," a fitting conclusion to a presidency that would end less than a month later.[19] Standing on the barbette of the flagship *Connecticut*'s aft twelve-inch turret, Roosevelt reminded the assembled officers and men that they had made history. "Other nations," he (in effect) bragged, would "have to follow you."[20] In his very last official business as commander in chief, Roosevelt reminded his successor William Howard Taft never to divide the fleet. It was, he told Taft, his "closing legacy" and one, he wrote to another, plainly shown by "the history of all wars up to and including the latest."[21] In typical Rooseveltian fashion, the Great White Fleet had been both history making and made by history.

Leaving Speculative History for Present Politics

Roosevelt's mitigation of the Japan crisis and the part the world cruise played in it may well have originated in his undergraduate education at Harvard in the late 1870s. Though Roosevelt's time at Harvard produced his first scholarly book of history on the naval aspects of the War of 1812, he had nevertheless taken precisely one course in history as an undergraduate. More importantly, it was at Harvard that young Roosevelt first encountered Teutonic germ theory, which held that a superior Anglo-Saxon race had emerged out of the Germanic forest, fended off Rome, invaded England, and from there jumped to the shores of North America, where the Virginia and Massachusetts settlers—descendants of this Teutonic "germ"—waged savage frontier warfare with Native American peoples. To Roosevelt and many other social Darwinists who accepted this premise, nations or races—Roosevelt often used the two interchangeably—progressed through a series of stages from barbarism to savagery and, ultimately, civilization.[22] These ideas had some cachet among professional historians working in that era, such as Herbert Baxter Adams and Edward Augustus Freeman, though by the time Roosevelt espoused it in his presidential rhetoric—if not his earlier scholarship—it was decidedly out of fashion among academic historians.[23] Of course, Teutonic germ theory was rooted in a hierarchically racist worldview, privileging the superiority of some peoples over others, the vast majority.

As president, Roosevelt viewed Japanese-American relations through the lens of Teutonic germ theory—that is, seeing the United States as a young but ascendant leader of "the civilization of the white races" facing an Asian race whose "touchiness" Roosevelt believed was a response to Anglo-American unwillingness "to admit them to association and citizenship." Japan, Roosevelt admitted, was "a most formidable military power."[24] He did not relegate the Japanese to the level of the Filipinos or Puerto Ricans, supposedly in need of America's imperial paternalism. Nevertheless, and though he chafed at the "outrages" Californians had wrought on Japanese immigrants, he concluded that "fundamentally their attitude is proper."[25] Roosevelt's worldview thus colored by Teutonic germ theory was one of constant struggle and conflict as nations of the world competed to emerge the victor. In the end, Roosevelt believed the most civilized nations would triumph, provided they did not neglect preparation, which for Roosevelt was both military and masculine in nature. Roosevelt's response, of which the world cruise was clearly one part, to the Japanese was, in his words, "to act with sufficient courtesy" and also "with sufficient resolve." But here, he told former British prime minister Arthur Balfour in March 1908, he was "leaving speculative history for present politics." That the one informed the other was, of course, not coincidental.[26]

Thus, it was quite natural in the course of the battle fleet's voyage for Roosevelt to make public pronouncements that linked this American brand of Teutonism to American navalism. When, at the Jamestown Tercentennial's opening day, Roosevelt linked the founding of America to the growth of "this mighty Republic" that had built the battleship fleet just offshore, it was no mere leap of the imagination. Roosevelt was using the past to make potent claims for the present. When the president returned to the fair on 10 June, just weeks before he settled on the world cruise, he stood before a replica of his mother's house in Georgia. Quite likely having in mind his Confederate uncles, he held forth on the "honor" and "triumphs" of "our battleships and great armored cruisers." Their names drawn from the states of the Union, these vessels marked "a common possession of all of us."[27] That he also referred to English "stock" as "an inheritance in which all of us share" was probably not coincidental.[28] In Roosevelt's mind, the racial origins of the United States were woven into the nation's ascendance in the new century, with the Navy now the instrument of that rise to world power.

When Roosevelt traveled to the Naval War College in June 1908 to preside over the Newport battleship conference, his primary concern was a dispassionate discussion of battleship design, but the speech he framed for public consumption struck a familiar chord.[29] His eye was on "a first class navy." Roosevelt did not have to mention the Japanese by name when he referred to "many hundreds of thousands of immigrants" coming "from many different strata of cultivation, and civilization." Friction was common. Sometimes it led to war. Yet, with an eye toward posterity, Roosevelt observed that "to be a great people and make a great failure is as unattractive a spectacle as history affords. To be a great Nation," he believed, "can only be done by building up and maintaining at the highest point of efficiency the United States Navy."[30] In February 1909, just weeks before the battle fleet's return, he told an English friend, "My policy is three-fold: (1) to keep out the Japanese (2) to do it with the minimum of friction and the maximum of courtesy (3) to build up the navy."[31] In these ways, Roosevelt invoked a historical worldview rooted in social Darwinism and Teutonic germ theory to inform his view of the crisis with Japan. At Jamestown and Newport, his solution was naval. Send the fleet to the Pacific. Continue to build the Navy.

Washington's Maxim

Indeed, Jamestown and Newport were just two of many places where the president sounded the call for naval preparedness, which during the crisis with Japan had become something of a Rooseveltian watchword. With his focus on the upcoming naval appropriations battle set for the summer and fall of 1908, with the lessons of Tsushima and the shadow of

HMS *Dreadnought* on his mind, and now informed by a contentious and not altogether conclusive battleship conference at Newport, Roosevelt hoped that the West Coast cruise and the voyage across the Pacific might quiet his congressional opponents. The enthusiasm generated by the fleet's visits to San Diego, San Francisco—where an estimated one million people lined the shores of the bay—and Seattle, was "not accidental," argues one historian, but "to some degree" part of the president's "domestic political strategy."[32] In fanning popular enthusiasm for "preparedness"—what critics viewed as militarism and navalism run amok—Roosevelt was guided by the past. His military policy was in nature neo-Hamiltonian, which the political scientist Samuel P. Huntington defined as an international worldview of struggle and conflict in which "nations must maintain adequate armaments to back up their national policies," thus supporting "the military in their efforts to build up the nation's defenses."[33] As Roosevelt was fond of saying, his view could be summed up by George Washington's well-known maxim "that the surest way to avert war is to be prepared to meet it."[34]

To Roosevelt, naval preparedness was one of the plainest lessons the American past had to teach. In *The Naval War of 1812*, published in 1882, Roosevelt condemned the Jeffersonians for their lack of preparation. As late as 1907, he dismissed Thomas Jefferson as "the most incompetent chief executive we have ever had . . . not even excepting Buchanan."[35] Roosevelt romanticized the gallantry of the American frigate and sloop duels, the leadership of the Navy's officers, the bravery of its men, and the superior design of its ships, but he nevertheless drew historical lessons about the failure of American navalism in the early nineteenth century that had implications for the twentieth.[36] So too for the Monroe Doctrine, which had been "an empty boast," he remarked at Newport, until "the voyage of the sixteen battleships around South America" had shown the world "the reality" of it.[37] In his *Hero Tales from American History*, a book for boys that he published with Henry Cabot Lodge in 1895, Roosevelt recalled that "our statesmen and our people had been too short-sighted to build a big navy."[38] If Jefferson and Madison had been too short-sighted, so too were leaders in his own time; Roosevelt griped to Philander C. Knox just days before the fleet's return to Hampton Roads that the question of preparedness "is so obvious that it ought not to be necessary to dwell upon. But our people are shortsighted and have short memories."[39] Thus, Roosevelt linked the past to the making of military policy in the present, emphasizing the long arc of history, the need to remind the American people of it, and the fallacy of a future that relied too much on emergency mobilization in an age of modern, industrialized war.

By Roosevelt's second term, his understanding of the historical dimensions of American military policy had long solidified. *The Naval War of 1812*, as Michael Crawford contends, underscored early on the young politician's nascent navalism, which "would see fruition decades later during his presidency in what some would call 'Teddy Roosevelt's navy.'"[40] His views on military policy, rooted in Washington's maxim and, in particular, the federalism of Alexander Hamilton, had crystalized. He deemed Hamilton "the most brilliant statesman that ever lived" and the *Federalist Papers* "a book which ranks among the ablest and best which have ever been written."[41] In many ways, Roosevelt's own calls for naval preparedness throughout the cruise of the battle fleet echoed Hamilton's plea in *Federalist* 11. "A few ships-of-the-line," as "Publius" put it in 1787, would surely fall short by Rooseveltian standards. Nevertheless, we might easily imagine the president underlining and dog-earing the notion that such a fleet would free the United States from the "wanton intermeddlings" of other nations that would otherwise have "nothing to fear from us."[42] When Roosevelt had set about in 1891 to publish a short history of New York City, his historical treatment of the Constitution not coincidentally referred to the federal ship *Hamilton*, a thirty-two-gun frigate in miniature, leading the 1788 ratification parade down Broadway.[43] Here was a bit of naval pomp and circumstance from the federalist era of which the Jamestown Exposition and the subsequent voyage of the Great White Fleet were but modern, Rooseveltian equivalents. Roosevelt's sense of fanfare in the forming of a body politic and of nationalism under the banner of military preparedness, a strengthened presidency, and what he admitted was his own "refusal to accept the strict and limited constitutional . . . view" were influenced in significant ways by the president's interpretation of the nation's founding and the failures of Jeffersonian naval policy during the War of 1812.[44]

The Man behind the Gun

The War of 1812 had convinced Roosevelt not only of the virtues of preparedness and the folly of its opposite but also of the enduring, perhaps eternal, importance of training, physical and mental discipline, and a broader fighting ethos. Roosevelt believed these characteristics of the naval officer and the enlisted man, in fundamental ways, transcended the technological changes transforming the nature of war on land and sea and, more importantly, formed the antidote to what he deemed a crisis of masculinity in fighting spirit that plagued modern industrial societies like the United States.

Roosevelt understood that great changes were transforming everything from the instruments of naval warfare to the very character of the American people and that his own view of America's ascent to the top of civilized nations was neither preordained nor eternal. In July 1907, just weeks after he committed to the world cruise, Roosevelt admitted to the German ambassador "certain ominous signs of frivolity" in American society, signs "of a lack of sense of proportion in ideals, and of inordinate love of ease and of pleasure, and an overemphasis upon merely material well-being." To another, he attributed such afflictions to a "luxurious and in some respects enervating and demoralizing industrial civilization."[45] Americans, he worried, were becoming soft, lazy, and materialistic. Highly sophisticated societies, Roosevelt observed, were subject to "decadence," and he cited historical examples from Rome to Spain bolstered by his reading of Tacitus, Gibbon, Macaulay, and others.[46] Here again, Roosevelt's views of military culture and military preparedness intersected with not only the apparently abject lesson of the Jeffersonians but also Roosevelt's longer view of Anglo-Saxon dominance now threatened by the very wealth and power that civilization conferred on nations of privileged racial stock.

For Roosevelt, the antidote could be found in history, in the premodern—in other words, in the set of ideals he framed in 1899 as "the strenuous life," in his own self-image as Rough Rider and cowboy, and, not least, in the fighting man.[47] At sea, this took the form of the modern naval officer filled with the youthful, reformist, pot-stirring, fighting ethos of a Sims, a Cameron Winslow, or an Albert Key, who collectively led the insurgency against the bureau system and the mixed-caliber battleship. "The line officer, the fighting man," Roosevelt remarked to Secretary of the Navy Charles J. Bonaparte, "is the pivotal man in the navy. . . . He is the man who does the vital work."[48] He once referred to a pair of destroyer lieutenants, for example, as "thorough gamecocks."[49] There was also a place in Roosevelt's vision of the fighting man for the uplifted, civilized, now largely Americanized enlisted corps, whose training, discipline, preparation, and efficiency piqued Roosevelt's Progressivism and underscored the role of working-class masculinity in the triumph of American sea power.

For all Roosevelt's reverence for Mahan or even Robley D. "Fighting Bob" Evans (who had commanded the battle fleet on its first leg to California before being having to be relieved because of illness), Roosevelt demonstrated, time and again, a proclivity to privilege the perspectives of certain junior officers who quickly recognized in Roosevelt an important and influential advocate for their views on naval reform from battleship design to naval administration and officer promotion. Here again, Roosevelt's view of history underscored his estimation of the issues at hand. Roosevelt's naval ideal was rooted in the heritage of John Paul Jones during the American Revolution, Thomas Macdonough during the War of 1812, and William B. Cushing and David Glasgow Farragut during the Civil War. These men had exhibited bravery and fortitude under fire and so were, in Roosevelt's mind, inspirational leaders whether for the young boys for whom he and Lodge wrote their *Hero Tales from American History* or for the midshipmen at the U.S. Naval Academy who listened to Roosevelt's 1906 Annapolis speech marking Jones' reinterment.[50] In *The Naval War of 1812*, Roosevelt contended that Macdonough's "skill, seamanship, quick eye, readiness of resource, and indomitable pluck, are beyond all praise."[51] In his *Hero Tales from American History*, he regaled his youthful readers with Farragut's "great feats on the Gulf coast," clearly reveling in "the hurly-burly of the night battle . . . below New Orleans." When the reader "becomes a voter," Roosevelt instructed, "he should have learned the lesson that the United States . . . should always have a first class navy."[52] Roosevelt was certainly no Luddite, yet the crucial element for him remained the human one, an essential feature of naval warfare no matter the age.[53]

Even as Roosevelt's fighting man permitted the gentleman officer—and the nation more broadly—to exhibit Victorian restraint backed always by the threat of overwhelming force, his articulation of the strenuous life also hearkened to a working-class definition of masculinity, one that celebrated the enlisted man's toughness and physicality. After spending time on board the battleship *Louisiana* in November 1906, Roosevelt wrote to his Secretary of the Navy about the enlisted men's "character and fine physique" and "their attitude as self-respecting American citizens" less than a year after a Bureau of Navigation decision requiring that all American enlisted personnel be citizens of the United States.[54] Roosevelt, in fact, was impressed by the Progressive influence of naval service on young men, citing their fine hygiene, health, and strength. "Certainly no class of our citizens of any kind produces a higher grade of citizenship" than the sailors of the U.S. Navy, he told Bonaparte.[55] Roosevelt was particularly fond of the "man behind the gun," the "gun-pointers," whose performance had been so much the focus of Sims' work and an impetus for the world cruise. Thus, the battle fleet's gunnery drills at Magdalena Bay, Mexico, in March 1908 and its exercises at Manila Bay in November—which Adm. Charles Sperry told an excited Roosevelt became a "perpetual war game"—were part of a larger sense that part of what the Navy cultivated was vigorous, well-trained, and civilized men.[56]

Roosevelt's idealization of the American navy's fighting men also permitted him to define those outside it as either effeminate or aged. In July 1907, Adm. Willard H. Brownson, the erstwhile chief of the Bureau of Navigation, resigned his commission after Roosevelt overruled him and permitted fleet surgeons to command hospital ships. This resulted in an embarrassing public spectacle for the Navy, and Roosevelt belittled the officer for his "smallness" and "pettishness." He likened Brownson's intransigent disagreement to insubordination, to "a mental attitude that would discredit a spiteful school girl."[57] Roosevelt reserved similar scolding for members of Congress who opposed his brand of navalism. Senator Eugene Hale, chairman of the Senate Naval Affairs Committee, was often the focus of Roosevelt's ire; he privately called Hale a "conscienceless voluptuary" and a "physical coward without one scrap of patriotism."[58] Of course it was men like Hale, Tillman, and Foss—the targets of Roosevelt's gendered attacks—who opposed his expanded battleship program in the 1908 debates over the naval bill.

Moreover, Roosevelt's conception of the fighting man's youthful vigor shone a harsh light on the actual state of the service's aged officer corps, and it was on these grounds that Roosevelt slowly began to build momentum to reform the promotion system according to merit rather than seniority and to replace the inefficiencies of the bureau structure with a general staff. As Reckner observes, one legacy of the world cruise is that it exposed the age and fragile health of men like Evans, who at the time of the cruise was the only serving Civil War veteran in the Navy.[59] No one—let alone Roosevelt—would impugn Evans' fighting reputation, but clearly his days on a flagship's bridge had come and gone, and to replace him there was only Admiral Sperry, who apparently commanded under the unfortunate sobriquet "Coffin Face."[60] Though reforms in naval administration and promotion would not bear fruit until the Great War, Roosevelt had put his significant influence behind the measures.[61] He thus countered what he deemed to be the enervating and emasculating influence of modern, industrialized society with the muscular preparedness of the fighting man, a seagoing version of the strenuous life the president so publicly espoused in his rhetoric and in his own self-image. At sea, his models were historical, men whose bravery and coolness under fire were timeless examples that, at least on the surface, defied technological transformations in naval warfare during the nineteenth century.

The Sound of Trumpet and Horn

Roosevelt, perhaps more profoundly than any other president before him, crafted a self-image that pervaded American popular culture, part Rough Rider and Western rancher, part trust-busting Progressive, always bespectacled, mustachioed, and toothy-grinned. Magazines like *Judge*,

Outlook, and *Puck* satirized him—and more than once his face appeared in caricature as the figurehead on the bow of a battleship. Whatever the caricature, he was a larger-than-life figure, and he could deftly construct an image to political gain. When, at the end of his presidency he was asked for a commemorative Big Stick to be auctioned off for the benefit of an orphan asylum, he was "very glad indeed to take advantage of an opportunity to assist."[62] When it came to naval affairs, of course, Roosevelt was a master at using the Navy and crafting naval heritage to garner popular enthusiasm to bolster his navalist agenda. "A blast upon his bugle trumpet," Rear Adm. Stephen B. Luce once remarked, "is worth a thousand men."[63] Throughout the world cruise, Roosevelt micromanaged publicity, deciding what newspaper correspondents would accompany the fleet, and when bad press (such as the Brownson affair or leaks regarding questions of battleship design) emerged, he moved quickly to damage-control mode. By November 1908, for example, he ordered the Secretary of the Navy to quiet his officers: "Under no circumstances," Roosevelt declared, "is any officer to discuss before the public . . . any question of naval policy without submitting what he wishes to say to the Secretary, or . . . to the President."[64] In Roosevelt, the Navy had a champion in the White House who reveled in the political battles but also understood how naval heritage and naval pageantry could mold public opinion to his cause.

The departure and return of the battle fleet illustrate Roosevelt's propensity for public spectacle. Famously the bride at every wedding, the corpse at every funeral, and the baby at every christening (as his daughter Alice once observed), Roosevelt may well have yearned also to be the admiral at every naval review or the lieutenant in every boarding party. Recalling Cushing's raid on the Confederate ram *Albemarle*, Roosevelt admitted that "had I been in his shoes, there were mighty few admirals with whom . . . I should have thought it worthwhile to change positions."[65] As the fleet steamed out of Hampton Roads in December 1907, Roosevelt could barely contain his enthusiasm. "Did you ever see such a fleet? Isn't it magnificent? Oughtn't we all feel proud?" he reportedly exclaimed. Reckner paints a picture of Roosevelt on board the *Mayflower* in the fleet's wake, loath to give up the moment. To be commander in chief was not nearly as glorious—at least on this day—as embodying the fighting man himself.[66] It was quintessential Roosevelt.

When the fleet steamed over the horizon, it voyaged quite literally out of the American past. It left behind Hampton Roads, whose waters, waxed one exposition book, honored "the hardy mariners who braved the dangers of the deep to establish the colony." The doors of the turreted "Battle of Hampton Roads" cyclorama were now shuttered. It was all that remained of what had been "by all odds, the most successful amusement venture" along the exposition's "War Path."[67] As the historian Michael Kammen argues, Jamestown and other expositions like it were part of a much larger cultural turn in the United States toward heritage, myth, and tradition; Roosevelt masterfully wove the past into a national origin story that intersected with his own views toward Japan and the naval preparedness he deemed necessary to meet the threat.[68] The Jamestown Exposition was by all accounts an economic bust, but its most successful aspects were naval. Postcards show an American battleship whose searchlight shines on the Virginia Company's ships under the banner "Light on the Past." Another depicts the "handshake of centuries": John Smith and Theodore Roosevelt, arms outstretched, reaching across time. Here was an apt metaphor for the ways Roosevelt's rhetoric, his presence, and his framing of history could merge past with present, seeming to elide time itself. The fair, remarked one promoter, "was conceived for the purpose of accentuating the historical, or reviving patriotism by a retrospect of our glorious past, and the contemplation of our present prestige and prowess as symbolized in the splendid exhibit of our Army and Navy. Can anyone say that the attention of the whole country was not drawn to things of the past?"[69]

The Great White Fleet returned to Hampton Roads in much the same way it had left, in a flurry of ceremonial gunpowder, though this time, as Roosevelt told the assembled officers and men, it had been the history *maker*. "I could not ask for a finer concluding scene to my administration," he recalled.[70] There was Roosevelt atop the *Connecticut's* turret, epaulets and blue jackets crowded before him. Less than a month before, the president's naval bill calling for four dreadnoughts in the coming year's appropriation—what Reckner deemed the "highest priority" of Roosevelt's naval policy—had emerged largely victorious in Congress, setting a new precedent of two battleships that year.[71] To be sure, it was not the four vessels on which Roosevelt "had set my heart," but he had been satisfied, nevertheless, that his political wrangling would keep the United States on par in the naval arms race ushered by the advent of the dreadnought.[72] On 13 February 1909, just a week before the return of the fleet, Roosevelt wrote to his son: "I think I have won out as regards the Japanese-California trouble." He had persuaded Japanese ambassador Kogorō Takahira "to make an address on Lincoln's birthday, for I knew that with our queer, sentimental people this would have a good effect."[73] The fleet returned on the 22nd, the birthday of Roosevelt's other political hero.

On 27 December 1912, less than two months after the Bull Moose candidate lost his third-party bid for the White House and nearly four years since the close of the fleet's cruise, Theodore Roosevelt addressed the annual gathering of the American Historical Association (AHA), of which he was now president, in Boston. His address, titled "History as Literature," spoke to philosophical debates within the growing historical profession. He wished particularly to emphasize the importance of what he called "vision and imagination" in historical writing. As he had once written to a friend and fellow writer, "it is good to hear the sound of trumpet and horn." More than just mastering facts, meticulously and painstakingly gathered, Roosevelt declared, the historian must "put flesh and blood on dry bones, to make dead men living before our eyes."[74]

That Roosevelt should now consider posterity following his recent electoral loss is hardly surprising. On more than one occasion, Roosevelt's address to his fellow historians considered "those great expressions of the historian *and the statesman* [italics added]." He was likely thinking of himself and his own life when he concluded his address: "Great thoughts match and inspire heroic deeds. Some day the historians will tell us of these things. Some day, too, they will tell our children of the age and the land in which we now live.... When the tale is finally told," he ended, "I believe that ... we shall yet in the end prove our faith by our works, and show in our lives our belief that righteousness exalteth a nation."[75] If, as Roosevelt said, one's faith in one's righteousness would be ultimately and historically manifest in one's works, then few moments apparently mattered to him quite so much as the voyage of the Atlantic Fleet battleships around the world. At the time of Roosevelt's address before the AHA, he was hard at work on his own autobiography, which he published the following year. The cruise of the Great White Fleet, he wrote therein, was "the most important service I rendered to peace." Yet he also admitted his "prime purpose" had been to "impress the American people." This, he boasted, had been "fully achieved."[76] A few pages later, in the final pages of his presidential memoir, Roosevelt chose to include a picture of himself on the deck of a battleship, not ambling alongside the gaunt-faced Fighting Bob Evans but among a cadre of youthful sailors, "the gun pointers of the U.S. battleship *Missouri*."

Notes

Epigraphs: James Fenimore Cooper, *The Two Admirals: A Tale, New Edition* (New York: Stringer and Townsend, 1852), 1:154; and TR to Ethel Roosevelt, on board USS *Mississippi*, 1 October 1907, in *The Letters of Theodore Roosevelt*, ed. Elting E. Morison (Cambridge, Mass.: Harvard University Press, 1951–1954), 5:813.

1. *New York Daily Tribune*, 27 April 1907, 2; on the Jamestown Tercentennial Exposition, see *The Official Blue Book of the Jamestown Ter-centennial Exposition* (Norfolk, Va.: Colonial, 1907); on world's fairs and empire, see Robert W. Rydell, *All The World's a Fair: Visions of Empire at American International Expositions, 1876–1916* (Chicago: University of Chicago Press, 1984).
2. Theodore Roosevelt, "At the Opening of the Jamestown Exposition, April 26, 1907," in *Presidential Addresses and State Papers* (New York: Review of Reviews, 1910), 6:1214.
3. *New York Daily Tribune*, 27 April 1907, 2.
4. Richard W. Turk, *The Ambiguous Relationship: Theodore Roosevelt and Alfred Thayer Mahan* (Westport, Conn.: Greenwood, 1987).
5. Roosevelt, "Speech at Mobile, Alabama, October 23, 1905," *Presidential Addresses*, 4:517.
6. Thomas Bailey, "The World Cruise of the American Battleship Fleet, 1907–1909," *Pacific Historical Review* 1 (December 1932): 389–423. On the Great White Fleet, James R. Reckner, *Teddy Roosevelt's Great White Fleet* (Annapolis, Md.: Naval Institute Press, 1988); Kenneth Wimmel, *Theodore Roosevelt and the Great White Fleet: American Sea Power Comes of Age* (London: Brassey's, 1998).
7. Charles E. Neu, *An Uncertain Friendship: Theodore Roosevelt and Japan, 1906–1909* (Cambridge, Mass.: Harvard University Press, 1967).

8. On Roosevelt's estimation of the Japanese crisis, see, for example, TR to Elihu Root, 13 July 1907, Morison, *Letters of Theodore Roosevelt*, 5:717; TR to Hermann Speck von Sternberg, 16 July 1907, Morison, 5:721; TR to Charlemagne Tower, 19 November 1907, Morison, 5:853; TR to Kermit Roosevelt, 19 April 1908, Morison, 6:1012–13; TR to Kermit Roosevelt, 23 January 1909, Morison, 6:1481; TR to Cecil Arthur Spring Rice, 21 December 1907, Morison, 6:869.

9. Morison, 6:1342n2.

10. Elting E. Morison, *Admiral Sims and the Modern American Navy* (New York: Russell & Russell, 1942), 156–75.

11. Paul E. Pedisich, *Congress Buys a Navy: Politics, Economics, and the Rise of American Naval Power, 1881–1921* (Annapolis, Md.: Naval Institute Press, 2016), 161–78.

12. Reckner, *Roosevelt's Great White Fleet*, 9–11.

13. Some early examples are Bailey, "World Cruise of the American Battleship Fleet," 398–400, 403; Harold Sprout and Margaret Sprout, *The Rise of American Naval Power, 1776–1918* (Princeton, N.J.: Princeton University Press, 1939), 259–285; and William Reynolds Braisted, *The United States Navy in the Pacific, 1897–1909* (New York: Greenwood, 1958), 223–32.

14. TR to Root, 13 July 1907.

15. Reckner, *Roosevelt's Great White Fleet*, 13; Theodore Roosevelt, *An Autobiography* (New York: Macmillan, 1913), 564; Henry J. Hendrix, *Theodore Roosevelt's Naval Diplomacy: The U.S. Navy and the Birth of the American Century* (Annapolis, Md.: Naval Institute Press, 2009), 168.

16. See, for example, Reckner, *Roosevelt's Great White Fleet*, x–xi.

17. Reckner, xi.

18. James R. Holmes, "A Striking Thing," *Naval War College Review* 61, no. 1 (Winter 2009): 5.

19. *New York Times*, 23 February 1909.

20. Franklin Matthews, *Back to Hampton Roads* (New York: B. W. Huebsch, 1909), 292.

21. TR to William Howard Taft, 3 March 1909, Morison, *Letters of Theodore Roosevelt*, 6:1543; TR to George E. Foss, 18 February 1909, Morison, 6:1526.

22. On Roosevelt and Teutonic germ theory, see Jean M. Yarbrough, *Theodore Roosevelt and the American Political Tradition* (Lawrence: University Press of Kansas, 2014), 10–49; Richard Slotkin, *Gunfighter Nation: The Myth of the Frontier in Twentieth-Century America* (New York: Atheneum, 1992), 29–62; and Gail Bederman, *Manliness and Civilization: A Cultural History of Gender and Race in the United States, 1880–1917* (Chicago: University of Chicago Press, 1995), 178–84.

23. Peter Novick, *That Noble Dream: The "Objectivity Question" and the American Historical Profession* (New York: Cambridge University Press), 87–88.

24. TR to Arthur James Balfour, 5 March 1908, Morison, *Letters of Theodore Roosevelt*, 6:960; TR to Philander C. Knox, 8 February 1909, Morison, 6:1511.

25. TR to John Sparks, 20 December 1907, Morison, 6:869; TR to Arthur Hamilton Lee, 26 December 1907, Morison, 6:874.

26. TR to Balfour, 5 March 1908.

27. Theodore Roosevelt, "At the Georgia State Building, Jamestown Exposition, June 10, 1907," *Presidential Addresses*, 6:1306.

28. Roosevelt, "Opening of the Jamestown Exposition."

29. On the purely naval dimensions of the Newport battleship conference, see John B. Hattendorf, B. Mitchell Simpson III, and John R. Wadleigh, *Sailors and Scholars: The Centennial History of the U.S. Naval War College* (Newport, R.I.: Naval War College Press, 1984), 61–65.

30. Roosevelt, "To the Conference of Officers at the Naval War College, Newport, Rhode Island, July 22, 1908," *Presidential Addresses*, 7:1771.

31. TR to Arthur Hamilton Lee, 7 February 1909, Morison, *Letters of Theodore Roosevelt*, 6:1508.

32. Hendrix, *Theodore Roosevelt's Naval Diplomacy*, 159.

33. Samuel P. Huntington, *The Soldier and the State: The Theory and Politics of Civil-Military Relations* (Cambridge, Mass.: Belknap Press of Harvard University Press, 1957), 270–72.

34. Roosevelt, "Opening of the Jamestown Exposition."

35. TR to William Henry Moody, 21 September 1907, Morison, *Letters of Theodore Roosevelt*, 5:803.

36. Theodore Roosevelt, *The Naval War of 1812, or the History of the United States Navy during the Last War with Great Britain, Part II* (New York: G. P. Putnam's Sons, 1900), 134–35, 189–90.

37. Roosevelt, "Conference of Officers at the Naval War College."

38. Henry Cabot Lodge and Theodore Roosevelt, *Hero Tales from American History* (New York: Century, 1896), 309.

39. TR to Knox, 8 February 1909.

40. Michael J. Crawford, "The Lasting Influence of Theodore Roosevelt's *Naval War of 1812*," *International Journal of Naval History* 1 (April 2002), www.ijnhonline.org/issues/volume-1-2002/apr-2002-vol-1-issue-1/ (accessed 16 January 2019).

41. Theodore Roosevelt, *Historic Towns: New York* (New York: Longmans, Green, 1891), 149–50.

42. "The Federalist Papers: No. 11," *The Avalon Project: Documents in Law, History, and Diplomacy*, http://avalon.law.yale.edu/18th_century/fed11.asp (accessed 21 January 2019).

43. Roosevelt, *Historic Towns*, 152.

44. TR to Kermit Roosevelt, 23 January 1909.

45. TR to von Sternberg, 16 July 1907.

46. TR to Balfour, 5 March 1908.

47. On Roosevelt and masculinity, see Bederman, *Manliness and Civilization*, 190–96; Kristin L. Hoganson, *Fighting for American Manhood: How Gender*

Politics Provoked the Spanish-American and Philippine-American Wars (New Haven, Conn.: Yale University Press, 1998), 143–45, 151–53.

48. TR to Charles Joseph Bonaparte, 28 November 1906, Morison, *Letters of Theodore Roosevelt*, 5:514.

49. Roosevelt, *Autobiography*, 566.

50. Theodore Roosevelt, "On the Occasion of the Reinternment of the Remains of John Paul Jones at Annapolis, Maryland, April 24, 1906," *Presidential Addresses*, 5:731–38; Roosevelt, *Naval War of 1812*, 134–35; TR to Frederic Remington, 28 October 1908, Morison, *Letters of Theodore Roosevelt*, 6:1322; Lodge and Roosevelt, *Hero Tales from American History*, 309.

51. Roosevelt, *Naval War of 1812*, 135.

52. Lodge and Roosevelt, *Hero Tales from American History*, 309.

53. On Roosevelt and military technology, see Matthew M. Oyos, "Theodore Roosevelt and the Implements of War," *Journal of Military History* 60 (October 1996): 645–54.

54. Frederick S. Harrod, *Manning the New Navy: The Development of the Modern Naval Enlisted Force, 1899–1940* (Westport, Conn.: Greenwood, 1978), 55.

55. TR to Bonaparte, 28 November 1906.

56. On the fleet's drills and exercises, see Reckner, *Teddy Roosevelt's Great White Fleet*, 51–52, 111–12, 138–39; TR to Charles Stillman Sperry, 5 December 1908, Morison, *Letters of Theodore Roosevelt*, 6:1411.

57. TR to Hart Lyman, 18 December 1907, Morison, *Letters of Theodore Roosevelt*, 6:876.

58. TR to Root, 13 July 1907.

59. Reckner, *Roosevelt's Great White Fleet*, xi, 35.

60. Reckner, 82.

61. On reforms in naval promotion, see Donald Chisholm, *Waiting for Dead Men's Shoes: Origins and Development of the U.S. Navy's Officer Personnel System, 1793–1941* (Stanford, Calif.: Stanford University Press, 2002), 553–92.

62. TR to Frederic Charles Winkler, 1 March 1909, Morison, *Letters of Theodore Roosevelt*, 6:1540.

63. Morison, *Admiral Sims*, 177.

64. TR to Victor Howard Metcalf, 26 November 1908, Morison, *Letters of Theodore Roosevelt*, 6:1383.

65. TR to Remington, 28 October 1908.

66. Reckner, *Roosevelt's Great White Fleet*, 23.

67. *Official Blue Book of the Jamestown Ter-centennial*, 33, 682.

68. Michael Kammen, *Mystic Chords of Memory: The Transformation of Tradition in American Culture* (New York: Vintage Books, 1991), 299–300.

69. *Official Blue Book of the Jamestown Ter-centennial*, 774.

70. Edmund Morris, *Theodore Rex* (New York: Random House, 2001), 549.

71. Reckner, *Roosevelt's Great White Fleet*, 110; on the congressional debate and the 1909 naval appropriations battle, see Pedisich, *Congress Buys a Navy*, 161–78.

72. TR to Kermit Roosevelt, 23 January 1909.
73. TR to Theodore Roosevelt Jr., 13 February 1909, Morison, *Letters of Theodore Roosevelt*, 6:1520.
74. TR to George Meredith, 9 January 1908, Morison, 6:901; Roosevelt, "History as Literature," *American Historical Review* 18 (April 1913): 479.
75. Roosevelt, "History as Literature," 488–89.
76. Roosevelt, *Autobiography*, 563–64, 573.

11

LEGACY

The Influence of Theodore Roosevelt on Franklin D. Roosevelt's Career and Worldview

Craig L. Symonds

One interested observer of Theodore Roosevelt's improbable ascendency to the White House and his management of national affairs was his fifth cousin once removed Franklin Roosevelt, who was twenty-five years his junior. The age difference, combined with "Cousin Ted's" larger-than-life personality and rapid ascent to national prominence, made Theodore Roosevelt a natural role model for the young and handsome Franklin. Late in life, Franklin declared that Theodore Roosevelt had been the "greatest man I ever knew." His adulation led him to adopt several aspects of Roosevelt's personal and public demeanor, including the wearing of pince-nez eyeglasses and several of Theodore's signature phrases, including his occasional declaration that he was "dee-lighted."[1]

The startling similarity between the political trajectories of the two men has led many observers, both contemporary and historical, to conclude that Democrat Franklin charted his rise to the presidency by relying on the template of the Republican Theodore. When he was only twenty-five, FDR confided to a group of friends that he planned to get himself elected to the New York State Assembly, win an appointment as Assistant Secretary of the Navy, and then become governor of New York. These were precisely the stepping-stones that had marked Theodore's rise to power. Perhaps Franklin would have risen to high office and embraced progressive and internationalist values independently, but the existence and example of the first President Roosevelt provided him, if not quite a road map, then at least an inspiration.[2]

That Theodore was a Republican and Franklin a Democrat was for both men due less to ideological distinctions than to habit and convenience. Party affiliation at the turn of the twentieth century was more like membership in one of Harvard's dining clubs: it determined your friendship circle, your business connections, and your political allies. Being a Democrat was a family tradition for Franklin, whose father had supported Grover Cleveland and had consequently been offered an ambassadorship, which he declined. In spite of that, Franklin prioritized family loyalty over party membership in his enthusiasm for "Cousin Ted." This was evident on the night in 1897 when TR, then Assistant Secretary of the Navy, presented an evening lecture at Groton School, where fifteen-year-old FDR was a student. A proud Franklin wrote home that "Cousin Theodore gave us a splendid talk on his adventures when he was on the Police Board . . . telling us killing stories about policemen and their doings in New York." "Cousin Theodore" returned to Groton a year later as a hero of the Spanish-American War, and once again Franklin basked in his reflected aura. When two years later TR appeared on the national Republican ticket as McKinley's running mate, Franklin, by then a freshman at Harvard, was an enthusiastic champion of his distant kinsman. He joined the Harvard Republican Club, and the future Democratic president participated in a torchlight parade through Cambridge and Boston in support of the Republican ticket.[3]

––––––––

FDR's enthusiasm for his distant relative was not merely a product of family pride. Among their shared values was a belief that government had both the authority and the responsibility to work proactively to improve the lives of American citizens. For the young FDR, this progressive outlook merged with a sense of noblesse oblige. It was the particular duty of those "born in a good position," he wrote in one of his school essays, to "do their duty by the community." Given that, Franklin Roosevelt applauded and celebrated many of the progressive accomplishments of TR's presidency, including his advocacy of protecting nature through conservation. Both men were naturalists at heart, with interests in birds, animals, and taxidermy, though Franklin was never the indefatigable hunter that Theodore had been.[4]

Another similarity was their mutual love of the Navy, an enthusiasm that was genuine, even inherent, in both men. TR's *The Naval War of 1812* was published the year Franklin was born, and Franklin read it (probably more than once) as a boy. On this issue, however, the example of his distant cousin was as much coincidental as suggestive. As a youth, Franklin built model ships, visited and explored whaling ships at New Bedford, Massachusetts, and listened raptly to stories from his uncles about the China trade. His mother dressed him from the age of eight in a bespoke sailor suit that she had ordered from England. When Franklin was nine, his father, James, bought the fifty-foot motorized sailing yacht *Half Moon*, named for the vessel that Henry Hudson had used to explore the river that ran past the family home at Hyde Park, and before he was ten Franklin had learned to pilot that vessel by both motor and under sail. As a teenager, he sailed the rough waters of the North Atlantic off Campobello Island at the helm of a twenty-one-foot knockabout called the *New Moon*. In school, he drew sketches of sailing ships in the margins of his notebook. Though Theodore had attended Harvard, Franklin aspired to go to the Naval Academy, and he almost certainly had more sea time than most of those who applied, having sailed as a passenger across the Atlantic and back eight times before he was fifteen. He later claimed, without providing details, that he missed going to Annapolis "by a week," noting only that his parents had objected. Instead of Annapolis, Franklin followed Theodore to Harvard, though even there he kept a small runabout handy.[5]

In addition to belief in activist government and a love of the Navy, the two men also shared a conviction that the United States had an important role to play on the world stage. Theodore's corollary to the Monroe Doctrine, his offer to mediate the Russo-Japanese War, and his decision to send the Great White Fleet on its famous voyage were all evidence of the senior Roosevelt's determination to push the United States into the forefront of world politics. Similarly, both as Assistant Secretary of the Navy under Woodrow Wilson and then as president, FDR sought to leverage the power of the nation, both military and economic, to secure a stable world order with the United States as the lynchpin.[6]

None of these shared values, however, inspired FDR to become a Republican. His adherence to the Democrats was partly paternal inheritance, but it was also pragmatic. When FDR graduated from Harvard in 1903, TR was in the White House, and young Franklin knew that as a mere distant cousin he could not count on Theodore's support if any of the president's four sons (or either of his two sons-in-law) decided to enter New York politics. Franklin's best chance for political advancement, therefore, was within the Democratic Party. As Geoffrey Ward has put it, "party loyalty was never more than . . . a vehicle for personal power" for either of the Roosevelts. FDR was what might be called a Pragmatic Progressive. While he sincerely embraced progressive values, he did so with a practical eye cocked toward public opinion to see what policies drew popular support and were likely to advance his ambitions.[7]

The connection between the two men deepened when at age twenty-four, Franklin Roosevelt married Theodore's young niece Eleanor, daughter of the president's younger brother Elliott. The marriage of the handsome and ebullient Franklin to the shy and solemn Eleanor baffled some of their friends at the time and has puzzled some historians since. Certainly, Eleanor had a fine mind and a compassionate outlook that encouraged Franklin to see beyond his circle of Groton-Harvard-Columbia classmates. She also had a kind of innocent sweetness. Photographs of the young couple portray a beaming Franklin and a demure Eleanor whose weak chin had not yet become a prominent feature and whose glorious hair was often piled up in the style popularized by the illustrator Charles Dana Gibson. It is likely that the twenty-one-year-old Franklin was genuinely smitten by this thoughtful, unassuming, and amiable nineteen-year-old woman. That has not, however, discouraged some from conjecturing that at least part of Eleanor's attraction for Franklin was that it brought him into the presidential orbit. It allowed Franklin to call the president not "Cousin

Ted" but "Uncle Ted." The president himself gave the bride away at their wedding, and his larger-than-life presence all but hijacked the event. The ceremony began late because of the crowd's eagerness to see the president, and once the vows were spoken everyone followed the president into the library, leaving the wedding couple standing alone. As Eleanor recalled the moment, "We simply followed the crowd and listened with the rest."[8]

Once the young couple returned from their European honeymoon, Franklin made his initial foray into politics. His plan was to run for the New York State Assembly, but political circumstances in New York led him to bypass the Assembly and seek a State Senate seat. Concerned about how Theodore might react to his candidacy, he asked Eleanor to approach her Aunt Anna, known as "Bamie," to find out her brother's attitude. FDR was not seeking his endorsement or expecting Theodore to campaign for him—that would be asking too much; he simply wanted to know if the still-popular ex-president (who had left office the year before) would campaign against him. Theodore told her, "Franklin ought to go into politics without the least regard as to where I speak or don't speak." FDR may have broached the topic himself at a reception in June 1910 when Theodore and his party returned from an African safari. If so, TR apparently gave FDR his blessing, for Franklin soon threw his hat into the ring.[9]

During the ensuing campaign, the twenty-eight-year-old Franklin took maximum advantage of his kinsman's popularity. He frequently began speeches by acknowledging to audiences "I'm not Teddy," thus managing to associate himself with the ex-president while simultaneously establishing his independence. After one such introduction, he later claimed, a boy in the audience responded by declaring that he knew FDR wasn't Teddy because "you don't show your teeth." That elicited a hearty laugh from the audience during which Franklin did show his teeth.[10]

After winning his State Senate seat, Franklin continued to mirror TR, most notably by leading the resistance against the Tammany Hall establishment machine in Albany in much the same way that Theodore had fought Jay Gould and his cronies. He proved an annoying thorn in the side of the Tammany machine but was not quite the firebrand that Theodore had been. FDR talked about demolishing "the machine" and establishing "good government," but he introduced few bills to bring it about—an example of how his pragmatic side occasionally diluted his progressivism. At this point in his life, he was less a genuine crusader than an ambitious privileged son seeking a place for himself.[11]

———

FDR had cheered when TR won the vice presidency, and he had publicly supported him for president in 1904 against the Democratic candidate, Alton B. Parker. In 1912, however, when Theodore tried to retake the presidency from his own handpicked successor, FDR campaigned enthusiastically for Woodrow Wilson, and his efforts helped Wilson become the first Democrat to carry New York in twenty years. That put FDR in line for a position in the new administration. There was talk about his becoming assistant secretary of the treasury or collector of the Port of New York, but there was only one job he had in mind, and it came to him the way many things did in his life: through his friendships and connections. Franklin had met Wilson's choice as Secretary of the Navy, Josephus Daniels of North Carolina, at the Democratic convention in June. In Washington for the inauguration early in 1913, he encountered Daniels in the lobby of the Willard Hotel, where Daniels asked him, "How would you like to come to Washington as Assistant Secretary of the Navy?" FDR was overjoyed: "How would I like it?" he exclaimed, employing another of TR's signature words to answer: "I'd like it bully well." Whether his determination to secure that particular position was one more example of Theodore's influence or a product of Franklin's lifelong love of things naval—very likely it was both—FDR joined the administration in March. TR wrote to FDR to congratulate him: "It is interesting to see that you are in another place which I myself once held. I am sure you will enjoy yourself to the full."[12]

———

He did. FDR loved his tenure as assistant secretary, hobnobbing with admirals and receiving the seventeen-gun salute to which he was entitled whenever he boarded a Navy ship. He even designed a special assistant secretary's flag that was to fly on any ship he boarded. From his first days in the job, FDR measured himself against TR's tenure in that position. Early on, when Daniels happened to be out of the office, Franklin archly told a reporter, "There's a Roosevelt on the job today," and, in a deliberate reference to the time fifteen years earlier when Theodore had ordered Commo. George Dewey to prepare for offensive operations in the Philippines, he added: "You remember what happened the last time a Roosevelt occupied a similar position?"[13]

FDR did not, of course, order the fleet into action, but like Theodore he quickly established himself as a champion of preparedness in general and in particular of a powerful, modern fleet, one that would allow the United States to play a significant role in international politics. "Our national defense," he asserted, "must extend all over the western hemisphere, must go a thousand miles out into sea, must embrace the Philippines and over the seas wherever commerce may be." Reflecting the views of Rear Adm. Alfred Thayer Mahan, he insisted that "we must have battleships." On all these issues, his views were virtually indistinguishable from those of the first Roosevelt. They were not, however, the views of either the Wilson administration or his immediate boss, Josephus Daniels.[14]

In that respect, FDR sometimes walked a fine line between advocacy and loyalty. Though the government was building two battleships a year, FDR was convinced that that was insufficient, and while Daniels was off on an inspection trip on the Gulf Coast he took it upon himself to release a memo that emphasized the Navy's unreadiness for war. His objective was to jolt the public, and thus the administration, into adopting a more vigorous preparedness program, but he had not cleared the memo with Daniels, and it made the Navy Department look bad. Upon his return, Daniels let FDR know that he had gone too far, and in a subsequent appearance before the House Naval Affairs Committee, FDR was every bit a team player. Two battleships a year, he assured the congressmen, was just right.[15]

Nevertheless, rather than react with anger to this and other of FDR's enthusiasms, Daniels responded mostly with benign tolerance, much as Secretary of the Navy John D. Long had done with TR. Daniels had known he would be getting a Roosevelt when he asked FDR to take the job, and he accepted his indiscretions with avuncular amusement. If, however, TR had appreciated the discretion that Long had granted him—"Long is just a dear," TR had written to his friend Henry Cabot Lodge—FDR did not always fully appreciate Daniels' forbearance. In letters home to Eleanor, he portrayed his boss as a doddering old Southerner (Daniels was fifty-one) who hardly knew what to do all day and yet took all day to do it. He even developed an unflattering impersonation of Daniels, which he occasionally shared with serving senior officers.[16]

FDR may have been impressed in spite of himself, however, by Daniels' deft handling of several incidents concerning civil-military relations during the first year of the Wilson presidency. In 1913, California passed a law barring Japanese Americans from owning land. When Japan lodged a formal protest on 9 May, several of the Navy's senior officers concluded that war with Japan was imminent, and the Navy's General Board issued orders for the cruisers of the Asiatic fleet to concentrate in the Philippines. Theodore would very likely have applauded that decision, but the former president was then off exploring the Amazon basin. Perhaps with Cousin Ted in mind, Franklin Roosevelt emotionally sided with the admirals. He may even have entertained the notion that if the crisis did lead to war, he could (like Theodore) resign his post and join the fight in uniform, thus further enhancing his national political profile.

Daniels, however, saw the board's reaction as not only needlessly escalatory but a challenge to civilian control of the military. The secretary pointedly informed Rear Adm. Bradley A. Fiske, who headed the General Board of the Navy, that no ships were to move without his direct orders, and he took the issue to the president. Wilson backed Daniels, establishing the secretary as the de facto as well as the de jure commander of the Navy. Daniels even hinted that he might abolish the General Board altogether if the Navy did not adhere to administration policy. The admirals—and the assistant secretary—got the message.[17]

Though Franklin characterized his boss as something of a dinosaur, Daniels quietly changed the Navy in a number of important ways. The least popular of the changes, certainly within the officer corps, was

General Order No. 99, which Daniels issued on 1 July 1914 prohibiting "the use or introduction for drinking purposes of alcoholic liquors on board any naval vessel, or within any navy yard or station." The daily grog ration for enlisted men had ended during the Civil War, and now the wardroom too went dry. Daniels saw this only partly as a temperance issue; his principal objection was that it was undemocratic that officers could drink wine with their meals while sailors were denied access to beer or liquor. Daniels made other changes too. He got officers out of their dress whites for shipboard duty and added more civilian faculty to the Naval Academy, including (shockingly to some) naming a civilian professor to head the English Department. He eliminated the Navy's tradition of going to sea only in good weather, insisting that the fleet should maneuver in winter as well as in summer. It was FDR himself who signed the order that officers of the deck would henceforth give helm orders as "left" and "right" instead of the traditional, and sometimes confusing, "starboard" and "larboard." In the process, Daniels modeled for FDR the ways in which patient diplomacy and attention to detail can effect change as efficiently as boisterous advocacy.[18]

In 1914, as war was breaking out in Europe, the United States faced its own, much smaller crisis along its southern border. When Mexican authorities in Tampico arrested nine American sailors from the USS *Dolphin* for entering a restricted area, the American naval commander on the scene, Rear Adm. Henry Mayo, demanded and obtained their immediate release. That was not enough for Mayo. Without consulting the Navy Department, he demanded a formal apology, the raising of the American flag on shore, and a twenty-one-gun salute. Such demands were fully consistent with nineteenth-century practices of naval powers when dealing with second-tier nations, the kind of demands that TR might have made. The Mexican government, however, refused to accept the humiliation, and Wilson, acting boldly in this case, ordered the Navy to occupy Vera Cruz.[19]

Franklin Roosevelt was on the American West Coast at the time and took it upon himself to make a number of bellicose public statements in the belief that he was acting in line with administration policy. Once again, he imagined that if the incident led to war, he could resign his position and become a warrior as Uncle Ted had done. Instead, Daniels recalled him to Washington. While en route there, FDR continued to tell reporters that the incident almost certainly meant war and that the Navy was ready. Previously FDR had gotten in trouble for saying the Navy was not ready; now he got into trouble for asserting that it was. Daniels sat him down and explained—again—the difference between loyal support and independent advocacy.

On most issues, however, FDR and Daniels worked well together. On at least one occasion, they were able to combine their stewardship of the Navy with their shared abhorrence of corrupt business practices. Daniels was more annoyed than surprised when, after inviting bids for steel plate for new battleships, all the sealed bids came back with exactly the same dollar figure. He let the companies know this was unacceptable and ordered them to rebid. Again the bids were identical. Daniels then deputized FDR to approach a Canadian company for a bid, which came in much lower. That compelled the American companies to lower their bids as well. This kind of hardball proved useful more than once and was another lesson for the young assistant secretary.[20]

———

By the summer of 1914, Franklin was growing bored with the job of Assistant Secretary of the Navy. Never fully comfortable with being second in command, he was eager for new challenges. He had been on the job for fifteen months, and Theodore had held the office for only thirteen months before heading off to Cuba and his famous "crowded hour" on Kettle Hill. FDR still lacked a moment of military heroism, but he was in a hurry, and he planned a run for the governorship of New York in the fall of 1914. When the stars failed to align for that ambition, he set his sights on Elihu Root's Senate seat. Daniels tried to talk him out of making the bid, not only to keep him in the Navy Department but because he thought it was a bad political move. He was right. FDR lost the Democratic primary to the Tammany candidate, James W. Gerard, by a nearly three-to-one margin.

By then, Europe was at war. Once again both Franklin and Theodore preached American preparedness, each of them convinced that the United States would eventually have to join the fight. Theodore was particularly pointed. He was beside himself that Wilson, whom he accused of "abject cowardice and weakness," did not respond more forcefully to German depredations in Belgium and on the high seas. FDR, as part of the administration, could not be as vocal as TR, though he did what he could. He urged Wilson to bring the fleet from Guantanamo Bay, Cuba, up to Hampton Roads so that it could be readied for active service. Wilson thought this too alarmist and turned him down. FDR was pleased when, following the *Lusitania* incident in 1915, Wilson finally sent a stiff note to the Germans promising to hold them strictly accountable. TR did not think the note went far enough and continued to complain about Wilson's unwillingness to take a bold stand. Secretary of State William Jennings Bryan, in contrast, thought it went much too far and resigned in protest, prompting FDR to write to Eleanor, "What d'y'think of W. Jay B.? . . . I'm disgusted clear through." To both TR and FDR, Bryan was an artifact of a bygone era.[21]

Franklin would not, however, break with the president and may even have appreciated Wilson's middle ground position. In a sycophantic note, he wrote to Wilson, "I want to tell you simply that you have been in my thoughts during these days, and that I realize to the full all that you have had to go through—I need not repeat to you my own earlier loyalty and devotion—that I hope you know. But I feel most strongly that the Nation approves and sustains your course and that it is American in the highest sense." Had he seen that note, TR would very likely have sniffed scornfully.[22]

Quite apart from the controversy over American readiness for war, FDR was delighted to do a favor for his famous kinsman that spring. The previous fall, TR had urged New York voters to back an anti-Tammany Democrat rather than the Republican boss of Albany, William J. Barnes, implying that Barnes had engaged in secret deals with the Tammany machine. A furious Barnes sued him for libel. TR insisted that it was not libel, because Barnes was in fact corrupt. His problem was that few politicians in New York were willing to testify about Barnes's corrupt practices. FDR happily did so, explaining to the jury how Barnes had repeatedly sided with Tammany during FDR's years in the State Senate. TR won the case and was grateful, writing to Franklin, "I shall never forget the capital way in which you gave your testimony."[23]

Two years later, when the United States entered the European war, Franklin saw another opportunity to burnish his resume with active service in uniform. Theodore was convinced that it was exactly what he had to do. "You must resign," the ex-president told him. "You must get into uniform at once!" At the same time, however, both Daniels and, more importantly, the president told FDR that he was now needed in the Navy Department more than ever. Wilson's motive, at least in part, was that he found it useful to have a Roosevelt in his administration at a time when another Roosevelt was charging him with irresponsible tardiness for having failed to prepare adequately for war. The request of a president would not have deterred Theodore from going to war, but FDR remained at his desk. It marked Franklin's first deviation from the template of Theodore's career path.[24]

FDR soon came to regret it. By the end of the year, all four of TR's sons were in uniform—two of them had been decorated for gallantry—and here he was, still occupying a desk and providing political cover for Wilson. Only in the last months of the war did he manage to convince Daniels that he should be allowed at least to visit the front. He crossed the ocean on the initial cruise of the destroyer USS *Dyer*, with a troop convoy. A midocean storm broke some deck plates, and there was a mad scramble during a presumed U-boat attack that proved to be a false alarm. Once in Europe, FDR toured the front, making several stops that included brief service with a U.S. Navy battery of fourteen-inch guns that had been bolted to railroad flatcars for long-range bombardment of the German lines. If it was not exactly a charge up San Juan Hill, it at least allowed Franklin to claim later that he had seen war. He left Europe determined to resign when he reached Washington and get into uniform as soon as possible.[25]

He never got the chance. En route back to America on the ocean liner *Leviathan* he fell ill, first with double pneumonia and then with the

Spanish flu, a pandemic so severe that it killed more people worldwide than the war. Franklin survived, but his life was changed nonetheless. He was so ill that upon his return Eleanor unpacked his suitcases for him— to discover in one of them a packet of love letters from Lucy Mercer, Eleanor's own secretary. Betrayed and heartbroken, Eleanor offered Franklin his freedom. Franklin's mother, Sara, would not hear of it, and FDR's political advisor, Louis Howe, warned him that as a divorced man he could never expect to become president. FDR foreswore his relationship with Lucy (a pledge he subsequently violated), and the married couple agreed to stay together. Despite that, their relationship would never be the same.

By the time FDR recovered physically from his illness and went to see Wilson to tender his resignation and ask for a commission, it was, in the president's words, "too late." Wilson had been informed just that week that Germany had sent out peace feelers; the war was within days of ending. FDR never experienced his "crowded hour." Instead, he had to settle for that trip across the Atlantic on convoy duty and his inspection of a naval battery near the front. The slightness of his exposure did not deter him from assuring a war-averse audience in 1936, "I have seen war. I have seen war on land and sea. I have seen blood running from the wounded. . . . I have seen children starving. I have seen the agony of mothers and wives. I hate war."[26]

Whether or not FDR's proximity to the battlefront had in fact burnished his political reputation, the Democratic Party concluded that it would be useful to have a Roosevelt on its national ticket, and in 1920 FDR found himself nominated for the vice presidency on a ticket with the colorless governor of Ohio, James Cox. He was back on track, and at the age of only thirty-eight, four years younger than Theodore had been when he ran for vice president with William McKinley in 1900. Did he envisage the possibility that circumstances could lift him, as they had Theodore, to the top job? Whatever he may have imagined in the dark hours of the night, the Democratic ticket went down to ignominious defeat that fall, garnering a mere 36 percent of the popular vote and winning only one state outside the old Confederacy.

The major turning point in the life and the political career of Franklin Roosevelt, the moment that moved him finally and irrevocably off the template of Theodore's trajectory to the White House, came on 11 August 1921. That morning, after a typically energetic day of sailing, swimming, and hiking at the family summer home on Campobello Island, FDR awoke unable to use his legs. After several misdiagnoses of a bad cold, a blood clot, and a spinal lesion, it was finally, and correctly, diagnosed as polio: infantile paralysis.[27]

It is tempting to compare Franklin's struggle with polio to Theodore's determination to overcome his youthful case of asthma, but it is a false comparison. Theodore defeated his asthma, very likely by simply growing out of it, but in the popular history—and in his own mind—by dint of determination and personal courage, building up his body until he became the epitome of the vigorous outdoorsman. That success had an important side effect: it solidified his belief that individual effort and determination could overcome almost any obstacle, and it contributed to a boisterous self-confidence that he brought to both politics and policy. Just as he enjoyed beeline hikes—following a compass bearing regardless of the physical obstacles—so too did he often choose the direct path in his public life. TR's triumph over disability also encouraged him to believe that others too could overcome obstacles if they simply worked at it hard enough.

It was very different for Franklin. He did work hard to overmaster his disease—far harder, in fact, than Theodore had to work to overcome his. FDR's doctors were worried by his trying to force his withered legs to do things they simply could not. Sheer will, however, could not overcome paralysis. He could not defeat his disease as Theodore had; instead, he was compelled to live with it. He became dependent on others (especially Eleanor) to help him do even the most mundane things, like going to the bathroom. The confident, even flippant youth who had coasted through college and charmed his way through society now developed an empathy for those who were similarly dependent. After August 1921, Franklin Roosevelt was a different man. Up to 1921 he had mirrored his distant relative's almost worshipful admiration for the individual hero—the "man in the arena"—who achieved improbable victories, often against daunting odds. It was a worldview that Theodore had never outgrown; by the end of his life—he died in 1919—it was possible to discern a neofascist strain in his political philosophy. FDR, too, was a youthful admirer of extraordinary heroes, from John Paul Jones to Stephen Decatur to Theodore himself, but after 1921 his affliction begat a greater appreciation of the kind of heroism that consisted of enduring the quotidian demands of simple survival.[28]

Another factor that developed FDR's empathy was witnessing the impact on ordinary Americans of the economic and social catastrophe that was the Great Depression. Perhaps Theodore, too, would have been moved by the widespread pain that characterized much of the 1930s; he was not immune to the needs of everyday Americans. But it is certain that it affected Franklin. "The duty of the State toward the citizen is the duty of the servant to its master," he declared soon after the Depression began when he was governor of New York. "Government can't sit back and expect private charity or even local government to take care of it. . . . People aren't cattle!"[29]

As president, he proved willing to experiment with the ways in which government could relieve Americans of their distress. His New Deal program owed much to Theodore's New Nationalism, though he also borrowed aspects of Wilson's New Freedom, which emphasized government regulation rather than centralized planning. FDR embraced both ideas, and his New Deal included, on one hand, national programs on health care and social insurance for the elderly and on the other, government oversight of commerce and banking and a regulatory commission to oversee the stock market. Both Roosevelts bore a special animus toward financial corruption, especially by corporations. If FDR's New Deal was more idiosyncratic and less systematic than TR's New Nationalism, they sought similar ends.[30]

But while the objectives of the two Roosevelts retained a certain congruency, the processes employed by the younger Roosevelt to achieve them were markedly different. Theodore had often pursued his agenda by seizing the moment, taking the lead, and charging ahead, relying on eventual success to validate his actions. He famously sent the Great White Fleet on its way without full congressional funding and effectively seized the Panama Canal Zone while others debated the wisdom, morality, and even the constitutionality of doing so. As he boasted later, "I took the Canal Zone and let Congress debate; and while the debate goes on, the canal does also." If that claim slightly exaggerates the precise role he played, it reflects his view of how a dynamic and efficient leader can, and should, overcome inertia and opposition. In contrast, the second President Roosevelt was more likely to nudge things along in the direction he believed best and patiently (at least to outward appearances) wait for public opinion to catch up with him. Only then would he make a full public commitment. "Patient" was not a word that many used to describe the first President Roosevelt.[31]

There were other differences too. Theodore seemed genuinely to enjoy the give-and-take of political brawling; at public events he dominated both the agenda and the conversation as he had dominated festivities at the wedding of Franklin and Eleanor. If he disagreed with someone, he was willing to say so in unmistakable terms. Franklin himself was no shrinking violet—he too loved being the center of attention—yet he avoided direct confrontation, practicing a studied conviviality and deploying his smile and charm when necessary. He would listen with apparent sympathy to the advocates of one policy or another, nodding agreeably—a friend later recalled that he had the habit of saying "Yes, of course" to everyone—and then after his visitor had left, was as likely as not to ignore whatever advice had been offered. That led some disillusioned visitors to conclude that FDR was duplicitous, when in fact he simply dreaded open disagreement.[32]

In foreign policy as in domestic policy, FDR sought many of the same objectives as TR had, but here too he was less direct and more nuanced in his approach. When war broke out in Europe in 1914, TR had manifested a willingness, even an urgency, to get America involved, repeatedly proclaiming that the cautious, in his view craven, Wilson did not do enough to stop German aggression. At the time, FDR had silently cheered him on, occasionally causing his boss, Secretary Daniels, to sigh in frustration. Yet when war came to Europe again in 1939, FDR found himself playing

Wilson's role, pledging that he would keep the United States out of the conflict. FDR's neutrality was fundamentally different from Wilson's, however; whereas Wilson had asked Americans to be neutral in thought as well as in deed, FDR declared his open sympathy for the British and worked hard to get them the arms and supplies they needed, most notably through the Lend-Lease program, on which he expended much political capital. Still, he did not campaign as Theodore might have done to make the United States an active belligerent.

Part of the difference was FDR's determination not to outrun public opinion, but in addition, the two men had different sensitivities about war as a molder of national character. In 1914, TR had informed an audience that while war was "terrible and evil," it was also "grand and noble," and those who sought to maintain peace at the price of honor were unlikely to have either. It is inconceivable that he would have told an audience, as FDR did in 1936, "I hate war." TR might well have reacted to FDR's policy of neutrality from 1939 to 1941 as he had to Wilson's from 1914 to 1917, when he had declared that "to be neutral between right and wrong is to serve wrong."[33]

Theodore had been particularly infuriated by Wilson's measured response to the sinking of the *Lusitania* in 1915, accusing the president of "abject cowardice and weakness." FDR too, despite his official support of the administration, had been disappointed. A quarter-century later, however, when a German U-boat (the *U-69*) sank an American merchant steamer, the SS *Robin Moor*, in May 1940, FDR did not react the way both he and TR had urged Wilson to react in 1915. While the sinking of the *Robin Moor* was not accompanied by the heavy loss of life that the *Lusitania*'s had been, it was an undeniable casus belli if FDR had wanted to make an issue of it. It is not difficult to imagine how TR might have responded to the incident. FDR, however, knew he did not have the backing of the public for a declaration of war, and so, Wilson-like, he merely delivered a defiant message to Congress.[34]

FDR did, however, sponsor a vigorous preparedness program. As early as 1934 he had used $238 million of emergency public funds to authorize enough new warships to bring the United States up to the tonnages

allowed by the 1922 Washington Naval Arms Limitation Treaty. Four
years later, he backed another act authorizing the first of the big new *Iowa*-
class battleships, and two years after that, following the fall of France in
the summer of 1940, he fulsomely supported the Two-Ocean Navy Act,
which within three years would make the United States the greatest naval
power on earth. While by any measure this was a remarkable turnaround
in only six years, Theodore might well have sniffed, "About time!"

It would be several years before any of those newly authorized ships saw
service. In 1940 FDR deployed the few ships he did have on "neutrality
patrols" out into the Atlantic. Ostensibly, their purpose was to create a
security zone around the United States, but they also had the practical
effect of allowing U.S. Navy ships to keep the British informed of U-boat
activity in the western Atlantic. After the fall of France, FDR expanded
this security zone until it covered half the distance between the United
States and Britain, and that resulted in a largely clandestine, undeclared
naval war with German U-boats in the summer and fall of 1941. It was
the kind of half-measure that might have struck the more forthright TR
as pussyfooting.[35]

By 1940, FDR had served eight years as president. Tradition called for
him to step aside, but he was reluctant to do so; there was still so much to
do domestically, and the international situation was fraught with peril.
On the night in 1904 that TR had been elected to a full term as president
in his own right, he had announced publicly that he would not run again.
He had regretted it almost at once, and FDR was surely aware of that. He
remembered, too, that TR had subsequently sought to regain the White
House in 1912 but, having lost control of the party mechanism, failed.
History had moved on. It would not happen to the second Roosevelt.

———

Even after Pearl Harbor, FDR, now a war president, remained careful
and nuanced in his management of the Western alliance and of his own
military commanders. This was not the kind of war that could be won by
bold charges up defended hills; it required delicate negotiations among

allies overseas and thoughtful distribution of national assets at home. In his dealings with the Combined and Joint Chiefs, FDR was, in the words of Nigel Hamilton, "a model of tact." Because World War II was a coalition war, FDR had to manage America's allies—including both Winston Churchill and Joseph Stalin, not to mention Charles de Gaulle—as well as equally contentious American flag-rank officers, including Ernest J. King and Douglas MacArthur. All that required not only determination but subtlety, even subterfuge. When the disagreements grew tense, FDR defused things with a joke or a laugh. When circumstances or reverses compelled him to adjust, he sought other paths.[36]

It must remain pure speculation how TR might have fulfilled the role of commander in chief in a global coalition war, but it seems likely that he would have been more pugnacious, more assertive, and more nationalistic than FDR. The earlier Roosevelt might well have sought to confront issues directly, and the devil take the hindmost. The weapons that FDR used so adroitly—his charm, his soothing manner, his willingness to listen sympathetically, even a willingness to dissimulate or deceive if necessary—did not come easily to TR. Given that, it was probably a stroke of great good fortune that it was Franklin and not Theodore Roosevelt in the White House from 1941 to 1945.

For two-thirds of his life, FDR had modeled himself on the example of his cousin-uncle, doing all he could to promote himself as the heir of TR's fame and popularity. He had deployed the name of "Roosevelt" as a political tool at every opportunity, proclaiming himself "dee-lighted," and mirroring his kinsman's ascent to national prominence. Then in 1921, with TR two years in his grave, their paths, and to some extent their personalities too, diverged. FDR's struggle with his physical infirmity changed not only his daily habits and his relationships with others, but also his personality and worldview. Being so thoroughly dependent led him to empathize with others who were dependent as well. He would not have been the man he was without the example and inspiration of Theodore Roosevelt, but he might never have grown into the man he subsequently became without the intercession of infantile paralysis.

Notes

1. Geoffrey C. Ward, *A First-Class Temperament: The Emergence of Franklin Roosevelt, 1905–1928* (New York: Random House, 1989), 81, 83, 90.
2. Nathan Miller, *FDR: An Intimate History* (New York: Doubleday, 1983), 62–63; Ward, *A First-Class Temperament*, 153.
3. FDR to "Papa and Mama," 4 June 1897, in *F.D.R., His Personal Letters*, ed. Elliott Roosevelt (New York: Duell, Sloan and Pearce, 1970), 1:110; Robert Dallek, *Franklin D. Roosevelt: A Political Life* (New York: Viking, 2017), 25; James Tertius de Kay, *Roosevelt's Navy: The Education of a Warrior President, 1882–1920* (New York: Penguin, 2012), 25–26.
4. Arthur Meier Schlesinger Jr., *The Crisis of the Old Order, 1919–1933: The Age of Roosevelt* (Boston: Houghton Mifflin, 1957), 1:323–24.
5. Frank Freidel, *Franklin D. Roosevelt: A Rendezvous with Destiny* (Boston: Little, Brown, 1990), 10; H. W. Brands, *T.R.: The Last Romantic* (New York: Basic Books, 1997), 21–23; *Philadelphia Record*, 6 April 1913; Gene Edward Smith, *FDR* (New York: Random House, 2008), 23, 33.
6. Robert Dallek, *Franklin D. Roosevelt and American Foreign Policy, 1932–1945* (New York: Oxford University Press, 1995); James MacGregor Burns, *Roosevelt: The Soldier of Freedom* (New York: Harcourt Brace, 1970).
7. Ward, *First-Class Temperament*, 89, 93.
8. Freidel, *Franklin D. Roosevelt*, 12–13; Eleanor Roosevelt, *This Is My Story* (New York: Harper and Brothers, 1937), 126.
9. Ward, *First-Class Temperament*, 106.
10. Dallek, *A Political Life*, 43; Ward, *First-Class Temperament*, 119.
11. Dallek, *A Political Life*, 43–47; Ward, *First-Class Temperament*, 119, 168.
12. Dallek, *A Political Life*, 52–53; Ward, *First-Class Temperament*, 200.
13. Freidel, *Franklin D. Roosevelt*, 27; Ward, *First-Class Temperament*, 202.
14. Dallek, *A Political Life*, 60.
15. Smith, *FDR*, 126–27; U.S. Congress, *Reports of House Committee on Naval Affairs* (Washington, D.C.: U.S. Government Printing Office, 1915), 571, 572, 586.
16. Dallek, *A Political Life*, 97; Brands, *T.R.*, 313; Freidel, *Franklin D. Roosevelt*, 24.
17. Kenneth S. Davis, "No Talent for Subordination: FDR and Josephus Daniels," in *FDR and the Navy*, ed. Edward J. Marolda (New York: Palgrave Macmillan, 1998), 5–6; Smith, *FDR*, 106.
18. Smith, *FDR*, 105.
19. Ward, *First-Class Temperament*, 240–41.
20. Smith, *FDR*, 107.
21. Brands, *T.R.*, 756, 775; FDR to ER, 10 June 1915, quoted in Smith, *FDR*, 130, see also 136.
22. Ward, *First-Class Temperament*, 306.

23. Ward, 296–97.

24. Ward, 346.

25. Brands, *T.R.*, 113–15; Smith, *FDR*, 158; Ward, *First-Class Temperament*, 409.

26. Film of this speech, given at Chautauqua on 14 August 1936, is available on YouTube.

27. Ward, *First-Class Temperament*, 584–98.

28. Ward, 600–17.

29. Miller, *FDR*, 254–55.

30. Freidel, *Franklin D. Roosevelt*, 16, 24, 104, 142.

31. James F. Vivian, "The 'Taking' of the Panama Canal Zone: Myth and Reality," *Diplomatic History* (1 January 1980), 95–100; Ward, *First-Class Temperament*, 160–61, 304.

32. Brands, *T.R.*, 531; James T. Patterson, *Grand Expectations: The United States, 1945–1974* (New York: Oxford University Press, 1997), 222. The friend was William Phillips, who reported FDR's standard response in *Ventures in Diplomacy* (Boston: Beacon, 1952), 179–83.

33. Brands, *T.R.*, 752–54.

34. U.S. Department of State, *Foreign Relations of the United States*, 1915 supplement (Washington, D.C.: U.S. Government Printing Office, 1915), 436–38; Brands, *T.R.*, 756; Ward, *First-Class Temperament*, 305.

35. Patrick Abbazia, *Mr. Roosevelt's Navy: The Private War of the U.S. Atlantic Fleet, 1939–1942* (Annapolis, Md.: Naval Institute Press, 1975); T. R. Ferenback, *F.D.R.'s Undeclared Naval War, 1939–1941* (New York: David McKay, 1967); Thomas A. Bailey and Paul B. Ryan, *Hitler vs. Roosevelt: The Undeclared Naval War* (New York: Free Press, 1979).

36. Nigel Hamilton, *Commander in Chief: FDR's Battle with Churchill* (Boston: Mariner Books, 2016), 58.

ABOUT THE CONTRIBUTORS

SARAH GOLDBERGER is an adjunct professor in the Department of History at Salve Regina University, having previously taught as a lecturer at Old Dominion University. She holds a PhD in U.S. history from the University of Illinois at Chicago, specializing in southern history and public memory. She has supervised the archival research efforts surrounding the archaeological analysis of historical sites and restoration of National Historical Landmarks in Virginia. She has published on the memory of the American Revolution during the Civil War in the *Virginia Magazine of History and Biography* and contributed a chapter on the preservation of Yorktown in *Destination Dixie: Tourism and Southern History* (2012).

———

JAMES R. HOLMES is the J. C. Wylie Chair of Maritime Strategy at the U.S. Naval War College and formerly served on the faculty at the University of Georgia School of Public and International Affairs. He earned his PhD in international relations from the Fletcher School of Law and Diplomacy at Tufts University and is the author, coauthor, or coeditor of several books, including *Red Star over the Pacific: China's*

Rise and the Challenge to U.S. Maritime Strategy (2013); *Strategy in the Second Nuclear Age: Power, Ambition, and the Ultimate Weapon* (2012); *Chinese Naval Strategy in the 21st Century: The Turn to Mahan* (2012); and *Theodore Roosevelt and World Order: Police Power in International Relations* (2006). A former U.S. Navy surface warfare officer, he served as engineering and gunnery officer in the battleship USS *Wisconsin*. He was the last gunnery officer in history to fire a battleship's big guns in anger.

———

DAVID KOHNEN is the director of the John B. Hattendorf Center for Maritime Historical Research at the U.S. Naval War College. He earned his PhD in war studies at King's College, University of London, and is the editor of *21st Century Knox: Influence, Sea Power, and History for the Modern Era* (2016).

———

BRANDEN LITTLE is an associate professor of history at Weber State University. He researches humanitarian interventions during the era of World War I and the modern history of the U.S. Navy and Marine Corps. He earned a PhD in history from the University of California, Berkeley, and an MA in national security affairs from the Naval Postgraduate School. Little received prizes for his doctoral dissertation and master's thesis, and his articles have appeared in the *Journal of Military History* and *First World War Studies*.

———

JON SCOTT LOGEL is an associate professor in the War Gaming Department of the Center for Naval Warfare Studies at the U.S. Naval War College. A former U.S. Army officer, he holds a PhD in history from Syracuse University and previously taught in the Department of History at the U.S. Military Academy at West Point. He is the author of *Designing Gotham: West Point Engineers and the Rise of Modern New York, 1817–1898* (2016).

———

EDWARD J. MAROLDA has served as the director of naval history (acting) and senior historian of the Navy at the Naval Historical Center in Washington, D.C. He earned his PhD in American history from George Washington University and has taught at Georgetown University. He has authored, coauthored, or edited seventeen works, including *Theodore Roosevelt, the U.S. Navy, and the Spanish-American War* (2001); *FDR and the U.S. Navy* (1998); *By Sea, Air, and Land: An Illustrated History of the U.S. Navy and the War in Southeast Asia* (1994); and *Shield and Sword: The United States Navy and the Persian Gulf War* (2001), the latter of which received the Navy League's Theodore and Franklin D. Roosevelt Naval History Prize. In 2017, the Naval Historical Foundation awarded him the Dudley W. Knox Lifetime Achievement Award.

———

KEVIN D. McCRANIE is the Philip A. Crowl Professor of Comparative Strategy at the U.S. Naval War College. He earned his PhD in military history from Florida State University and is the author of *Admiral Lord Keith and the Naval War against Napoleon* (2006) and *Utmost Gallantry: The U.S. and Royal Navies at Sea in the War of 1812* (2011). His articles have appeared in *Naval History*, the *Journal of Military History*, *Naval War College Review*, and the *Northern Mariner.*

———

MATTHEW OYOS is a professor of history at Radford University. He received his PhD in history from the Ohio State University and was a postdoctoral fellow at the Triangle Institute for Security Studies, University of North Carolina at Chapel Hill. Among his publications are *In Command: Theodore Roosevelt and the American Military* (2018) and the centennial republication of Theodore Roosevelt's *The Rough Riders* (1998), to which he contributed the introduction.

———

JASON W. SMITH is an assistant professor of history at Southern Connecticut State University. He earned his PhD in history from Temple University and was the Class of 1957 postdoctoral fellow at the U.S. Naval Academy. His work has appeared in the *Journal of Military History*, *Environmental History*, *International Journal of Maritime History*, and *New England Quarterly*. He is the author of *To Master the Boundless Sea: The U.S. Navy, the Marine Environment, and the Cartography of Empire* (2018).

———

CRAIG L. SYMONDS is the Ernest J. King Professor of Maritime History at the U.S. Naval War College and also professor emeritus at the U.S. Naval Academy, where he taught history for thirty years and served as department chair. He earned his PhD in history from the University of Florida and is the author or editor of twenty-nine books, including *Decision at Sea: Five Naval Battles That Shaped American History* (2005); *Lincoln and His Admirals: Abraham Lincoln, the U.S. Navy, and the Civil War* (2008); *The Battle of Midway* (2011); *Neptune: The Allied Invasion of Europe and the D-Day Landings* (2014); and *World War II at Sea: A Global History* (2018). He has been awarded the Lincoln Prize, the Theodore and Franklin D. Roosevelt Naval History Prize, the John Lyman Book Award, the Samuel Eliot Morison Prize for Naval Literature, and the Dudley W. Knox Lifetime Achievement Award.

About the editors

JOHN B. HATTENDORF is the Ernest J. King Professor Emeritus of Maritime History and senior mentor, John B. Hattendorf Center for Maritime Historical Research, at the U.S. Naval War College. He served as the Ernest J. King Professor of Maritime History for thirty-two years, from 1984 to 2016. Additionally, he was chair of the Naval War College's Maritime History Department and director of the Naval War College Museum from 2003 to 2016. A former officer in the U.S. Navy, he earned his DPhil degree in history from the University of Oxford (DLitt, 2016) and is the author or editor of more than fifty books, including *Sailors and*

Scholars: The Centennial History of the U.S. Naval War College (1984) and *The Oxford Encyclopedia of Maritime History* (2007). He is the recipient of the Naval Historical Foundation's Dudley W. Knox Lifetime Achievement Award, the Navy League's Alfred Thayer Mahan Award for Literary Achievement, and the North American Society for Oceanic History's K. Jack Bauer Award for Achievement in Maritime History.

WILLIAM P. LEEMAN is an associate professor of history and a faculty fellow of the Pell Center for International Relations and Public Policy at Salve Regina University. He earned his PhD in history from Boston University and taught at the U.S. Military Academy at West Point from 2009 to 2011. He is the author of *The Long Road to Annapolis: The Founding of the Naval Academy and the Emerging American Republic* (2010), and his articles have appeared in the *New England Quarterly*, the *Historian*, the *New England Journal of History, Naval History, Rhode Island History*, and the *Hudson River Valley Review*.

INDEX

Note: The index uses "TR" for Theodore Roosevelt and "FDR" for Franklin Delano Roosevelt.

The Naval Institute Press is the book-publishing arm of the U.S. Naval Institute, a private, nonprofit, membership society for sea service professionals and others who share an interest in naval and maritime affairs. Established in 1873 at the U.S. Naval Academy in Annapolis, Maryland, where its offices remain today, the Naval Institute has members worldwide.

Members of the Naval Institute support the education programs of the society and receive the influential monthly magazine *Proceedings* or the colorful bimonthly magazine *Naval History* and discounts on fine nautical prints and on ship and aircraft photos. They also have access to the transcripts of the Institute's Oral History Program and get discounted admission to any of the Institute-sponsored seminars offered around the country.

The Naval Institute's book-publishing program, begun in 1898 with basic guides to naval practices, has broadened its scope to include books of more general interest. Now the Naval Institute Press publishes about seventy titles each year, ranging from how-to books on boating and navigation to battle histories, biographies, ship and aircraft guides, and novels. Institute members receive significant discounts on the Press' more than eight hundred books in print.

Full-time students are eligible for special half-price membership rates. Life memberships are also available.

For a free catalog describing Naval Institute Press books currently available, and for further information about joining the U.S. Naval Institute, please write to:

Member Services
U.S. Naval Institute
291 Wood Road
Annapolis, MD 21402-5034
Telephone: (800) 233-8764
Fax: (410) 571-1703
Web address: www.usni.org